Ancient Greek
Architects at Work
Problems of Structure
and Design

Ancient Greek Architects at Work

Problems of Structure and Design

J. J. COULTON

Cornell University Press
Ithaca, New York

First published 1977 by Cornell University Press

Published in the United Kingdom under the title *Greek Architects at Work*

International Standard Book Number: 0-8014-1077-0

Library of Congress Catalog Card Number: 76–44117

Printed in Great Britain by
The Camelot Press Ltd, Southampton

Contents

Plates

Figures

Preface

There are many points of view from which ancient Greek architecture may be studied—as a reflection, for instance, of economic and social conditions, as a succession of complex artefacts or aesthetic experiences, or as a source of inspiration for the architects of today. All these are of course valid approaches, but in this book I have tried to look at Greek architecture from the viewpoint of the ancient architects; I have tried to identify several of the problems which Greek architects must commonly have encountered in the course of their work, and to derive from the buildings themselves, and from such written evidence as there is, an idea of how these problems may have been tackled. Obviously the full range of Greek architects' thought is not covered, but I have tried to discuss a variety of aspects of their work; similarly some of the suggestions put forward here will probably require refinement, modification, or even rejection, but I have nevertheless thought it worthwhile, using the available evidence, both written and material, to draw a picture of the Greek architect's work which, although it may change from one period to another, is internally consistent at any given period. For without some such picture Greek architects are liable to appear schizophrenic—men who are not formally educated but nevertheless use the latest mathematical concepts in their elevations, men who in spite of a meticulous procedure of design are frequently forced to modify their buildings during construction, and so on. Certainly I believe that the architects deserve more prominence in the study of Greek architecture, for it is essentially the human intelligence of the architect which makes the difference between a beautiful building and a beautiful rock form.

The choice of illustrations to accompany the text perhaps requires a brief explanation. The existing state of most Greek buildings is so far from their original appearance that photographs can rarely convey the architects' intentions, and since comparatively small differences between buildings were important to my argument, it seemed desirable to remove distracting differences in draughtsmanship by redrawing most of the plans and elevations, even where existing versions were technically finer. At the same time this made it easier to maintain a uniform scale for each series of buildings which invite comparison. Many of the other drawings have been specially devised to illustrate points made in the text, and if ambition has sometimes outreached execution, I hope that intelligibility at least has not suffered.

Since some of the ideas presented here have been maturing for a considerable period, it is not always easy to make an appropriate acknowledgement of indebtedness. I should like, however, to thank my colleagues at Edinburgh for many fruitful and critical discussions, particularly Dr M. J. Angold, Mr K. M. Bury, Mr J. C. Higgitt, Dr R. Hillenbrand (who read an early draft of Chapter 1), Professor S. Piggott, Mr D. W. R. Ridgway, Mr D. B. Robinson, Mr E. C. Ruddock (who patiently answered my structural queries), Professor A. M. Snodgrass, and Dr T. F. Watkins. Many other friends have also contributed, whether wittingly or not, and I must mention particularly Dr M. A. R. Colledge, Dr J. R. Green, Dr J. G. F. Hind, Dr R. Mason, Professor H. A. Thompson, and Dr C. K. Williams. I owe a special debt of gratitude to Dr W. H. Plommer, whose teaching started the train of thought from which this book has emerged, and who, although disagreeing with me on some fundamental questions, was kind enough to read a complete draft of my text and to suggest many corrections and improvements; that I have not always heeded his advice is simply a measure of my obstinacy. Finally I must thank my wife who acted as guinea pig for much that I have written here, and who has assisted me immeasurably with some of the more tedious phases of the work.

J. J. Coulton
Edinburgh, January 1976

1

Architect, patron and project

Whatever his true responsibilities may be, the chief job of an architect today is generally felt to be the designing of buildings. Pictures of architects in the classical world, however, normally show them supervising work on the site, not seated at their drawing-boards;[1] for Plato, writing in the early fourth century B.C., what distinguished the architect was that he did not just work out what should be done, like an accountant, but also gave the necessary orders to the workmen until the building was finished,[2] and contemporary inscriptions emphasize the importance of his supervision. Indeed by derivation *architekton*, the Greek word translated here as architect, means chief builder, and some scholars have regarded the *architekton* simply as a master craftsman with no real responsibility for the design of buildings.[3] In the same passage, however, Plato takes as accepted that the *architekton* is not himself a workman but a director of workmen, and that he contributes theoretical knowledge not practical craftsmanship;[4] we shall therefore continue to translate the word as architect rather than master builder. Naturally the conditions of the Greek architect's life and work were different in many respects from those of his modern namesake, and we should perhaps look at these before going on to consider the more specifically architectural problems he had to face.

One of the difficulties in doing so is the scanty and fragmentary nature of the evidence. The names of over a hundred Greek architects are known from the period *c.* 650–50 B.C., but in no case can an architect's career be reliably reconstructed; and there are many aspects of the practice of architecture in ancient Greece where little more than an informed guess is possible. The story must be pieced together from the *Ten Books on Architecture*, written by the Roman architect Vitruvius in about 25 B.C., from brief references in works on other subjects, from inscriptions (often desperately incomplete) which record proposals or accounts for various building projects,[5] and from the buildings themselves. The evidence is generally fuller for the fourth and succeeding centuries. To some extent it may be applied backwards into the fifth and sixth centuries, but this must be done with caution. Considering the changes in Greek culture and society during the period we are concerned with, it would be surprising if the conditions of architectural practice remained constant, and in one important respect the period around 600 B.C. must have been very special.

For as we shall see (Chapter 2), the conventions of Greek monumental architecture developed fairly rapidly during the seventh and early sixth centuries, and the practice of architecture in the early stages, when there was no long tradition to rely on, must have been different in many respects from that in the fifth and fourth centuries when the conventions were centuries old.

From surviving inscriptions dealing with Greek building projects we learn that from the fourth century at least the architect was expected to exercise detailed control over matters of workmanship, inspecting each course of stone before the next was laid, approving the tightness of the joints and the quality of the metal clamps between blocks, and authorizing payments to the various workmen and contractors involved.[6] On any major building project there was thus always in attendance an architect, acting in part as clerk of the works. In addition to such matters of craftsmanship and administration, however, the architect was also responsible for technical decisions—the way in which unusually heavy blocks should be moved and lifted, the development of special foundations, the construction and operation of cranes, and so on.[7] Until the development of theoretical mechanics in the late fourth and early third centuries, there was no distinct concept of engineer as opposed to architect in Greek, and Eupalinos of Megara, who supervised the construction of a tunnel (cut from both ends to meet in the middle) at Samos in about 530 B.C., is called an *architekton* by Herodotos.[8] Even later, when a distinction could be made, it was not made rigidly. Vitruvius still expects that an architect will have to design siege machinery, fortifications and cranes, as well as temples and theatres, and his anecdotes show that Hellenistic architects covered a similar field.[9]

Nevertheless, this emphasis on the practical aspects of the Greek architect's work does not mean that he had no responsibility for design. Although Greek temples are strongly conventional in design, no two of them are quite the same, not even those which are believed to be works of the same architect; and although their design is basically simple, it is developed to extreme refinement and sophistication. Even in this restrictive field, therefore, design work was necessary, and the architect was the only man to do it. In those buildings which do not conform closely to an established type, the architect's responsibility for design must have been correspondingly greater.

The simplicity and conventional nature of Greek architecture may, however, explain in part why design would not seem such an important part of the practice of architecture. The basic plan of the normal Greek temple, a long hall with a portico round all four sides, can be traced directly back to the seventh, if not the eighth century (cf. Chapter 2), and a definitive monumental form both in plan and elevation had been worked out, for the Doric temple at least, by the early sixth century, to remain fundamentally unchanged for about half a millennium (cf. plate 1, figs.

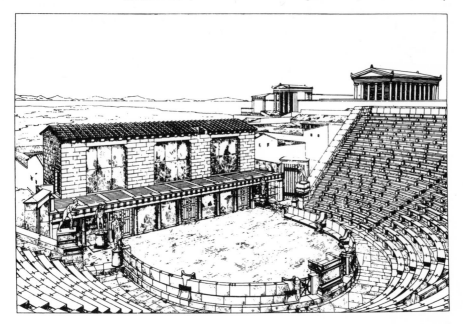

1   Theatre at Priene, late Hellenistic phase: restored perspective

11–12). The stoa, a general purpose public hall used in both secular and sacred contexts, was even simpler: basically a long, narrow building with a colonnade down one long side (plate 2). So too with other building types like the theatre (fig. 1); none of those which developed a monumental form before the Hellenistic period would have required an intricate design procedure, and most architects would not be producing something obviously new. Another reason for less emphasis on the architect's role as designer may be that design and execution were not distinct processes as they are today (cf. Chapter 3). It seems likely that only the general lines of a building would be decided definitely before construction began, and that much of the detailed design would take place as the building went up, in the light of the established conventions of architecture, the particular problems that emerged, and the architect's own decisions. Where the building was of a normal type, such a procedure would raise few difficulties, and it is noticeable that where an unusual type of building is attempted, there seem to be *ad hoc* solutions to some of the special formal problems that arose.

One fairly constant feature of architectural practice in Greece is that commissions were normally public ones. The tyrants of the sixth and fifth centuries may have had elaborate palaces, but the meagre evidence does not suggest it, and the practice of building elaborate houses for private citizens, requiring an architect as opposed to a builder, does not emerge much before the Hellenistic period.[10] A sign of the new attitude is the comment of Theophrastos[11] in the late fourth century that the Flatterer will say, on entering his patron's house, that it has been 'well architected' (this would presumably cover execution as well as design). The compliment to the patron may be a direct one, assuming that he will have overseen the work himself, or an indirect one, endorsing his discernment in choosing a good architect; but in either case the house is recognized as a fit field for the *architekton*.

There might still be a personal patron in other circumstances, however. When a city was ruled by a tyrant or king, he would presumably play the major part in initiating and controlling public building, even if he preferred, as some did, to work through the usual machinery of state; an architect might well be employed directly by such a ruler, therefore.[12] Outside his realm a monarch had to work through the usual machinery, and a democracy was often jealous of its right to control public building; the people of Ephesos refused Alexander's offer to pay for the temple of Artemis there on condition that he had his name inscribed on it.[13] This sort of patronage was naturally more widely available in the Hellenistic period with its rich monarchies, and several cities did accept large public buildings, complete with inscriptions, from foreign royalty.[14] In the early third century the Milesians accepted a 600-foot-long stoa donated by Antiochos, prince of Syria; and Antiochos may have provided an architect to lay out the building, for the plan finds its closest parallel in a building belonging to the same dynasty, the shop complex on the agora at Doura Europos on the Euphrates. The site of the stoa was, however, to be indicated by a Milesian architect, and the style of the colonnade forming its façade is similar to that of other colonnades at Miletos.[15] A closer relationship between donor and design is suggested by the two stoas built at Athens by Eumenes II and Attalos II, successive kings of Pergamon. The Athenians may have exercised some control over the siting and general form of the buildings, but the detailed design certainly, and the workmanship probably, is Pergamene (cf. pp. 137–9).[16]

There are also several cases where a private individual is known to have financed a public building.[17] Again such offers were not always well received,[18] and it is uncertain how far a private donor could control the design of his building, and so serve as the architect's patron. An architect may occasionally have been his own patron. The late-fourth-century Leonidaion at Olympia was, according to its inscription, 'made and dedicated' by Leonidas of Naxos; either verb might by itself mean only that he provided funds, but the use of both suggests a double activity. Its style is in most respects comparable to that of other buildings at Olympia, but it does show some East Greek features (fig. 2).[19] Three centuries later, Andronikos of Kyrrhos seems to have designed and paid for the Tower of the Winds at Athens.[20]

Normally, however, public building was more truly public,[21] and the architect's patron was the city-state or some similar body, whether the building concerned was secular or sacred. For sanctuaries normally belonged to one particular city-state, whether they were of local significance like the Akropolis at Athens, or of Panhellenic importance like Olympia; and their building projects would be controlled through the normal machinery of the city-state concerned. Subject to that control, other interested cities might put up small buildings at international sanctuaries like Olympia and Delphi, often supplying not only the money

2   Leonidaion at Olympia (late fourth century): Ionic order of outer portico

but architect, masons and materials as well. This was not a constant activity but such sanctuaries could to some extent act as a clearing house for architectural and technical ideas.

A typical public project might run something like this. An initial proposal to build would be made in the assembly (or equivalent), by a statesman like Perikles with a political purpose in mind, by somebody who wished to gain prestige by association with a notable building, or simply by a person who felt a special interest in the cult or project concerned.[22] The assembly would discuss the desirability of the proposal and the way it could be financed and might suggest modifications. Then if the proposal was approved, a supervising committee would be appointed, and an architect selected to draw up a specification. The committee would organize a work-force and construction would start, either by letting the work out in contracts or by hiring workmen directly. As work went on, the architect, with or without members of the supervising committee, would inspect it, and authorize payments; the money was usually drawn from a separate finance committee. In all these stages there were variations, however, depending on the nature of the job and the structure of the state or other body responsible.

We have seen how the money for a project might all come from a single individual, but this can never have been normal. Other known sources of money for monumental building are the spoils of battle and the proceeds of a particularly good year in a city's mines,[23] and a sanctuary of international importance could count on contributions from all over the Greek world and beyond; both the sixth-century and the fourth-century temples of Apollo at Delphi were financed in this way.[24] For the vast majority of projects, however, these special sources could not have been drawn on, which leaves two main possibilities as the normal means of raising money: that it was drawn from the regular funds of the state or sanctuary, or that it was subscribed more or less voluntarily by the private citizens of the city. We know that under Perikles (c. 450–429 B.C.) the great buildings of Athens were financed from public funds, from the 460 talents or more which the Athenians collected annually from their 'allies'.[25] Athens' position at this time was a very special one, however, and private contributions were made too.

It is difficult to estimate the annual budget of a normal Greek city at any period, but such evidence as there is suggests that it was small, particularly in the archaic period.[26] It is hard to imagine the state income of Selinous in Sicily being sufficient for the two normal temples, the four large ones and the colossal one that were constructed between c. 550 and 450 B.C.[27] On the other hand, there is ample evidence for private contributions towards public building projects at least from the fourth century on, and inscriptions were often set up listing the contributors and their donations.[28] There is little evidence of this system in the fifth century,[29] and none in the sixth, when the idea of permanent civic records had scarcely developed; but if personal and family prestige could be relied on in the Hellenistic period, it is likely that the method was effectively applied earlier on as well. The Athenian practice whereby rich individuals were called on to undertake such public duties as the maintenance of a trireme in the navy, or the production of drama at a state festival, is simply the formalization of such a method, and shows that it was preferable, instead of imposing direct taxation, to rely on the rich to carry out their responsibilities generously by involving their sense of honour and prestige. In the archaic period when prestige-loving aristocrats held most of the city's wealth, their financial support, whether as individuals, as families, or as clans, must have been vital.

It is by no means certain how far the Greeks were able to estimate accurately the cost of monumental building, and in some cases, perhaps in most, they did not expect to have all the money available before building began.[30] The next stage was therefore to arrange the supervision of the project, which a large public body could hardly do directly. In the sixth century a single man seems often to have undertaken the supervision, but later the job was done by a committee. Sometimes, especially in large sanctuaries, there was a standing committee in charge of maintenance and construction which could take control;[31] sometimes officials originally appointed for a different purpose were put in charge;[32] but normally a special committee was appointed.[33] Membership of such committees would change regularly, and as a result the proposer of a project might well not be among its supervisors. The same variation applies to the appointment of an architect; there might already be one working for the city or sanctuary,[34] but for a large project a new architect was normally chosen, sometimes by the supervising committee, sometimes by the assembly.[35] In Athens the Council would approve, and if necessary modify, the full preliminary design, but that may not have been normal.[36] Architects rarely, if ever, competed for commissions, perhaps because there was little financial reward.

Construction could be organized in three basic ways: by contract for a particular part of the work at an agreed price, by piecework at an agreed rate for a particular type of work, or simply by paying daily wages. The accounts for the Erechtheion at Athens in the years 409/8 to 406/5 B.C.[37] show that work there was based predominantly on day wages, and this may have been generally true of Periklean buildings too.[38] Piecework was the predominant system at Didyma in the third and second centuries.[39] But contract work seems to have suited the requirements of most Greek building projects, and, particularly if there was difficulty in getting work completed, it had the advantage of binding the worker to his agreed piece of work—at least if he wanted payment for it.[40]

The size of the contracts varied enormously. In the fourth-century temple of Asklepios at Epidauros they range from 9800 drachmas for the ceiling, doors and other woodwork to $\frac{1}{2}$ drachma for painting serpents as decoration.[41] Where the contracts were small, the authorities must have dealt directly with the craftsmen, so that close official supervision of the work, and a sophisticated system of public accounting would be needed, just as they were in a project based on piecework or day wages. With large contracts, however, where the contractor could certainly not have done the work himself, the supervision and accounting could be simplified, for the contractor would have hired and paid the actual craftsmen, and procured the materials and equipment. This may be one reason why the early work on the temple of Asklepios, when the administrative machinery was newly created, was all iet out in large contracts.

The advantages of letting work in large contracts would have been even greater in the sixth century, for it is doubtful if any Greek city of that period had the administrative machinery to supervise a project in detail, as was normal in the fourth century. Herodotos says that the contract price for rebuilding the temple of Apollo at Delphi (burnt in 548 B.C.) was 300 talents.[42] This suggests that the whole project was let out as a single contract, for such a round number is unlikely to result from the addition of many small contracts. The single contract was probably taken up by the Alkmaionids, an aristocratic Athenian family who were in exile at the appropriate time; they were certainly responsible for construction from an early stage, for elsewhere Herodotos says that they substituted marble for the *poros* (limestone) specified in the main façade;[43] that would have been impossible if construction had proceeded very far. It has been argued that the 300 talents was an estimate not a contract, since such a contract would have no parallel in later project organization. A contract is what Herodotos calls it, however, and some support for the view suggested here is given by the story of how Phalaris made himself tyrant of Akragas (*c.* 570–565 B.C.) by undertaking the construction of the temple of Zeus on the akropolis of the city.[44] He was entrusted with 200 talents, perhaps the contract price for the whole temple, and used this to hire a large body of men and get together plenty of construction material on the akropolis, all without raising suspicion; but instead of building a temple, he fortified the akropolis and seized the city. Phalaris is called the supervisor, but he seems to have been bound by a contract, and Theron, who later gained power by the same trick, certainly was; both men were, like the Alkmaionids, aristocrats.[45]

There is, therefore, some probability that building programmes in the archaic period were organized rather differently from the later ones which we know more about. The importance of aristocratic individuals and families, as providers of funds, as contractors for (and so as supervisors of) whole buildings, and presumably also as instigators of building, was very much greater, and the architect must have dealt more often with the individual or family concerned than with the state.[46] The touchiness of the Athenian assembly when Themistokles and Perikles seemed to be continuing this aristocratic tradition is understandable, and the Athenian organization of building work on a day-wage basis would have been due to the state simply taking on the role of contractor, and so dealing directly with the craftsmen on the same basis as the aristocrat in the sixth century. The difficulty of doing this in a city with no large pool of skilled labour may have led to the modified contract system which we see in the fourth century. This modified system kept most of the benefits of both the earlier ones.[47]

This then was the varying background against which Greek architects worked; in considering their probable importance in the development of Greek architecture, their social status and education are of some relevance. Few will probably argue that Greek architects belonged either to the lowest grade of society or to the wealthiest aristocracy; but within those limits there is considerable scope for difference of opinion, and there are at least two points of view for which there is some evidence. The scholars who believe that architects were essentially master craftsmen suppose that they were trained by a sort of apprenticeship in traditional building, and rose from the ranks of the actual builders; the view taken here, however, is that architects were on the whole distinct from builders, that they were normally educated men, trained by what they had read as well as by their practical interests and experience.

The main evidence for the first view is the conventional nature of Greek architecture, which suggests a traditional craft design; this is supported by the wages paid to architects, normally 1–2 drachmas a day, little more than a skilled craftsman,[48] by the insignificant duties which Hellenistic city architects were often called on to perform (cf. below p. 29), and by the extreme rarity of buildings signed by their architects whereas sculptors commonly signed their statues.[49] There are also one or two cases where an architect at the sanctuary of Delos seems to have served earlier as a contractor,[50] and rather more numerous instances of men practising as both architects and sculptors. This rather surprising combination of skills is found in both the sixth and the fourth centuries,[51] and since the obvious common factor is the technical skill in handling and shaping stone which may be required in both fields, it suggests that architects may have worked with stone.

The evidence for the second view seems to be stronger, however, although one must obviously allow for the possibility that not all architects were of the same status and education. Certainly the earliest monumental architects cannot have been just humble craftsmen trained in traditional skills, for during the seventh century, as we shall see (Chapter 2), a large number of new techniques was introduced and the temple changed radically in form and structure. Although the new type of architecture was much more expensive than the old, it nevertheless spread rapidly throughout the Greek world. Its prestige must have been very great, and the men who could produce it can hardly have been without prestige themselves. The architects of the first stone temple of Apollo at Delphi were regarded as legendary figures,[52] almost on a par with Daidalos, and the late seventh to early sixth century is the time when practical matters had the highest status in Greek society; Thales, the first of the Greek philosophers, is represented by Herodotos as an eminently practical man, and Euthykartidas, a Naxian sculptor of c. 600 B.C., carved a life-sized marble statue as his own dedication to Apollo and so must have been able to support himself for the year or so required to make it.[53] As already mentioned, the training of the earliest architects cannot have been as traditional master-builders; it is argued in Chapter 2 that many of the new techniques were derived from the eastern Mediterranean, particularly from Egypt, and if architects learnt a lot of their skills in Egypt, they would not be the only Greeks to have done so. It has long been maintained that this was true of the first Greek monumental sculptors, and in the early sixth century both Thales and Solon of Athens visited Egypt.[54] But since the first architects did not blindly follow either the Egyptians or their own predecessors, they must to a considerable extent have educated themselves.

An important development in the middle of the sixth century was the writing of the first architectural treatises, a tradition which was continued down through the Hellenistic period. None of them has survived, but Vitruvius mentions a work on the temple of Hera at Samos by Theodoros and one on the temple of Artemis at Ephesos by Chersiphron and Metagenes, both projects belonging to the years around the middle of the sixth century.[55] These must have been among the earliest prose works in Greek, for the first philosophical work in prose was written by Anaximandros of Miletos at just about the same time; earlier works, even on such prosaic subjects as agriculture, astronomy or the nature of matter, had been in verse. The Ionian school of philosophy in the sixth century had an interest in the practical as well as the abstract, and by the end of the century had begun the systematic collection of historical and geographical information.[56] It is presumably not merely coincidental, therefore, that the first Greeks to write about architecture were working in Ionian cities; the date at which they did so suggests that they were well up with the intellectual trends of the time.

Although these architectural works are lost, it seems likely that the detailed information about the two temples preserved in later authors is derived from them. If so, we can be sure that they were not just the preliminary specifications for the buildings, as has sometimes been argued, for we learn of the problems that arose during construction.[57] The emphasis seems to have been on the technical problems involved. Theodoros is credited with the invention of the square, the level, and the lathe, and a lathe was indeed used for the bases of the columns at Samos;[58] all three devices must have been known before (the first two are obviously essential for monumental architecture in dressed stone), and so Theodoros was probably the first to describe them. At Ephesos we hear mainly of the methods of transporting and setting in place the very large blocks involved.[59] In addition to technical matters, however, a description of the buildings, both in terms of absolute size and of the rules of proportion used, was probably included.[60]

The tradition of writing such treatises continued throughout the fifth century, but we know nothing of their contents; the work by Pytheos, architect of the temple of Athena at Priene and the Mausoleion at Halikarnassos in the mid fourth century, is quoted by Vitruvius, however; in addition to (presumably) explaining the design of his masterpieces, he made theoretical criticisms of the Doric order, and expressed emphatic views on architectural education.[61] The range of these treatises seems therefore to become more theoretical, less technical, and in the Hellenistic period Hermogenes, also quoted by Vitruvius, took up the criticisms of the Doric order, and also set out the justification for his developments in temple design.[62]

The existence of these treatises shows that throughout the classical and Hellenistic periods architects were sufficiently educated and self-conscious about their work to write about it. Their training was also apparently based to some extent upon the written works of earlier architects, for Xenophon makes Sokrates ask the sophist Euthydemos, who has made a collection of technical treatises, whether he is thinking of becoming an architect, a piece of sarcasm which would be pointless if architects did not learn from such treatises.[63]. There is also evidence from the fourth century onwards that they had a more general liberal education. The speech by Philon of Eleusis, giving an account of his Arsenal at Piraeus (c. 340 B.C.), was accepted as a masterpiece of eloquence,[64] so he must have been an educated man, while Pytheos proposes a particularly high ideal of education for architects by stating that they should be all-round experts who beat the specialists in every field.[65] Within the widening field of monumental architecture in the Hellenistic period there may have been more scope for a training through experience rather than education, but Vitruvius, who often reflects Hellenistic ideas, insists on a wide-ranging education for architects, although not at a specialist level.[66] There was, however, no officially prescribed training or certification at any period.

Education, of course, is only one aspect of social status; wealth and social connections are others. Of the social connections of architects we know virtually nothing; Vitruvius says[67] that 'the ancients' normally chose architects of good family but he may be biased. In the few cases where we know the occupation of an architect's father, the father too was an architect; this need hardly surprise us in view of the general custom of son following father in Greece, and Vitruvius tells us that it had normally been true of architects, although not apparently of himself.[68] Of architects' wealth we know little more. Kallikrates in the 440s B.C. undertook the construction of the new Long Wall, running about six kilometres from Athens to Piraeus,[69] and in the fourth century Philon of Eleusis was among the rich, though not the very rich, of Athens.[70] In the Hellenistic period

Hermogenes was sufficiently important to change a proposed temple from the Doric to the Ionic order, and some architects apparently paid for the buildings they designed.[71]

The more or less liberal education and adequate status and wealth of Greek architects seems inconsistent with the low payments they received. However, these payments were probably not an economic salary, but a conventional living allowance, comparable to those paid for other state duties;[72] the chief motive for an architect accepting responsibility for a new temple would be the prestige he would gain by ensuring that it was a credit to his city. He would probably be a man of naturally practical turn of mind who did not need to work full-time for a living, and who took every opportunity to extend his knowledge, both by collecting technical treatises like Euthydemos, and by looking at, learning about and discussing existing temples and any construction work in progress. This would not be just for the love of knowledge, but to gain a position of respect among his acquaintances and in the city at large as a man whose advice on practical matters was worth listening to. Prestige in one form or another accounts for much in Greek life, and it is worth remembering that Greek generals were equally non-professional, but could none the less be brilliant.

If architectural training was gained largely through reading and discussion rather than by practical experience, it would explain how local men could emerge as architects to meet a specific demand. For in spite of the general uniformity of Greek architecture, local styles are discernible at all periods and in matters which must have been the province of architects rather than craftsmen.[73] Although the architects of whom we hear in the written sources did travel a certain amount, they rarely went outside their own region. Thus a Corinthian architect might work at Delphi but not at Ephesos; an Ephesian architect might work at Miletos but not at Athens. There are exceptions, of course, perhaps more numerous in the archaic and Hellenistic periods.[74] If architects were trained by apprenticeship, therefore, it is hard to see how a man like Libon of Elis, architect of the temple of Zeus at Olympia (c. 470–457 B.C.), could have learned his job. Small treasuries and perhaps other public works, through which he might have gained some practical experience, had been built at Olympia in the recent past, but a large temple would raise many problems of design and construction not met with in such buildings, and we know of no large temple in the neighbourhood during the preceding thirty years. Similarly the outburst of building at Athens after c. 450 B.C. involved at least four major architects, yet it is doubtful whether there had been any serious temple building at Athens since the Persian Wars.[75] Nothing certain is known of the origin of these architects, but with the exception of Iktinos' reputed design of the temple of Apollo at Bassai (Arcadia),[76] all their work was in Athens, Attica and Delos (now under direct Athenian control). What is more, although each of them had to some extent a personal style, there are sufficient common elements to constitute a Periklean style which does not develop out of the immediately preceding work of Libon at Olympia.

With the late fifth century we come to the first detailed records on stone of a building project,[77] and in these we meet for the first time architects who supervised work on a building which they had not themselves designed. Work on the Erechtheion at Athens had apparently stopped for a short period, and was resumed in 409/8 B.C. The architect who served in 409/8 was replaced in 408/7 by another who may also have served only for a year. Both were Athenian citizens, and both were paid a drachma a day, the same as the skilled workmen.[78] Other architects serving in the sanctuaries of Eleusis, Delphi and Delos in the fourth and third centuries seem also to be involved chiefly in supervising and were normally paid 1–2 drachmas a day.[79] It has therefore been argued that a distinction should be drawn between designing architects, men of some status who initiated work on major projects, and supervising architects, who might design minor buildings but normally executed the designs of others; the latter were simply master craftsmen, and paid accordingly.

Certainly those who supervised work on the Erechtheion could have done virtually no design work, for the building was nearly complete by 409/8 B.C., and even the cornice was to a large extent half worked. We normally find, however, that where a building took a long time to complete, the parts set in place late are late in style as well (fig. 3), suggesting that the 'supervising' architect also did some design work.[80] Equally the designing architect might supervise construction for a number of years;

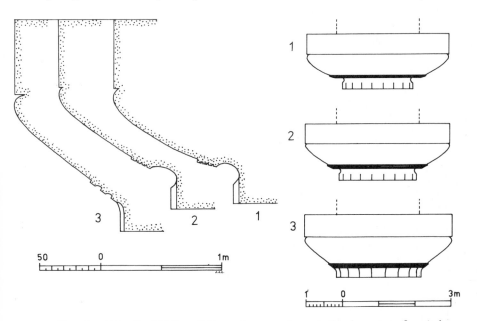

3 Temple of Apollo ('GT') at Selinous (c. 530–460 B.C.): development of capital forms during period of construction

this was certainly true of Chersiphron and Metagenes at Ephesos, and it is most reasonable to suppose that Theodotos, the architect who supervised the temple of Asklepios at Epidauros from start to finish (at a drachma a day), was also its designer.[81] In fact a separate supervising architect, not responsible for the fundamental design, seems to have been appointed only when a project dragged on for more than a generation (in which case it was inevitable), or when there had been an interruption which might well have led to (or been caused by) the departure of the original architect.[82]

Two or more architects sometimes worked on a building together rather than successively, particularly in the sixth century and on colossal buildings; four architects are named for the archaic Olympieion at Athens which got no further than the stylobate to take the columns, and the Hellenistic temple at Didyma was laid out by Daphnis and Paionios together,[83] but there is no real indication of how the work was divided. From the fourth century onwards the title *hyparchitekton* (underarchitect) is sometimes found; the underarchitect seems to have taken on the day-to-day supervision, while the architect was responsible for general standards and final inspections.[84]

If architects normally supervised the construction of the buildings they designed, responsibility for a major project might well mean a lifetime's employment. But the temple of Zeus at Olympia was finished in about 15 years, and as far as we know there was as little major building activity in the area in the following 30 years as there had been in the 30 years before the project. What did Libon do for the rest of his life? Only in rare circumstances, for instance in Athens during the second half of the fifth century, was building activity so prolonged and extensive that an architect could hope to find a similar commission when the old one was complete. The evidence suggests that architects appointed to supervise a project already under way, although they might serve several years, did not serve for a working lifetime either.[85] Those who believe that Greek architects were essentially master craftsmen, and that the payment of 1–2 drachmas a day was a full economic salary, suppose that they returned to their craft of stone-masonry or house-building. If the architect was a man of independent means, however, as suggested here, ceasing to work on a project would mean an end to arduous responsibilities rather than the loss of desirable employment and wages. This would certainly better account for the fairly rapid turnover of supervising architects when the project itself was continuing, and the honours paid to Agathon, supervising architect at Delphi in the 330s B.C., and to his son and grandsons, suggest that the family was of some standing.[86] At all events it is clear that architecture could not normally be regarded as a lifetime's profession, at least before the Hellenistic period.

The situation in the Hellenistic period may have been different. The rich new kingdoms would provide opportunities for more permanent patronage; new cities of the Greek type, each requiring its temples and civic buildings, were founded as a matter of policy across large areas of Anatolia and the Near East; and even in the older cities the range and extent of monumental building was increasingly stretched to include such things as gymnasia, market buildings and even houses. Thus the scope for architectural practice was radically increased.

A new development in the Hellenistic period was for cities to retain an official architect, a position which may not have been secure, but which was for an unlimited period. In earlier inscriptions references to 'the architect' are all concerned with projects already begun, for which a particular architect would already have been appointed.[87] Athens, as usual in matters of administration, adopted the practice first. In an inscription[88] of 337/6 B.C., 'the architects salaried in the city' are asked to prepare plans for the fortification of Piraeus, and even earlier, in 346 B.C., we hear of 'the architect' who arranges special seats at the theatre for ambassadors and city benefactors.[89] This official is not distinguished in any way, but later there was an 'architect in charge of the sanctuaries'.[90] In the late fourth century, Vitruvius tells us, the Rhodians retained an architect of some standing for an appropriate yearly payment,[91] and other cities seem to have followed suit.[92] The duties we hear of are mainly minor: arranging for the cutting of inscriptions, indicating where they may be set up, supervising repairs to statues, and so on; but there were more important duties, too. At Kyzikos there were three city architects to look after the public buildings and equipment.[93] At Aspendos in the second century A.D., Zenon is described as 'architect of the theatre and the city's works',[94] and there is no reason to suppose that city architects in the Hellenistic period did not also design civic buildings when required. Since the architect was also an engineer, however, one of his most important duties might be organizing defensive works for the city. That was why the Rhodians retained Diognetos, and the Olbians (probably) sent for an architect from Byzantion for the same purpose.[95]

References to city architects are comparatively few, and it is hard to determine their status separately. Diognetos of Rhodes was, according to Vitruvius, a man of repute, and the charlatan who replaced him was an educated charlatan. There is in fact no reason to believe that city architects were in general different from any other kind of architect, and the minor responsibilities mentioned above can be regarded as equivalent to the responsibilities for inspecting clamps and jointing undertaken by the architects who designed temples. As we shall see, the methods of designing which were developed during the Hellenistic period brought the work of the Greek architect much closer to that of his modern namesake. Although there were clearly substantial differences between architectural practice then and now, Cicero, writing in the late first century B.C., links architecture with medicine and teaching as appropriate pursuits for those of suitable standing[96]—an assessment which would not be wildly inapposite today.

2

The problem of beginning

Between about 1100 and 700 B.C. there was no truly monumental architecture in Greece. Little building of any sort has survived from this period, and what there is consists of houses and small shrines, competently built in many cases, but with no attempt at elaboration and using simply the locally available materials.[1] Building activity seems to have increased both in scale and intensity from the middle of the eighth century onwards; but not before the seventh century do we find a truly monumental architecture—that is, buildings intended to impress and endure, not just to perform a function. Yet by the beginning of the sixth century the basic forms of Doric architecture had been created, and there were large temples built throughout of carefully dressed stone, except for an elaborately tiled roof. This rapid development of a monumental architecture where previously there had been only a folk architecture raises problems for modern archaeologists; it must also have raised many problems for Greek builders of that time, who were suddenly called upon to cope with a whole range of matters which had not previously had to be considered.

The idea of monumentality was not entirely new to Greece, however. During the course of the eighth century a tradition had grown up in Athens and some other places of marking important graves with elaborately decorated pots up to 1·5 m high, a tradition which shows the desire for an impressive and (as far as possible) lasting memorial.[2] At about the same time there was a marked growth of interest in the heroic past of Greece. The *Iliad* and the *Odyssey* were composed; legendary scenes were probably depicted on pottery; and hero cults were established at many Bronze Age tombs and settlements.[3] An interest in the remains of the past might well have inspired the people of the late eighth century to emulate the architectural achievements of the Bronze Age—the corbelled vaults of the circular *tholos* tombs and the regular megalithic masonry (cf. fig. 9). But there were serious difficulties in following these heroic precedents. The palaces and settlements of the Bronze Age were, with a few possible exceptions, ruins which the Greeks of the eighth century, hardly experts in archaeological interpretation, would find difficult to understand,[4] while the great tombs, which could be more readily appreciated, had no place in the religious and social conditions of the time. Thus the remains of Bronze Age architecture could not really supply helpful models for the eighth-century architects to follow. But there was an even more serious problem. The monumental architecture of the Bronze Age was a tradition dead for three centuries and more. However inspiring these ruins might be, there was no means of knowing how they had been made. What tools would be required? How were the huge blocks moved and put into place? Was it simply that the men of old could lift easily what two men of later times could barely lever from the ground,[5] so that two of them could raise the huge stones used in Bronze Age tombs and fortifications?

Thus although there are some signs of a desire for monumental architecture in the eighth century, the desire could not easily be fulfilled. The best example of the growing architectural ambition is the first temple of Hera at Samos, built probably in the first half of the eighth century (fig. 4).[6] It was over a hundred feet long, but consisted simply of a narrow hall open at one end, with a row of posts down the middle to support a thatched or a flat clay roof. The base for the cult statue (the shelter of which was one of the main functions of a normal Greek temple) had therefore to be displaced to one side. Some time afterwards a portico of wooden posts was added round all four sides of the original hall, each post standing on a roughly circular stone base. This surrounding portico, perhaps the earliest one known, is of great significance from the point of view of design, since it is the forerunner of the porticoes of stone columns which form the most impressive and characteristic element of later Greek temples. The portico does not appear to have any structural value, and with a depth of only 1·30 m it could not provide much useful shelter for visiting pilgrims; nor could it have had much religious significance to an eighth-century Greek. Perhaps it was inspired by the frequent mention of porticoes in epic descriptions of palaces, for although the actual Bronze Age palaces, from which those descriptions had been derived, used porticoes in quite a different way, Samos was far away from those palaces both in time and space, so that a misinterpretation would be easy.[7]

In spite of its size and its portico, however, this temple was technically similar to other buildings of the period. The walls were of coursed masonry, but the faces were not smoothly dressed, and the joints were tight only at the faces; the walls were built up of two distinct skins of stones with

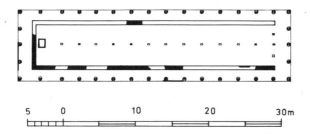

4   First temple of Hera at Samos (early eighth century): restored plan

little binding. Neither posts nor roof were of durable materials. The delay in outgrowing these technical limitations is illustrated by the second temple of Hera at the same site (fig. 5), built a century or so later, in the mid seventh century.[8] The surrounding portico was included from the start, and the awkward central row of columns was omitted, but although the walls were more smoothly dressed and their courses more regular,[9] they still consisted of two skins, with joints tight only at the faces (plate 3); the colonnade was still of wooden posts; and the roof was still of thatch or clay. In fact in all buildings before the seventh century roofs were of thatch or clay,[10] supported, where necessary, on simple wooden posts. The stones were small enough to be manœuvred into position by hand, sometimes with the aid of a crowbar,[11] and the working of stone was normally limited to the improvement of jointing at the wall faces and the production of roughly formed cylindrical post bases, all of which could be done with a mason's pick-hammer. More regular ashlars were used in parts of the ninth-century fortifications of Smyrna, but it is noteworthy that they were sawn to shape like Mycenaean masonry, not chisel-dressed like later Greek work.[12]

This lack of technical development is rather surprising, for Greece was by no means isolated or stagnant during this period. By the early eighth century there was a Greek trading settlement in north Syria, and shortly afterwards a Greek colony was established off the west coast of Italy,[13] the first of a whole series of colonies founded in the later eighth and seventh centuries on the coast of Sicily and south Italy. Levantine art was already influencing Greek pottery and metalwork in the eighth century,[14] but although there is some evidence of Near Eastern influence on Greek architecture, it does not seem to have been effective before the late seventh century, by which time Greek architecture was well on the way to being monumental. The reason is presumably that the architecture of that area did not impress the Greeks or provide them with the sort of models they could use; nor was it an all stone architecture as Greek architecture was later to become.

One explanation for this delay, followed by rapid development in the later seventh century, is that the Greeks reacted to the stimulus and technical skill of Egyptian architecture. In about 660 B.C. the Egyptian king (or pharaoh) Psamtik I, known to the Greeks as Psammetichos, gained control of his country from the Assyrians with the help of Ionian and Carian mercenaries. From then on there was close contact between Greece and Egypt, with Greek finds at the trading town of Naukratis (western Egypt) going back at least to 620 B.C.[15] Thus from the mid seventh century onwards, the Greeks could have seen the massive works of pharaonic architecture in dressed stone, and, more important, they could have learnt from the busy architectural programmes of Psamtik and his successors how such buildings were put up.[16]

Certainly Egyptian architecture would have provided the best model for

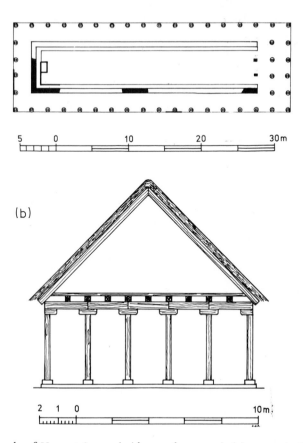

5 Second temple of Hera at Samos (mid seventh century): (a) restored plan; (b) hypothetical elevation

what Greek architecture later became, since both depend on accurately cut megalithic masonry, and although the details differ, there is a considerable similarity in proportion and general effect between an early Doric colonnade and some Egyptian ones: in both cases stone columns about six diameters high, crowned with a square abacus, carry a smooth architrave roughly square in section, above which rises a further vertical face ending in a strong projection (cf. plate 4).[17] A Greek could even see how these effects might be applied to the type of temple already developed in Greece, for although major Egyptian temples were quite different, there are several small Egyptian shrines which consist of a walled inner hall surrounded by a portico of columns or square pillars.[18]

The rapid development of a monumental sculpture in Greece from the mid seventh century onwards has often been explained in similar terms,[19]

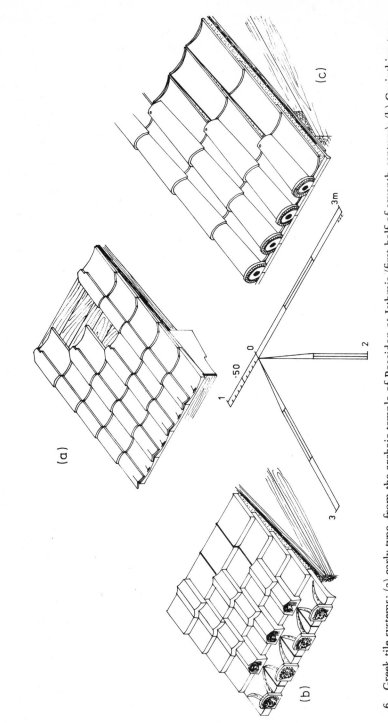

(a)

(b)

(c)

.50

0

1

2

3

3m

6 Greek tile systems: (a) early type, from the archaic temple of Poseidon at Isthmia (first half of seventh century); (b) Corinthian type, from the temple of Apollo at Thermon (c. 630 B.C.); (c) Lakonian type, from the temple of Hera at Olympia (c. 600 B.C.)

and the two arts demand many of the same skills and often occur together.[20] In architecture, however, some important initial steps may have been taken earlier. Both archaeology and literary tradition[21] suggest that monumental architecture began in the northeast Peloponnese (Corinthia and the Argolid). Seventh-century temples at Corinth and nearby Isthmia[22] had tiled roofs and walls built partly at least of carefully dressed ashlar masonry, and other early remains have been found at Tiryns, Mycenae and the Argive Heraion.[23] These last are not securely dated, but the temples at Corinth and Isthmia are both said to belong early in the century. Full supporting evidence has not yet been published, but if so, important stone-working techniques, such as the ability to quarry stones to a specific size, and to work them to a regular rectangular shape, must antedate contact with Egypt, and may have been developed independently in Greece.[24]

Apart from their use of squared stone blocks, the technique of these two temples does not resemble anything outside Greece. The blocks are quite small, and have rope-grooves cut down each end and across the bottom to help lift and manœuvre them, a feature with no obvious source inside or outside Greece, and used in no later Greek building. The use of tiles is also remarkable, for there is no immediate precedent in or out of Greece. The tiles at Corinth and Isthmia must nevertheless be some steps away from the start of the technique. For Greek roof tiles were normally of two types: roughly flat pan-tiles which formed the main roof covering, and narrower cover-tiles which protected the joints between rows of pan-tiles (fig. 6b, c). In these early sets,[25] however, the pan-tiles and cover-tiles, although conceived as distinct elements, are made in one piece (fig. 6a); there are also special tiles for the eaves, ridge and hips of the roof.

Flat roof tiles of terracotta and of schist, used like slates, have been found in some Early Bronze Age buildings,[26] and more elaborately shaped tiles were perhaps used in the Late Bronze Age.[27] But tiled roofs can never have been normal at any time in the Bronze Age, and there is no sign of tile manufacture in the four centuries between 1100 and 700 B.C.; and since by 700 B.C. any Bronze Age tiled roofs would have collapsed, it would be hard for seventh-century builders to draw inspiration from that source. Tiled roofs depended on the technique of mass-producing clay objects in moulds, which was introduced into Greece from the Levant in about 700 B.C.[28] But there were no tiled roofs in the Levant, and the idea was probably an original Greek invention (or re-invention).[29] Tiles, of course, formed a more permanent roof than thatch or clay, and at the same time they not only allowed, but encouraged the characteristically Greek low-pitched pediment, for Greek tiles were not normally fastened to the roof, but were kept in place by their weight, sometimes with a clay bedding, so they would not stay in position on a steep roof.

Virtually nothing of the early temple at Isthmia was found in situ, and some features of its plan are uncertain. It seems to have had a surrounding portico, like the temples at Samos, but the form given to its colonnade is

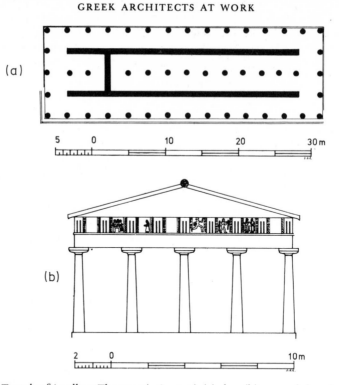

7   Temple of Apollo at Thermon (*c.* 630 B.C.): (a) plan; (b) restored elevation

unknown. In about 630 B.C., however, a temple at Thermon in Aitolia (north-west Greece) was built under Corinthian influence (fig. 7), and this preserves rather more evidence of its outward appearance.[30] Here again there was a long, narrow hall, surrounded by a portico (in this case with 5 × 15 columns), and in general arrangement the chief development from the earlier temples is the false porch at the rear; this rear porch (*opisthodomos*) is a feature of almost all later Greek temples, and makes the rear façade of the inner building exactly the same as the front façade, so that even within the outer portico there is no obvious frontal emphasis in the design.

The columns of the temple originally stood on separate stone blocks, which were much later joined up to make a continuous platform. No remains of the columns were found, so they were probably wooden. But the diameter and spacing are indicated by the slightly raised area about 0·65 m in diameter on the stone base block where each column stood. Such large columns can hardly be justified on structural grounds, since the column spacing was only 2·70 m on the ends (2·80 m along the flanks). Compare these proportions with those of the two temples at Samos, where the spacing was about the same, about 2·50 m, but the supports were only about 0·35 m thick.

The beams carried by these columns were probably also wooden, but remains have survived of a frieze which probably ran above them. The excavators found a number of painted terracotta slabs about 0·88 m high and 0·99 m wide, which probably belonged to a frieze of alternating square panels (metopes) and grooved triglyphs such as is found in later stone architecture. The triglyphs were not found, but fragments have been found at Thermon of rather later triglyphs made also of terracotta.[31] Above the frieze came a simple terracotta cornice of considerable projection, and then a tiled roof, elaborately decorated (fig. 6b). The columns, the painted frieze and the ornamented roof all show that the architect here was aiming at something more than mere structural efficiency, and although the temple at Isthmia *may* have been similar, there is a strong contrast with the earlier temples at Samos.

At this stage in fact it first becomes reasonable to speak in terms of the Greek orders—that is, the conventional decorative systems which characterize later Greek and Roman architecture. The metopes at Thermon provide some of the earliest evidence for the development of the Doric order, which dominated mainland Greece for the next five hundred years or more. East of the Aegaean the development of monumental architecture seems to have been roughly similar; large dressed stone blocks and carved stone decoration appear in the late seventh and early sixth centuries B.C., and terracotta is an important decorative material in the early stages. But the details of the story are different, and the Ionic order, which dominated the eastern Aegaean area, seems to have crystallized as a fixed conventional system fifty to eighty years later than the formation of the Doric order.[32] The dating of the various stages is also rather clearer in mainland Greece, so that the remainder of this chapter will deal only with the Doric order.

The origins of the Doric order have been much argued over. The most widespread theory is that it represents the translation into stone of traditional forms in wood which derived naturally from the wooden structure. Thus Vitruvius explained the triglyphs of the Doric frieze as representing the ends of the main roof beams and the slab-like mutules of the cornice as representing the rafters.[33] There is a wide variety of explanations of this sort covering more or less every detail of the Doric order, but they all seem to be open to a number of objections. First, although no doubt all the proposed archetypal Doric orders could be built out of wood in the way suggested, none of them seems to arise naturally out of the simple wooden structures of a primitive society. They involve beams carefully sawn to shape—often apparently specially sawn into two pieces so that they can be joined together again by the thin planks necessary to explain other features of the system. Yet one would expect primitive builders to be as sparing as possible with the saw.[34] Secondly the proportions of the Doric order as reconstructed in supposed wooden prototypes are still monumental proportions. Compare, for example, the suggested restoration of the temple of Apollo at Thermon (fig. 7b), which

8   Model of temple or house from Perachora (*c.* 750–725 B.C.): restored drawing

embodies the sort of proportions one must give to a wooden Doric
prototype, with a restoration of the second temple of Hera at Samos (fig.
5b), where the size and spacing of the posts are indicated by the surviving
remains and the drawing shows the sort of proportions natural in a simple
wooden post-and-lintel structure.[35] Yet there is no indication of such
intentionally monumental construction much before the mid seventh
century.[36] Thirdly, the forms making up the Doric order appear ready
developed. Early Doric architecture is not as consistent and rigid as it
became later, but the 'correct' forms appear to be at least as early as the
variations, and the earliest surviving examples of each element are
immediately recognizable for what they are. Yet earlier clay models of
houses and temples show no more indications of the Doric order than any

other primitive building would (for example, fig. 8). The earliest vase-painting to show (apparently) Doric columns also dates from the mid seventh century.[37]

The evidence seems to suggest, therefore, that the Doric order was not the result of a slow development, and there is no reason to believe that it represents a coherent structural system in any material. Rather it was the invention of a builder or a number of builders in the north-east Peloponnese who, around the middle of the seventh century, were trying to create a monumental style in architecture.[38] We need not believe that all their inspiration came from a single source, and indeed it would obviously be misguided to be too categorical about what in fact inspired the invention, for we are dealing with the psychology of anonymous men dead for two and a half thousand years. But we can point to certain sources which would have been available to Greeks of this period, and which may well have been influential.

The early Doric capital, for instance, finds close parallels in Greek architecture of the Bronze Age. As we have seen the Greeks of the seventh century B.C. were very conscious of their heroic past, and one of the monuments surviving from it which Corinthian and Argive builders could certainly have seen is the Lion Gate at Mycenae;[39] above the gateway there is a triangular slab carved with two lions rampant and between them a column with a capital quite similar in shape to an early Doric one. Even more similar were the capitals of the half-columns flanking the door of the Treasury of Atreus (fig. 9), a massive corbelled tomb of the late fourteenth century B.C., for like many early Doric capitals these had a ring of leaf ornament round the neck. But although the Treasury of Atreus would have been known to the people of the seventh century, and is still substantially intact today, its decorative façade was found in fragments in the nineteenth century and it is not so certain that a recognizable capital could have been seen in the seventh century.[40]

The façade of another such tomb had fluted half-columns flanking its door and could have inspired the fluting typical of Greek columns.[41] It is again uncertain that they were visible in the seventh century, however, and functional column shafts in Greek Bronze Age architecture were wooden,[42] and so would not have survived to the seventh century to provide a model. In fact Doric columns taper upwards like Egyptian columns, not downwards like those of the Bronze Age, and the number of flutes in most early Doric columns is sixteen,[43] an easy number to produce, but also the number commonly used in Egypt.[44]

The Doric architrave, roughly square in section, and crowned by a continuous projecting band (laenia), also has parallels in Egypt, although strictly the projecting band there belongs to the cornice. However, the peg-like projections on the Doric architrave (and also the cornice) have no precedents in Egypt or Bronze Age Greece, and are probably derived from functional pegs in wooden construction, although that need not mean that

9   'Treasury of Atreus' at Mycenae (*c.* 1300 B.C.): restored elevation of façade

such pegs appeared in primitive architecture in those particular positions. Similarly the alternating frieze of triglyphs and metopes may have been placed so as to be reminiscent of a wooden structure with repeated beam ends; but it cannot be taken as a literal translation from wood, as Vitruvius suggests,[45] for the beams implied are too massive, and the ceiling level too low.

The earliest surviving Doric friezes all have decorated metope slabs, and from the first the intention may have been decorative, similar in its organization to the panelled decoration on slightly earlier Greek pottery.[46] The idea of using painted terracotta slabs may have been taken from Assyria, where this Mesopotamian technique had been adopted.[47] The split rosette frieze common in Bronze Age architecture shows some similarities to the triglyph frieze,[48] but the closest formal precedent to the latter occurs on a sarcophagus from Egypt made in the late thirteenth century and re-used in the eleventh; along the sides slightly projecting grooved members alternate with flat panels carved with hieroglyphics, the whole forming a simplified and perhaps imperfectly understood version of a common Old Kingdom sarcophagus type. This particular sarcophagus can hardly have been visible at the appropriate time, but other versions of the same motif occur on later sarcophagi.[49] At all events, in looking for the origins of the Doric frieze, we may well have to take into account quite different explanations for its position, its intention, its material and its form.

The earliest tiled roofs were without ornament, but in the temple of Apollo at Thermon the eaves were decorated with modelled and painted heads of women and lions (fig. 6b), and there was a large disc with a gorgon's head masking the end of the ridge pole at the apex of the roof.[50] Later these decorative roof terracottas became even more complex. In mainland Greece they reached their greatest elaboration in the late seventh and early sixth centuries, but for long after that rich terracotta embellishments were popular in Sicily, south Italy and Etruria; even in mainland Greece the eaves and ridge were usually given some sort of decorative treatment.[51]

It is interesting that the first new material to which Greek builders turned in their search for a more monumental mode of expression was terracotta, for it was a material with which the Greeks were already extremely proficient, able to produce large, colourful and crisply shaped objects.[52] The use of terracotta was thus a very natural reaction from builders not yet familiar with monumental techniques, but trying to achieve monumental effects. The most long-lasting aspect of this experimentation with terracotta was the adoption of tiled roofs; terracotta friezes and other architectural elements went out of fashion when dressed stone came into use for the entire structure of a temple, but although marble tiles were used on some particularly prestigious buildings, terracotta tiles remained the normal roofing material throughout antiquity (fig. 6b, c; cf. Fig. 15).

(a)

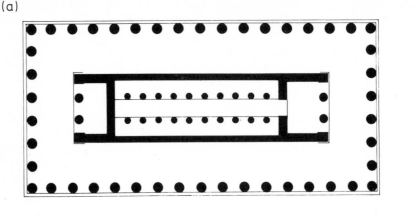

(b)

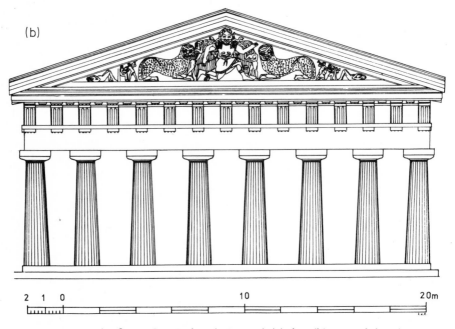

10   Temple of Artemis at Kerkyra (*c*. 600 B.C.): (a) plan; (b) restored elevation

The first steps towards a monumental architecture seem therefore to
have been taken largely by using techniques already available in Greece.
Whether or not the example of Egypt provided the initial stimulus for this
process, it must surely have assisted it, for even in the fifth century
Herodotos found Egyptian architecture extremely impressive. Greek

architectural techniques were most similar to Egyptian in the late seventh and early sixth centuries, when accurately cut masonry replaced wood and terracotta almost entirely; but that is no argument against the earlier importance of Egypt, for it would naturally have taken the Greeks some time to recognize and learn the relevant skills. There was probably a considerable period when they regarded Egypt as a useful source of ideas and information in this as in other fields.[53]

The last stages of the transition are illustrated by the temples of Hera at Olympia and Artemis at Kerkyra, both built around 600 B.C. (figs. 10, 11).[54] At Olympia the upper parts of the building were of wood and mud brick, and are lost, but the platform and lower walls are remarkably well preserved. At Kerkyra on the other hand the platform and walls have disappeared almost entirely, but the upper parts are well represented, and show that the whole building was of stone. Both buildings are considerably bigger than anything that had gone before, covering an area of about 1000 square metres—that is, about twice the area of the second temple of Hera at Samos or the temple of Apollo at Thermon. The inner nucleus of each consists of a rectangular hall (cella), with a porch in front (pronaos) and a matching false porch behind (the opisthodomos); and all round this inner building runs a portico of substantial columns.

There is no doubt that in the portico of the temple of Artemis at Kerkyra the Doric order appeared in its full form. Enough has survived to show that there were fluted columns carrying Doric capitals of the normal early type, an architrave crowned by the usual Doric details, a frieze of grooved triglyphs and plain metopes, and a projecting cornice decorated with the plank-like mutules and pegs. The differences between this and later examples of the order consist almost entirely of changes in the various proportions to produce a more harmonious effect (cf. figs. 11, 25, 29, 46). Above the cornice of the temple of Artemis came the tiled roof with its elaborately painted and moulded terracotta decoration, but the crowning glory of the temple was its sculptured pediment. The low triangle formed by the gable was filled with relief sculpture, the greater part of which consisted of a running gorgon 2·79 m high, flanked by two panthers; all three fierce faces turn towards whoever approaches the temple and the purpose of the sculpture was not just decorative but to frighten off evil influences as well.

The temple of Hera at Olympia had roof terracottas as elaborate as those at Kerkyra (fig. 6c), but there was no sculptured pediment. So too although the platform and lower walls of the temple were of dressed stone, the columns were apparently wooden and the upper walls mud brick. The limited use of dressed stone was probably a matter of economics rather than of date, however; the development of monumental architecture in Greece was not precisely like a dose of hemlock, producing a slow petrifaction that worked steadily up from the ground, and there is no doubt that the architect of the temple of Hera was master of the new

(a)

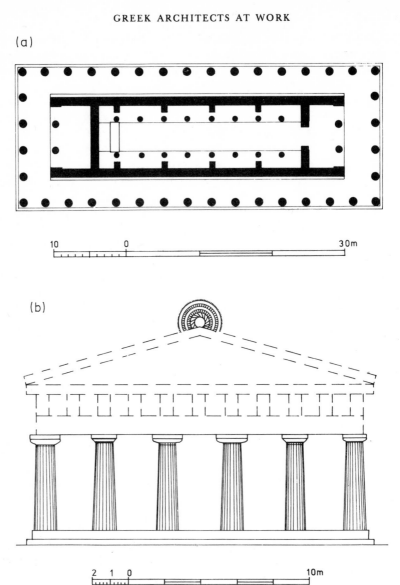

(b)

11 Temple of Hera at Olympia (*c.* 600 B.C.): (a) plan; (b) restored elevation

techniques demanded by building in dressed stone. Nor is there any doubt that he was aiming at a monumental effect, for the diameter of the columns varied from 1·0 m to 1·28 m for a span of about 3·56 or 3·26 m. The upper parts of the temple are lost, but the stone columns which, quite soon after the construction of the temple, were gradually put in to replace the wooden ones, are of normal Doric form,[55] and the fact that the space between the corner columns and their neighbours is less than that between the other columns suggests that there was also a Doric frieze, for such a reduction in the column spacing at the angles was normal in mainland Doric temples (cf. pp. 60-2).

Even if there was already a Doric frieze, and perhaps also other features of the Doric order, in the temple of Apollo at Thermon it is not so much the form of these two early-sixth-century temples that shows a break with the past; it is rather the techniques of construction, and it may be of value to look briefly at the operations required in the construction of an early Doric temple,[56] and to see how far they raised new problems for Greek builders, and where the solutions to them may have been learnt.

Megalithic masonry in dressed stone, as practised by the Greeks, requires the production of stone blocks to specific sizes. It would be hopelessly uneconomic to deliver to the site all the stone in blocks of the largest size that the building required (usually the architrave blocks), yet there were some positions where nothing smaller would do. No quarry workings datable between 1100 and 700 B.C. have been recognized in Greece, but the stones used in buildings of that period suggest that there was no attempt to quarry blocks directly to a specific size or shape, and few blocks, if any, of a specific size and shape would be needed.[57] Some attempt was presumably made to produce roughly suitable sizes, but the control cannot have been close; the shapes probably depended mainly on the way the stone broke, so that different kinds of rock would produce walls with very different appearances.[58] At least from the later sixth century, Greek quarries worked to a very different system. Blocks were cut from the quarry to suit the size ordered by the builders, and even column drums were sometimes quarried in already cylindrical form. A channel was cut round the block required to a depth equal to the desired block height; the block was then detached from its bed with wedges.[59] Egyptian quarries were worked in the same way,[60] but the technique may well have been learnt elsewhere, for it had spread to other parts of the Near East too,[61] and would probably have been adopted by the Corinthians for the ashlar masonry of the early temples at Corinth and Isthmia.

No block from these temples weighs more than 500 kg but by the end of the seventh century the Greeks were handling blocks of up to 40 tons, raising quite new difficulties. The Egyptians of the third and second millennia B.C. used sledges on rollers rather than waggons on wheels for overland transport of heavy blocks, and so too did the Assyrians.[62] But by the fifth century at least, the Greeks normally used waggons.[63] Indeed four-wheeled waggons had been known from at least the ninth century B.C.;[64] and that is how Homer expected a heavy stone to be transported, although he was clearly unfamiliar with the handling of colossal blocks.[65] Sledges and rollers were certainly used sometimes,[66] and some of the blocks used in the sixth century, weighing well over twenty tons, would probably have been beyond the powers of a waggon; but the special devices described by

Vitruvius for moving such blocks seem to derive from the waggon principle rather than the sledge and rollers.[67]

The change to an architecture of dressed stone would also make new demands on the accuracy of measurement and levelling. It is difficult to test the accuracy with which builders of the ninth and eighth centuries worked, for their buildings are often badly preserved, and in many cases it cannot be taken as axiomatic that they were aiming at regularity, that they were really trying to make all angles right angles and all pairs of opposite sides equal.[68] Certainly a high degree of accuracy does not seem to be basic to the kind of effect created by premonumental architecture, and would be wasted in materials such as rubble masonry and mud brick. On the other hand, the sharp lines of dressed stonework make accuracy and regularity aesthetically desirable, and regularity was certainly an aim of later architects (cf. pp. 97–8). In the temple of Hera at Olympia no irregularities in the shape of the rectangular platform were noticed by the excavators, but in the temple of Artemis at Kerkyra the foundation trench (virtually all that is left of the platform and walls) is about 0·30 m wider at the east end than at the west. Very considerable irregularities occur in the column spacing of the temple of Hera, and there are rather smaller variations between the surviving triglyphs and metopes of the temple of Artemis. But in spite of these irregularities the accuracy of laying out in sixth-century Greek architecture is high, and suggests that measuring-rods rather than cords were used for setting out distances; for shorter measurements quite finely divided rules were known both in Egypt and Mesopotamia, but no Greek measuring instrument has survived.[69]

The Egyptians probably obtained levels over a large area by flooding it with water and working from the water level, but they also used an instrument consisting of an A-shaped frame with a plumb-line hung from the apex; the line would coincide with a mark on the cross-bar when the two feet were on a horizontal surface.[70] Flooding a site with water would have been impracticable in Greece, and was not apparently tried, but the A-shaped level was used, both for testing the level of a single block (for which it is best suited) and also for testing extensive surfaces.[71]

Greater precision would also be needed in setting out and working to shape the individual blocks of a structure, now that the blocks ran from side to side of the wall. For that the builders would also need to use, and to use with great accuracy, the mason's square. This they must already have learnt by the time of the early temples at Corinth and Isthmia, however, and in any case it was probably a matter of refining a well-known technique, not learning a new one.

In normal Greek masonry, only the horizontal joint faces are dressed to a plane, while the vertical faces have the centre part worked back more or less roughly so that only a comparatively narrow band round the sides and top of each face makes contact with the next block (fig. 12c).[72] This treatment of the vertical joint faces, called *anathyrosis* because the effect is something like the frame of a door (*thyra*), is found in the earliest Greek monumental architecture, including the temples of Hera at Olympia and Artemis at Kerkyra, but it does not occur in Egypt or the Bronze Age architecture of Greece. In Egypt both horizontal and vertical joint faces were normally dressed accurately to a plane, so that adjacent blocks made contact over the whole of each joint face. In Bronze Age Greece on the other hand (as also in premonumental Greek architecture and that of the Near East) walls were commonly made up of two skins of masonry with the joints tight only at the visible faces.[73]

In some early instances of *anathyrosis* the vertical joint faces met only at the edges, with the rest of the face roughly concave.[74] This is as if the old technique used in two-skinned walls were being applied to monumental architecture, where the blocks ran right through from side to side of the wall; each single block was simply treated like the two separate blocks of the old type of wall. However, this method meant that any dressing of the wall faces after the blocks were laid would tend to destroy the quality of the joints by removing the only part of the blocks which actually made contact; thus it was obviously better to have the joints making contact over a band round each joint face, not just at the extreme edges—in fact, the normal technique of *anathyrosis* (fig. 12c). The final dressing would then remove only part of the contact band. Edge *anathyrosis*, as we may call it, thus forms a natural and reasonable transitional stage between the premonumental methods and the normal band *anathyrosis*, but it was not a necessary one.

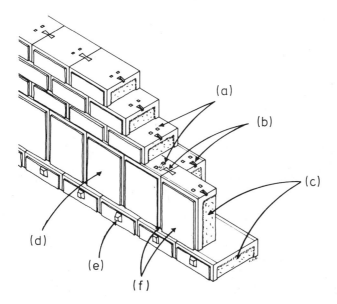

12   Features of early Greek monumental masonry: (a) U-shaped hole; (b) dove-tail clamp; (c) band anathyrosis; (d) orthostate; (e) handling boss; (f) preliminary dressing

Already in the mid seventh century column bases were cut with a horizontal joint face consisting of a smooth band surrounding a slightly sunken central area.[75]

The joint faces were normally prepared before the blocks were raised into position, so that the next problem would be to lift the new heavy architectural elements. The rapid increase in the weights handled would present new problems to the Greeks in lifting just as it did in horizontal transport (cf. pp. 45–6). Although some lifting of heavy stones was done by the Assyrians and their neighbours, it was rarely to the top of a building. The most obvious source of expertise was therefore again Egypt, with its all-stone architecture.[76] The favourite Egyptian method was to build temporary ramps of earth up which the stones could be dragged on rollers to the required level; when one course was completed the ramp would simply be raised to the level of the next one. During the sixth century this method was certainly used sometimes in Greece[77] and was probably normal for heavy blocks. It was probably not until the end of the century that the Greeks began to use pulleys and winches for heavy lifting, but another Egyptian device, a sort of rocking sledge, may have been used. If a block of stone was loaded onto such a rocker, and wooden beams of suitable size were placed under alternate ends of it, then, as it was rocked backwards and forwards, rocker and stone would gradually rise.[78] But the use of the rocker for lifting building blocks is uncertain, and since it would leave no evidence, is likely to remain uncertain.

Knobs of stone left on the blocks of unfinished Greek buildings (fig. 12e) have usually been interpreted as intended to take loops of rope attached to a hoist of some sort, but their shape and position are often unsatisfactory for such an explanation, and suggest that they were left to give purchase to levers used to move the blocks firmly into position. Similar knobs are found on some Egyptian buildings, apparently for the same purpose. In many early monumental buildings (including the temples of Hera at Olympia and Artemis at Kerkyra) U-shaped holes were cut in the top of the blocks (fig. 12a). These also imply the use of levers rather than hoists, for they rarely occur over the centre of gravity of a block. Here again there are parallels in Egypt, for similar holes in heavy stone sarcophagus lids were apparently used with levers to manœuvre them into position.

The walls of the early temple at Isthmia seem to have consisted of roughly uniform courses from bottom to top, but in the temple of Hera at Olympia the lowest course of the outer wall faces consists of slabs set on edge (orthostates; cf. fig. 12d). This use of orthostates is characteristic of Greek architecture, and seems to have been borrowed from the Near East, where similar slabs, either sculptured or plain, often form a dado for walls of mud brick or rubble.[79]

In premonumental Greek architecture mud seems to have been used sometimes as a binding medium in rubble masonry walls, but in their monumental architecture the Greeks, like the Egyptians, relied on the size

1 *Above* Temple of Hephaistos at Athens (*c.* 450–445 B.C.) from the north-west

2 *Below* Stoa of Attalos at Athens (*c.* 150 B.C., rebuilt 1953–6) from the north-west

3 *Above* Masonry of the first and second temples of Hera at Samos (early eighth and mid seventh centuries)

4 *Below* Dair al-Bahri: portico of shrine of Anubis (fifteenth century)

and good jointing of the dressed stone for the stability of their buildings. The Egyptians sometimes used a thin layer of mortar not as a cement but as a lubricant to help them slide heavy blocks into place;[80] the Greeks laid their blocks absolutely dry. In certain situations, however, some more positive way of holding the blocks in position did seem desirable, and clamps of various forms were used between adjacent blocks. The Egyptians had long used dovetail clamps, shaped like a bow-tie, and examples in wood, lead, stone, and copper have been found. Once more the Greeks borrowed directly from Egypt to start with, the dovetail clamp (fig. 12b) being the commonest type in the sixth century;[81] a variant type with a hooked piece of iron leaded into the usual dovetail cutting occurs in the temple of Artemis at Kerkyra and some other sixth-century buildings, and this form has parallels in the Near East[82] rather than Egypt. As with methods of lifting stones, however, the Greeks did not remain content with a borrowed technique, and new forms of iron clamp were in common use by the end of the century.

The last, and perhaps the most striking, similarity between the techniques of Greek and Egyptian architecture is the finishing process. Both Greek and Egyptian builders wanted their finished walls to present a smooth regular surface, with the face of each block in the same plane; and the columns, although built out of a number of separate blocks, should have an unbroken outline from top to bottom of the shaft. But how could this be achieved if the blocks were laid completely finished? For without the slight scope for adjustment which mortared joints provide, small but noticeable irregularities would be bound to occur. This problem simply did not arise in most premonumental architecture; the solution adopted by later Greek architects was the same as that used in Egypt, and since it is not an unavoidable way of building in stone, they presumably learnt it there. The separate blocks of platform, wall or column were laid with a small allowance of extra stone all round. The surfaces were then dressed only to the extent that was required for the setting of the following course; elsewhere narrow strips were dressed to the intended surface to provide points of reference for measuring and levelling (fig. 12f), and only when the building was finished was the whole of each wall face or each column dressed down as a single entity.[83] This procedure had the added advantage that any wear or slight damage to exposed faces during the course of construction would affect only the mantle of extra stone, and would disappear when the final dressing down was done.

It will be obvious how much the importance of Egypt to monumental architecture in Greece depends on the form and dating of the early temples at Corinth and Isthmia (p. 35). If they were built in the early seventh century and included some of the basic forms of the Doric order, then the role of Egypt was to reinforce, and perhaps accelerate, an already active process by providing some new skills and demonstrating what could be achieved with them.[84] If these early temples did not involve Doric forms, and particularly if their dates fall after *c.* 660 B.C., the importance of Egypt was probably much greater, providing a stimulus to patrons as well as architects, and helping them to overcome the technical and formal difficulties which had delayed the development of a monumental architecture. Even in this case, however, the process was an eclectic one. At no stage was Greek architecture intended as a copy of Egyptian architecture, and several other sources of ideas were tapped. Indeed the characteristic Greek temple was devised by the Greeks themselves, and their characteristic decorative systems, even if the elements were borrowed, were equally original in their combination of them—and indeed in the whole concept of an order. It was in the technical field that the Greeks borrowed most, but even there they were selective, and by the end of the sixth century they had discarded many of the borrowed techniques in favour of their own.

3

The problem of design

In discussing the formal and technical difficulties faced by the early Greek architects, one problem was omitted which falls rather between those categories—the problem of design. A man modelling a clay figure can start from any point he chooses, can to a certain extent modify the part formed first in the light of what he does next, and can even reject the whole form and start again without much loss; a painter is in much the same position. The sculptor working in marble is rather more constrained, for a serious mistake will be both irremediable and costly, but he can work gradually into the stone over the whole of his figure, so that the relation of the parts to each other can be clearly visualized at a stage when minor changes to any of them are still possible. The architect on the other hand must always start his buildings at the bottom, and cannot modify at all what he has built first in the light of what follows. Mistakes made at the start can therefore not be corrected, and they will also be ruinously expensive, for a monumental building will occupy many men for many years. For these reasons an architect more than any other artist needs a technique of design, a technique which will allow him to visualize the finished building beforehand with sufficient accuracy to ensure that the lower parts of the building will suit the parts which are to be put upon them, and that the whole building is satisfactory in form, function and structure. Design work in a rather different sense is also needed to communicate the architect's intention to the builders, for whereas a statue can in most cases be completed by one man with his own hands, this is normally impossible in architecture.[1]

Today we take for granted the techniques of scale drawing, of plan, elevation, and section, of perspective drawing and scale model, which an architect employs before beginning to build, but even with these techniques mistakes may arise which are due to the difficulty of visualizing beforehand exactly how a complex building will function, and how it will feel to the people who use it. The Greeks were not of course born with these techniques ready formed in their minds, and they can have derived little help with the problem of design from the traditions of architecture before the seventh century. For, as we have seen, these earlier buildings were simple in structure and function; they do not seem to have involved precise formal requirements either, and would thus not need any special design

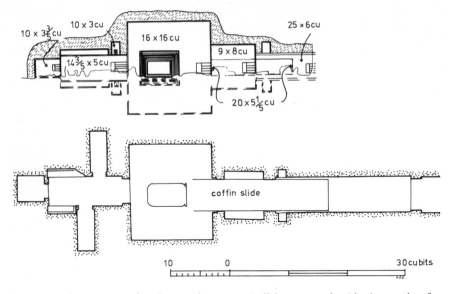

13   Turin papyrus plan (restored symmetrically) compared with the tomb of
Ramesses IV at Thebes (twelfth century)

technique. Design would, therefore, be another new problem of technique confronting the first Greek monumental architects, and they might reasonably have looked at the methods used in Egypt and the Near East, as we have suggested they did over other matters.

The idea of an architectural ground plan had certainly been developed in both Egypt and Mesopotamia, for examples have survived: two statues of Gudea of Lagash (*c.* 2200 B.C.) show him seated with a drawing table on his knees, equipped with stylus and ruler, and on one of these tables a plan is engraved (plate 5);[2] other less elaborate plans survive on clay tablets. Surviving Egyptian plans are mostly on limestone flakes,[3] but there is a papyrus plan of the tomb of Ramesses IV (twelfth century) which can be compared with the tomb as executed (fig. 13).[4] It is uncertain whether Gudea's plan was drawn accurately to scale, although his ruler is finely divided, as if for precise measurement. Similar rulers are known from Egypt,[5] but the plan of Ramesses' tomb is drawn only roughly to scale; the sizes of some rooms as drawn correspond neither with those specified in writing nor with those actually executed (cf. fig. 13 above and below). Furthermore, unlike Gudea's plan, the Egyptian plan makes no allowance for the thickness of the walls, and the intellectual clarity of the plan is confused by doors shown in elevation, as if folded down on to the floor. This combination of plan and elevation, a commonplace of Egyptian painting, was therefore not excluded from technical drawing.

Elevations are much rarer than plans, but true front and side elevations are shown in a drawing of a small Egyptian shrine, a work of carpentry rather than architecture.[6] They are drawn on squared papyrus, and this use of a square grid may have been a common tool of architectural design as it certainly was in pictorial design, since drawings of the human figure, based on a modular system of proportion, were normally set out on a grid of squares.[7] The cross-section of a house seems to be shown in the tomb of Dhutnufer at Thebes,[8] but there is no evidence of cross-sections used in a technical context.

An important limitation on architectural drawing both in Mesopotamia and Egypt is the restricted size of the drawing area. A papyrus sheet could not easily be made more than about 0·45 m square, and although several sheets were normally glued together to form rolls, the available area seems never to have been extended in both directions;[9] the papyrus for the plan of the tomb of Ramesses IV would have been about 0·45 × 1·50 m. In Mesopotamia plans were drawn on raw clay tablets,[10] for which the maximum size would be about 0·35 × 0·50 m; Gudea's drawing table is about 0·20 × 0·35 m. On this restricted drawing area a building of any size could only be drawn at a small scale, and details in plan and elevation could not effectively be shown. The constituent elements of both Egyptian and Mesopotamian architecture were conventional, but the ways in which they were grouped, often to form highly elaborate palaces and temple complexes, were not. Small scale plans, even if not minutely accurate, would therefore be of great value in organizing the various elements, in making sure that access was possible where required, and so on.

In Greek architecture, however, the whole temple plan was both simple and conventional, and the task of the architect was not to design elaborate complexes, but to refine proportions and details of form. Little help could therefore be derived from plans and elevations drawn on a limited area with instruments of limited precision, and it appears that Greek architects developed a technique of design which did not involve scale drawing. Certainly no plans or elevations of Greek architecture have survived, and there is no clear mention of them in Greek literature or building inscriptions before the Hellenistic period; nor have any instruments for technical drawing been found.[11]

In considering the problem of design we are again dealing with an archaeological problem which is by no means solved, but I have tried to set out the material for this chapter in such a way as to illustrate how, in my opinion, Greek architects faced up to a serious difficulty, rather than to argue at length for a particular viewpoint. The evidence in favour of this view will in fact emerge, but not in the order in which it would be presented for the purposes of argument. It should be remembered, however, that much of what is set out in the pages of this chapter may not be universally accepted.

The building inscriptions of the fifth and fourth centuries tell us something about the methods of design then in use, and much of this must be applicable, if in a simpler form, to the sixth century. Most of these inscriptions are specifications, contracts, and accounts, however, and deal with the construction of buildings rather than their conception; they therefore tell us more about the techniques used in communicating design than those used in creating it. Nevertheless it may be convenient to look first at this aspect of the problem before going on to see how the design was worked out. The most important element seems to have been a technical description called the *syngraphai*—specifications—which set out the general lines of the building with a good deal of detail on the way it was to be built. The information given there might be supplemented by further details in the individual contracts—also called *syngraphai*—specifying the work undertaken by each contractor.[12]

One example of the general specifications has survived almost intact, inscribed on a large marble stele. It deals with the naval arsenal built at Piraeus in about 340 B.C. by the architect Philon of Eleusis.[13] It is duly headed '*syngraphai*', and contains a clear general explanation of the design, sufficient for a fairly convincing restoration on paper (fig. 14), and detailed specifications for the lower parts, and it ends with general conditions for the contractors. Some crucial details are not given, however (for instance, the arrangement of the Doric frieze and the spacing of the inner columns), so that it does not give full instructions for the builders, and some clauses explain the design as well as specifying it; for instance the columns are to be placed so as to 'leave a twenty-foot wide passage for the public through the middle of the arsenal'. Such explanations would concern the clients—the Athenian people—rather than the builders, yet there is far too much technical detail for this to be simply a proposal put to the Athenian assembly. It seems in fact that no rigid distinction was made between the functions of a design; for the builders this description contained enough information to allow detailed contracts for the initial stages to be written and agreed; for the public it contained a coherent account of the form of

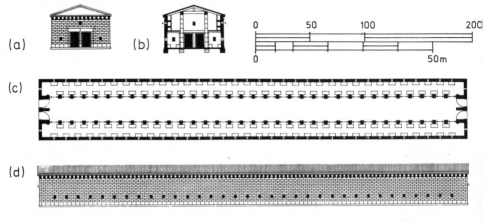

14   Arsenal of Philon at Piraeus restored (*c*. 340 B.C.): (a) front elevation; (b) cross-section; (c) plan; (d) side elevation

the building, with some explanation of its special features; and for the architect it probably served as an effective record of his ideas on the building so far. It was in fact simply 'the design'.

The Prostoon Inscription from Eleusis,[14] slightly earlier in date and less well preserved, gives a good idea of the terms of the individual contracts into which the general specification would be broken down. This time there is no indication of the general nature of the building, and the contracts are arranged according to the quarries from which the stone is to be taken. For each group of stones quarrying, transport, and dressing and setting are normally listed separately, with much repetition. A sample clause runs thus:

Stones to be quarried of Pentelic marble, length 17 feet, width 2 feet, thickness 1½ feet, to be trimmed straight and square on all sides and handed over for loading sound, white and unstained, and with appropriate surplus: in number 8. Stones to be transported from Pentelikon to Eleusis, length 17 feet, width 2 feet, thickness 1½ feet, and to be unloaded in the sanctuary sound and unbroken; in number 8. Eight Pentelic stones to be dressed, length 17 feet, width 2 feet, thickness 1½ feet, straight and square on all sides, and to be rubbed smooth, and to be hoisted and set on both of the thresholds, the joints being made tight and unbroken, and to be clamped and leaded, and to be dressed true on top.

As already mentioned, there is no reference to drawings, plans or elevations in *syngraphai* of either type; one might particularly have expected them in the Arsenal Inscription, for the arsenal did not follow a closely defined convention. The necessary detail is instead conveyed mainly by measurements and by technical terms such as 'triglyph' or 'Ionic cornice'. The architect himself was also available on the site to explain what he intended and to set out the necessary lines;[15] but where special detail was required, the architect would supply a *paradeigma* or an *anagrapheus*.

The meaning of *paradeigma* is clear—a specimen or example—but there has been argument over *anagrapheus*. *Grapho* in Greek can mean either 'write' or 'draw', and its compounds carry the same ambiguity; so *anagrapheus* could, it is argued, mean either a description or a delineation. The evidence suggests, however, that it meant a template, used particularly for blocks with complex mouldings which could be specified by a two-dimensional profile.[16] The *paradeigma* on the other hand was used for elements like triglyphs or capitals which required a design in three dimensions, and in cases where carved or painted decoration had to be shown. These specimens were often made of wood, stucco, or clay, even where they were to be copied in more permanent materials;[17] but in at least one case the material was stone, for the specimen capital was to be set in place in the actual building, along with the others.[18] In this case the specimen must obviously have been full size, and that is likely to have been normal, for the use of full-size specimens would be the easiest way of ensuring the uniformity which is so important to the effect of a Greek building. The

(a) Plan

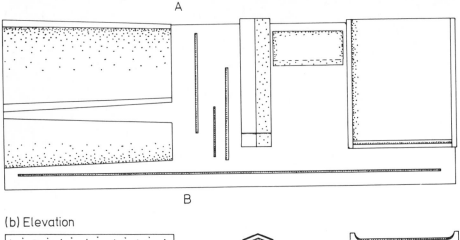

(b) Elevation

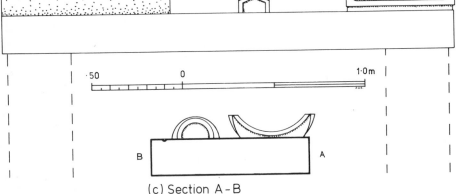

(c) Section A - B

15   Tile standard from Assos with Lakonian tiles to left and Corinthian tiles to right:
(a) plan; (b) elevation; (c) section

working masons could take whatever measurements they required directly with callipers, so avoiding any problems produced by coarsely divided or inaccurately standardized rulers.[19]

Both the nature of these specimens and the need for them are illustrated by the stone tile standards which have been found in three Greek cities (fig. 15).[20] One might have expected a written specification giving the essential dimensions, so that doubtful tiles could be measured at the works or on the site; instead full-size marble replicas of the normal tile types were set up at some central point, and the tiles would have to be brought to the standard, where they could be checked directly.

The use of full-size specimens in this way raises a question of the architect's responsibility for the design. There is evidence of specimens not made by the architect,[21] but none of specimens made by him (as one might expect if he was by training a craftsman); since questions of detail are so important to Greek architecture, does this not mean that the craftsmen who made the specimens were the real designers? The specimens certainly not made by the architect, however, are all of minor decorative details; there is no evidence of who made the architecturally important specimens such as capitals and triglyphs. Architects who were also sculptors, like Skopas of Paros, obviously could have made such specimens themselves, but did they? There is nothing Parian about Skopas' temple at Tegea,[22] and some of the forms of the Parthenon resemble those of the Propylaia (the work of a different architect, but probably built by the same workmen) much more closely than those of the temple of Apollo at Bassai (a work attributed to the architect of the Parthenon, but surely built by different workmen).[23] The responsibility for supplying specimens was the architect's, however, and as the man in charge of construction he would naturally approve, or even initiate, innovations, although he might not impose his own local style on another area. At the least, the architect must have determined the dimensions, probably also the proportions, of the part in question, so that it would fit its place in the whole building.

With one exception references to a *paradeigma* before the Hellenistic period involve only a single element or detail, and this is true also of the *anagrapheus*—naturally enough if it was really a template. The exception is not in an official inscription but in the passage of Herodotos discussed on p. 22 in which he remarks that the Alkmaionidai, in the late sixth century, made the temple of Apollo at Delphi better than the *paradeigma*.[24] This suggests that there was a scale model of the building as a whole. The most important change, however, was the change from limestone to marble, and since the material to be used could more easily be specified in words than by a model, Herodotos was probably using the word loosely and meant specification when he said specimen. For the word *paradeigma* does not carry the implications of small scale that model often carries in English, and there is no clear evidence that the concept of working to scale was current in Greece before the Hellenistic period.[25]

The procedure outlined above for transmitting design to the builders is based essentially on fourth-century documents. The more fragmentary evidence for the fifth century does not imply any major differences, but can the same procedure be presumed for the sixth and even seventh centuries? The use of specimens and templates is probably the simplest way of achieving the effect of uniformity which was already characteristic of sixth-century architecture, and so is likely to go back to an early period. Equally some form of specification/contract clearly underlies Herodotos' account of the Alkmaionidai at Delphi. It may well have been much simpler than Philon's description of his Arsenal, however, for if the construction of a whole temple was let as a single contract in the archaic period, as suggested on p. 22, far fewer details would need to be specified beforehand. The size, number of columns and materials would have to be set out in the contract, but the sizes of individual elements could be settled between contractor/supervisor and architect as work went on. Where we have documents, a tendency is certainly visible for later contracts between temple authorities and builders to become more detailed and restrictive,[26] so that it is reasonable to suppose that lost earlier contracts were simpler.

The use of specimens as a means of design might have been borrowed from Egypt, for there too complex capital forms are repeated many times along a colonnade; no positive evidence is known to me, however, for the use of specimens by Egyptian architects. Surviving Egyptian descriptions of buildings are boastful rather than technical, and so too are those of the Assyrian kings.[27] The closest parallels to the Greek technical descriptions are to be found in the Old Testament, where the specifications for Noah's Ark,[28] giving size, materials, construction and essential features, is much what one might expect of an early Greek specification. Hebrew culture is unlikely to have influenced Greek architecture in the seventh century directly, but both may have borrowed from a common source.

This brings us to the problem faced by an architect in the late seventh or early sixth century when required to build a stone temple of given size. If general plans and elevations drawn to scale are not mentioned in fourth-century building inscriptions, which are reasonably numerous and varied, it is unlikely that they were used then, and if they were not used in the fourth century, they can hardly have been used in the less sophisticated seventh and sixth centuries. The basic reasons for this rather surprising failure to adopt an already existing design technique have already been mentioned. The general form of a Greek temple was firmly established by convention and therefore needed no plan, while the ways in which one temple differed from others of the same period and area were subtle curvatures, slight variations in column size and spacing, small additional mouldings in new places, and so on, and the effect of these could not easily be demonstrated or appreciated at a small scale, particularly when the necessary drawing equipment was far from perfect. Scale drawings and scale models would therefore not be helpful. Indeed Greek architects normally used different proportions in buildings of different sizes (cf. pp. 86–8) and might well have found scale models positively misleading.

If the only preliminary design was a written specification with less detail than that for Philon's Arsenal, the architect would have to work out important details of the design as the building went up, and there is a fair amount of evidence that this is what happened. In the Arsenal Inscription the *paradeigma* is referred to in indefinite terms—'such *paradeigma* as the architect shall supply'—and the same is true of the specimens and templates referred to in other inscriptions.[29] Such phrases suggest that the specimens and templates did not yet exist, and we have seen (p. 27) that where a temple took a long time to complete, the parts built late are late in design. The initiating architect did not, it seems, supply a full set of specimens before construction started. Much later, Vitruvius' rules for

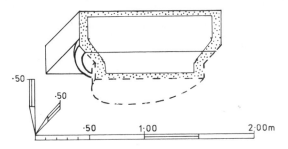

16 Temple of Hephaistos at Athens (*c.* 450–445 B.C.): roughed out Doric capital (its neck worked off before re-use), compared with finished profile (undotted): section with oblique projection

designing an Ionic colonnade suggest that each part was, or had once been, designed only after the preceding part was in place.[30]

In a Doric temple the points where the design of the upper parts is rigidly and inevitably controlled by what comes below are few, even if important. The columns do not have to be a specific height in order to allow an architrave of the desired height, nor does the architrave height predetermine the frieze height. Of course the relationship of all three controls the visual effect, but an architect wishing to change the accepted visual effect could radically alter the size and proportions of the columns, while still putting on them the normal architrave and frieze. The column height would directly affect building costs, and so might need to be decided from the start, but this is less true of other elements. The approximate size of each element would of course need to be decided a certain time before it was actually put in place, so that suitable blocks could be quarried and brought to the site. But since blocks were quarried as construction proceeded, and were always cut substantially larger than required (cf. fig. 16),[31] there was no inherent reason why the decisions on size or form need have been either absolutely precise or taken much in advance.

Very early on in construction, however, the architect would reach a stage where what he decided would inevitably control the effect which he might want to create at a later stage. The proportion which he gave to the stylobate, the rectangular platform on which the columns were to stand, would determine whether the columns on the front of the temple could have the same spacing as those on the flanks.[32] Equal spacing is only possible if the stylobate proportions have been properly calculated. How should this be done? Archaic temples have varying numbers of columns on the flanks and even on the fronts, so that there could be no question of sticking to a single 'correct' proportion for all temples. The first reaction seems to have been a simple and natural one: the proportion for the stylobate was given directly by the number of columns, so that if the temple was to have 6 × 16 columns, the desired stylobate width was divided by 6 and multiplied by 16 to find the appropriate length (or vice versa, if the

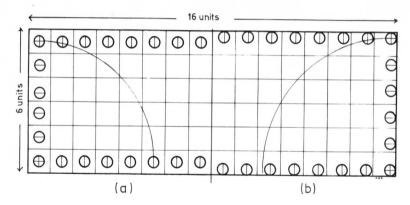

17 Hypothetical temple plan with 6 × 16 columns based on a grid of 6 × 16 squares:
(a) with columns centred in grid squares, giving equal front and flank intercolumniations; (b) with columns set at edge of stylobate, giving front intercolumniations
greater than flank ones

length was specified initially). This would give a uniform column spacing
all round if the stylobate projected half an intercolumniation beyond the
axis of the colonnades (fig. 17a). In fact it projects much less, however, with
the result that the front column spacing is substantially wider than that on
the flanks (fig. 17b).

Eventually, in the third or fourth quarter of the sixth century, the
formula was modified; the stylobate was lengthened so that (in the example
given) its proportions would be made 6 : 16½ or 6 : 17. There is of course
no theoretical justification for these modifications, but given the preferred
size and numbers of columns, they work fairly well. It was not apparently
until the early fifth century that architects decided to fix the
intercolumniation (for front *and* flanks) first and calculate the necessary
length and width from that. Since the client would presumably continue to
indicate the size of temple he wanted in terms of its length or width, the
architect would have to calculate from that an appropriate
intercolumniation, and then work back again from the intercolumniation
to an exact stylobate length and width; another stage in the preliminary
design process was therefore required.

Intimately connected with the equal spacing of front and flank
colonnades is the problem which arose over the triglyph frieze at the
corners of a Doric temple.[33] The Greeks insisted that there should be a
triglyph not a metope next to the angle. For structural reasons the axis of
the flank architrave had to come over the axis of the endmost column of the
front. The triglyph was set in the same vertical plane as the main outer face
of the architrave, but its width (from side to side) was normally much less
than the architrave thickness (from front to back). So if the endmost
triglyph of the front was to reach the corner of the frieze, its axis would
inevitably fall outside the axis of the flank architrave, and therefore outside

the axis of the endmost column of the front (fig. 18). As a result, either the frieze elements near the angles had to be stretched, so that the column spacing could remain uniform (cf. fig. 29b); or the column spacing next to the corner could be reduced so that the distribution of the frieze could remain uniform (cf. fig. 46a); or the two approaches could be combined in varying degrees. The first approach requires no special planning, since it would become obvious as the building went up how much wider than usual the triglyphs and metopes near the angle would need to be. But with the second approach, or any predetermined combination of the first and second, the desired arrangement of the frieze could only be achieved if at an earlier stage in construction the column spacing had been adjusted by precisely the right amount.

The connection between this triglyph problem and the problem of equal column spacing can be seen from a hypothetical illustration. If a stylobate is built with the right proportions to carry a uniformly spaced colonnade of 6 x 16 columns (compare the front and flank intercolumniation in fig. 19a), and it is then decided that the intercolumniations next to the angles should be contracted, the remaining intercolumniations will have to be extended. The total amount of the extension will be the same for the flanks as for the fronts, but since it has to be shared between thirteen normal flank intercolumniations but only three normal front intercolumniations, its effect will be greater on the fronts, with the result that the front intercolumniations will now be wider than those on the flanks (contrast the front and flank intercolumniations in fig. 19b). Although this is a

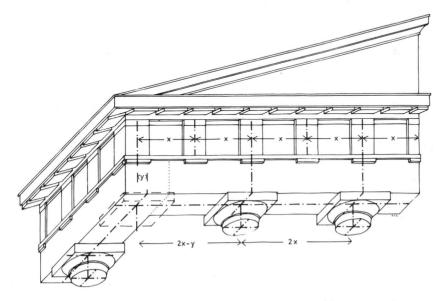

18   Angle contraction in the Doric order: elevation with oblique projection

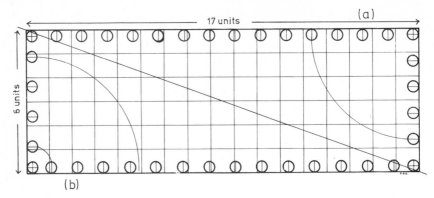

19 Hypothetical temple plan with 6 × 16 columns: (a) without angle contraction and with front and flank intercolumniations equal; (b) the same stylobate with angle contraction introduced, making front intercolumniations greater than flank ones

hypothetical situation, the archaic temples in Sicily and south Italy, where architects preferred to stretch the frieze elements near the angles rather than contracting the angle intercolumniations, do in fact normally have the flank columns more widely spaced than the front ones, while the reverse is true in the archaic temples of mainland Greece, where architects preferred a uniform frieze and contracted angle intercolumniations.

Angle contraction was used on the mainland from the early sixth century (cf. p. 45), and in the western colonies from c. 480 B.C.,[34] yet architects never seem to have reached a theoretical grasp of how much the contraction should be. Inspection of figure 18 shows that the axis of the endmost triglyph will fall outside the axis of the endmost column by an amount y equal to half the architrave thickness (front to back) minus half the triglyph width (side to side), which is therefore the amount of contraction required. Yet it is extremely rare for that to be the actual amount found. One reason why this rule was not developed may be that to apply it architects would need to know precisely the architrave thickness and triglyph width before the stylobate was laid (for the contracted intercolumniation would affect the jointing in the stylobate and the steps below it). We have just seen how slow they were to decide even the intercolumniation before the stylobate size. Vitruvius[35] gives a simpler rule: contraction = $\dfrac{\text{triglyph width}}{2}$; if the architrave thickness is twice the triglyph width (as it is often, but not invariably), this rule will produce the same effect as the correct one, but it is doubtful how far even this was applied.

Temple architects seem in fact to have paid no attention to the frieze or architrave in working out the positions of the columns, but to have related the normal intercolumniation to the stylobate width by a rule with a built-in allowance for angle contraction; for a six-column façade the stylobate width was divided into $5\frac{1}{3}$ parts, of which one was taken as the intercolumniation (or when the intercolumniation was decided first, the stylobate width was found by multiplying it by $5\frac{1}{3}$; cf. fig. 20a). The amount of angle contraction would vary, depending on the proportion of stylobate depth (front to back) to intercolumniation. Thus it was an *ad hoc* rule, the effect of which (and to a lesser extent that of Vitruvius' rule) depended on the proportional relationship of various parts of the building not directly controlled by it. The effect is predictable if the conventions are respected,

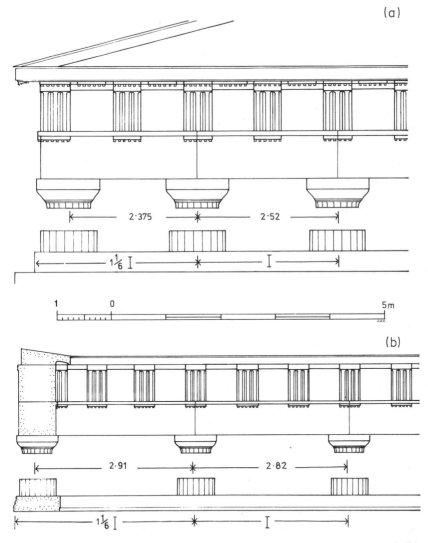

20   (a) angle contraction in the temple of Hephaistos at Athens (*c.* 450–445 B.C.); (b) the same formula producing increased angle intercolumniation in the Stoa at Brauron (*c.* 430–420 B.C.)

but if other conventional rules are changed, the result may be surprising. Thus in the sanctuary of Artemis at Brauron (Attica), a stoa was built (*c.* 430–420 B.C.) with three metopes above each intercolumniation instead of the usual two, so that the column diameter (and hence the stylobate depth) was much smaller than usual in relation to the intercolumniation. As a result, when the same rule was applied, and the stylobate for 11 columns was made equal to $10\frac{1}{3}$ intercolumniations,[36] the effect was not angle contraction but angle extension! In this case extension was preferable to contraction, for the colonnades met at a re-entrant, not an external angle, but it is doubtful if the effect was predicted in detail, since the extension is much too small to produce a regular frieze (fig. 20b).

The difficulty apparently caused to architects by the problem of uniform column spacing and the triglyph problem provides further evidence that they did not work out their designs in detail before starting construction, for neither problem is hard to deal with if the frieze is designed first (as can easily be done on a drawing-board). Greek architects were apparently slow to see the need to define precisely at an early stage parts of the building which would not actually be required until much later. This slowness was probably due in part to the fact that they were breaking new ground. In no earlier architecture known to them did the upper parts of a building make such precise demands upon the design of the lower parts, so that it was not immediately obvious what was required, and how it should be done. Indeed precise regularity was probably not at first considered of overriding importance; there were other matters which needed more urgent investigation.[37] Certainly archaic architecture shows less uniformity than later architecture both between one temple and another and between 'identical' elements of the same temple (cf. fig. 42).

The means adopted by Greek architects to cope with the need for planning are characteristic. Rules of proportion were formulated so that the appropriate size for each element could be derived from a dimension already decided. Rules of proportion are of course still used by architects (under the name of formulae) to determine, for instance, window area in terms of floor area, or beam section in terms of length and load. To Greek architects, however, they were important in formal as well as technical matters, and in many ways rules of proportion took the place of drawings, as a means of recording a design, and of transmitting accepted norms over a large area of space and time. They also provided a means of predicting the appearance of a building before it was built. For if the rules used in an existing temple were known (and as we have seen—pp. 24–5—books containing this sort of information were available in the mid sixth century; oral transmission of rules probably goes back further), then the same effect could be achieved by using the same rules again. More important, the effect could usually be altered in a predictable way by changing a specific rule. If a temple seemed too squat, the rule for column height could be altered; if it seemed top-heavy, the rules for architrave height and frieze height could

5 Statue of Gudea with a plan on his knees (*c.* 2200 B.C.). Paris, Louvre

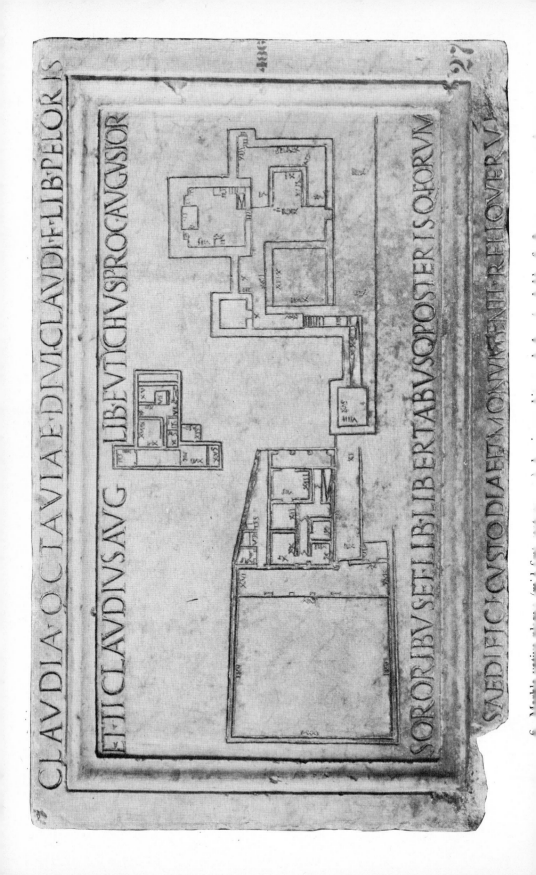

6. Marble cutting plan, ...

be changed. Experimentation of this sort seems to have been practised by the Hephaisteion Architect in fifth-century Athens,[38] and although some rules were long accepted it is doubtful if any architect simply took over *all* the rules for his temple from an existing one.

Rules of proportion have sometimes been credited with mystical significance, but in spite of the Greek obsession with numbers, architects seem normally to have regarded them in a more prosaic light.[39] The aim was to create an appearance which was satisfying in fact rather than in theory; if the appearance was found unsatisfactory, the rule was changed. Thus Vitruvius[40] tells us that the rules of proportion initially adopted for columns were based on the human body as an accepted model of strength and beauty; when later builders, however, 'having progressed in subtlety of taste', changed the rules to give more slender columns, no theoretical justification is suggested. Similarly Philon of Byzantion, in the late third century, compares the development, by trial and error, of effective rules of proportion for catapults with the similar development of architecture.[41]

Much is still unknown about the way the rules of proportion were applied, but some general principles seem discernible.[42] There is documentary evidence for the use of rational ratios like $1 : 10$, $1 : 4$, but little or none for irrational ratios like $1 : \sqrt{2}$, $1 : \pi$ or $1 : 1 \cdot 618 \ldots$ (the 'Golden Section');[43] and it would be hard to set out a series of irrational ratios which could be used for purposeful experimentation of the sort suggested above. The difficulty in finding simple ratios in actual buildings could be due to a tendency to apply them approximately so as to obtain simple measurements in feet.

There seems also to be an increasing concentration on the small elements of a building as the basis of the proportional system. The width and length of the stylobate seem initially to have been related to each other directly, and Pliny records that in early temples the column height was made one third of the width, a rule which fits some, though by no means all, early Doric temples.[44] Later the stylobate width and length were derived from the intercolumniation, and so too, in some cases, was the column height.[45] The final stage in this development is reached with Vitruvius' rules for Doric,[46] according to which a module was first derived and all the elements of the order, down to the smallest detail, were simple multiples or fractions of the module. The effect of this development is to allow the individual elements of the Doric order to be made regular and uniform, and to be related to each other by simple, convenient, and perhaps aesthetically satisfying ratios; but at the same time the simple, convenient, and perhaps aesthetically satisfying ratios which in early temples often related the major dimensions of length, width and column height, are liable to disappear.[47]

Various reasons can be suggested for the change. The early system is applicable only to temples; it would obviously be unreasonable to derive the column height of a stoa, which might have twenty, fifty or even a hundred columns, from its length, and from the mid sixth century stoas were gradually entering the field of monumental architecture. The intercolumniation is a more flexible unit of design where a variety of buildings is required. Even in temples it will assist the organization of work if the intercolumniation, which controls the size of more blocks than any other dimension, is uniform and defined at an early stage; and the system of small, defined contracts, requiring a more reliable preliminary design, will have encouraged the change. The modular system further simplifies the process of design, and its convenience has been appreciated by architects since Vitruvius almost to the exclusion of any other. Nevertheless, it has the effect of fossilizing the order, for if the system is to retain its advantages, the module must not become too small, nor the multiples and fractions of it too complex; as a result, gradual change of the sort referred to by Philon of Byzantion, and found in surviving buildings, becomes impossible. Compare the rigidity of Vitruvius' rule for architrave height in the Doric order with his rule for architrave height in the Ionic order, for which he uses a non-modular system.[48] Since the proportions given by a modular system create a clearly recognizable pattern, even if the module cannot be identified, it is possible to establish with some probability that a modular system was not used by Greek architects, at least before the late Hellenistic period.[49] It is much more likely that earlier architects used a system similar to the one set out by Vitruvius for the Ionic order.[50] In this the rules do not relate each element to a single common module, but form a sort of chain, so that each element is derived successively from a preceding one, usually the immediately preceding one. The ratios between successive parts are also more complex than in the modular system, and the ratios between widely separated parts may be very hard to calculate. Because of this structure, such a system gives more scope for experimentation and variation, and so fits better with the existing evidence of Greek architecture.

Vitruvius' rules for Ionic are arranged so that the colonnade could be designed as the building went up; the overall dimensions of each element are derived from something that would already exist if the building were under construction, while the details of each element are derived from its overall dimensions. As already noted, the language suggests that this successive procedure had in fact been used, and there is archaeological evidence that it was used in the layout of Doric temple plans. From a fairly early period it was normal for the side walls of the cella building to be aligned on the axes of the columns one in from each corner. Excavation of the Hephaisteion at Athens (c. 450–445 B.C.) has shown that instead of first building the cella in accordance with a predetermined plan and then adding the colonnade round it, the order was reversed; the foundations for the cella building were dug through the work chips which had built up as the stylobate and its foundations were being dressed (fig. 21). These excavations do not show how far construction had proceeded before the

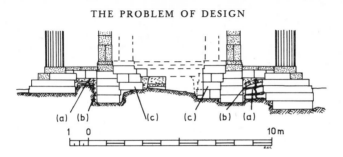

21 Temple of Hephaistos at Athens (c. 450–445 B.C.), cross-section: (a) masons' chips from work on outer order; (b) foundation trench for cella foundations; (c) foundations for inner colonnades built against cella foundations

cella foundations were laid out, but in other temples the evidence suggests that in spite of the inconvenience to the builders, the outer colonnade ran well ahead of the cella and its porches, and may sometimes have been substantially complete before the cella was begun.[51] In elevation too, the design of the cella porches depended on the outer colonnade, and the desired relationship could be best achieved if the outer colonnade already existed.

Examination of a detailed report on any Greek building will show that calculation is more useful than scale drawing in working out how the building looked and how the blocks went together; the same was probably true for an ancient architect trying to work out in detail what sizes he was to give the various elements, and here we may have an additional reason for the successive design procedure. For it is doubtful if any system of numeral notation was used by the Greeks when they first began monumental architecture.[52] The system most widely used in the fifth and fourth centuries (first attested in the sixth) was similar to the Roman one—if anything clumsier—and had no accepted way of writing fractions. It is even doubtful if there were widely used verbal expressions for fractions other than submultiples ($\frac{1}{5}$, $\frac{1}{6}$, $\frac{1}{7}$, and so on) before the Hellenistic period. This, taken with the Greek system of measurement, based on a foot divided into four palms each of four dactyls (fingers), meant that it was very difficult to calculate accurately the various dimensions of a building beforehand; for instance Vitruvius' rules make the architrave height for a 24-foot-high Ionic column one part in $12\frac{1}{2}$ of the column height; by calculation that would be 1 foot, 3 palms, 2 dactyls plus an amount which could not be written in numerals or measured with a normal ruler. Thus calculation beforehand almost inevitably meant approximation. Approximate calculations would presumably be made for the orders to be placed with the quarry, but where real precision was required it could more easily be achieved by working directly on the appropriate part of the building, as was done for the cella side walls. The extent to which an architect preferred to calculate beforehand and the accuracy of his approximations varied probably both from period to period and from architect to architect.

To some extent this difficulty in calculating out a design was removed in the Hellenistic period by the adoption of a handier numeral system which, although invented in the sixth century, was little used in mainland Greece before the late fourth. The twenty-four letters of the Greek alphabet, supplemented by three extra signs, were used to represent the units 1–9, the tens 10–90, and the hundreds 100–900, so that 888 was written ωπή instead of ΓHHHΓΔΔΔΓIII. Various ways of writing fractions with these alphabetic numerals were also developed, but the most common was the old Egyptian method of writing all fractions as a string of submultiples (for example, $\frac{7}{16}$ written as $\frac{1}{4}+\frac{1}{8}+\frac{1}{16}$), which would naturally lead to errors and approximations in calculation.

The Hellenistic period must have seen a major change in techniques of design, however. The alphabetic numerals and the modular system of proportion would make it easier to plan accurately beforehand using the traditional procedures, but the change in the whole emphasis of architecture during the Hellenistic period required something more profound. A wider range of buildings was given a monumental treatment—gymnasia, council chambers, innumerable stoas, and even houses; and although these might be conventional in broad terms, they were more complex and less consistent in plan than temples, for they would often need to combine a variety of elements within a single building. At the same time, where architects had previously been content to design buildings without formal relation to their surroundings (although not regardless of them),[53] they now became increasingly interested in combining several buildings to form larger units such as the sanctuary or the agora (compare fig. 22 and fig. 53); again, although the basic principles might be conventional, the individual schemes varied considerably. There would therefore be much more to be gained by drawing preliminary plans, even imperfect ones, than there had been with the simpler and more strongly conventional buildings of earlier periods; and indeed there is evidence that this was done.

Although, as already mentioned, Vitruvius' rules for temple design could be followed without the use of scale drawing, it is clear from the remarks on the nature of architecture in his first book that he took architectural drawing for granted.[54] The architect will make drawings to demonstrate the kind of building he intends, and later three specific types of drawing are listed as the elements of composition: the plan, the elevation, and the perspective drawing. Architectural drawings and drawing equipment have survived from the Roman period (plate 6),[55] so there is no doubting Vitruvius' word, and Roman architects would have needed plans even more than Hellenistic ones. Vitruvius is here quoting from a Greek source, however, and the words he uses for the three types of drawing are Greek words, so that we are not dealing with a Roman innovation.

Vitruvius' word for perspective, *skenographia*, first occurs in Aristotle, in the literal sense of scenery-painting, but Vitruvius claims elsewhere that some sort of perspective drawing, and some sort of theoretical discussion of it, already existed in the fifth century.[56] It was developed for theatrical scenery, however, and although an architect of the mid fourth century was said by some to have been also a scene-painter, there is no suggestion that the technique was useful to him as an architect.[57] In the first century B.C. there was a fashion at Rome and elsewhere for decorating rooms with

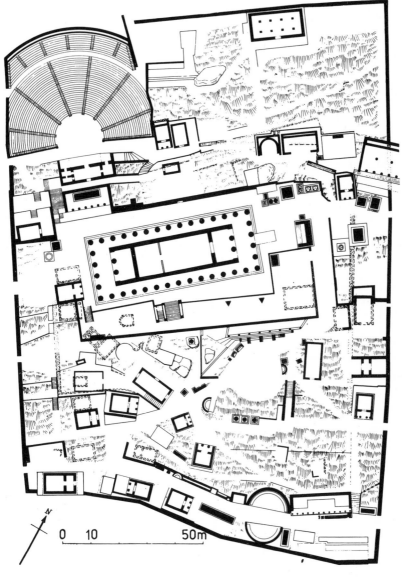

22 Plan of the sanctuary of Apollo at Delphi (mostly sixth and fifth centuries)

architectural perspectives which seem to recede into the wall,[58] and these show that by then the technique was sufficiently developed to be of use in architectural design (plate 7). When it reached that stage is uncertain, but architects are unlikely to have required perspective before the Hellenistic period, and some of the most successful Roman perspectives show a small circular shrine axially placed within a colonnaded court, and viewed down the axis—a composition based on late Hellenistic ideas.

One would expect plans and elevations to be used by architects rather earlier than perspectives, both because they are simpler to construct and because they are more useful in working out designs. Unfortunately Vitruvius' words for plan and elevation have not survived in earlier Greek. A ground plan may, however, be referred to in an inscription from Priene, where the word used is *hypographe*. A certain Hermogenes in the second century dedicated at the temple of Athena 'the *hypographe* of the temple [?],

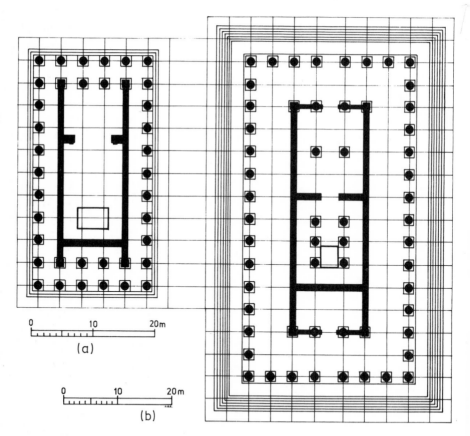

0   10   20m
(a)

0   10   20m
(b)

23   Ionic temple plans imposed on a uniform grid: (a) temple of Athena at Priene (*c.* 350–330 B.C.); (b) temple of Artemis at Magnesia (*c.* 130 B.C.) (central grid spacing = 1⅓ normal spacing)

which he also executed'.[59] The temple at Priene was completed more than a century earlier, and although it was repaired in the second century, it seems more likely that the temple concerned (if the word temple is correctly restored) was another one; this Hermogenes has often been identified with the influential architect of that name who was active in the second century, and who wrote commentaries on two of his temples.[60] Hermogenes' two most important innovations concerned the temple plan (cf. fig. 23b); he might reasonably have dedicated a carefully drawn temple plan, presumably on stone, to show posterity how his system worked. The choice of the word translated here as 'executed' is perhaps surprising, for it refers commonly to a major undertaking such as a building or large statue,[61] but it might be sufficiently explained if the plan were on stone, and particularly if plans were not common at the time. This word might be better explained if the dedication were a model, but that would probably strain the word *hypographe* which, as yet another compound of *grapho*, should mean rather a drawing.[62] However, *hypographe* is certainly not a technical term for a plan, since in a Delian inscription *hypographai* supplied by the architect are used to define details;[63] they should be drawings, but were perhaps, like the *paradeigma* and *anagrapheus*, at full size.[64]

Hermogenes worked in Ionia using the Ionic order, whereas the discussion so far has been based on mainland Greece and the Doric order for which the evidence, both archaeological and epigraphic, is far more plentiful. The evidence for Ionian design methods before the Hellenistic period is slender, but there is no reason to suppose that it was based on different procedures; it is for the Ionic order that Vitruvius specifies a successive system of proportion. Ionian architects seem nevertheless to have conceived their temples rather differently. The colonnade is from an early period more rigorously related to the plan of the cella building than in Doric, and it is the axes of the walls, not their outer faces (as in Doric), which are considered. In archaic temples the irregularity in flank column spacing suggests that the cella walls controlled the column placing, rather than vice versa (cf. fig. 27a, b), and in the Hellenistic temple at Didyma (*c.* 300 B.C. and later) the 'cella' and its porch were built before the outer colonnades.[65] From the fourth century onwards the irregular column spacing was tidied up, and the position of both columns and walls was based on the divisions of a uniform square grid (fig. 23a). This conception of the plan, impossible in Doric, could probably be achieved if the only plan used was the platform of the temple itself, but some of the more thorough and elaborate embodiments of it, like Hermogenes' temple of Artemis at Magnesia (*c.* 130 B.C.),[66] suggest that the plan was worked out on a drawing (fig. 23b; cf. fig. 27c). Vitruvius' insistence that an architect must be skilled at drawing may even go back to the fourth-century Ionian architect Pytheos.[67]

If architects used scale drawings in the Hellenistic period, they might reasonably have used scale models, and small models of siege machinery and artillery were certainly being used by about 300 B.C.[68] The evidence for small models in architecture is ambiguous, however. Most of it comes from Delos, where third-century inscriptions refer to 'the *paradeigma* of the Kynthion' and 'the *paradeigma* of the propylon'.[69] This could mean a model representing the whole building (and therefore a scale model), but it could also mean a specimen belonging to the building but representing only a part of it (and therefore a normal *paradeigma*). The latter seems more appropriate to the propylon, since the work in hand was repairs,[70] so a model of the whole building would be unnecessary. In fact, since a whitened board was used for it, the *paradeigma*, if general, must have been a plan not a model, and even that would not require whitening on both sides. The doors, however, were entirely replaced, and a board whitened on both sides might well be used for a specimen of their design and decoration.[71] If this argument is sound, then the *paradeigma* of the Kynthion could also be a specimen capital (for example) rather than a model of the whole building, a conclusion which is supported by the simple and unoriginal design of that sanctuary.[72]

In fact an architect normally uses scale models, not in working out a design or conveying instructions to the builders, but in demonstrating his ideas to his patron; they are thus most important when architects have to sell their projects in competition with each other. This practice, deplored by Vitruvius, and hardly attested in Greek architecture,[73] was common enough under the Roman empire, and it is in such a context that the use of scale models is most clearly indicated.[74]

There are two reasons why small models might have been adopted more quickly for catapult design than for architectural design. In designing a catapult the builder had to visualize not only the appearance, but also the working relationship of the parts, so that the design problem was more demanding than in architecture; at the same time there was, during the early Hellenistic period, much more radical experimentation in catapult design than in architectural design, so that convention was less helpful both to designer and patron. This gives additional significance to the instructions of Philon of Byzantion for scaling up or down from a model catapult.[75] A rod the length of the model's missile is divided like a cubit rod into six parts, one of which is divided into four parts. Another rod the length of the desired missile is similarly divided, and measurements taken off the model with the small rod are applied to the new machine with the large rod. This, says Philon, is a widely useful method, and more accurate than multiplying and dividing by means of dividers. The way he describes this method suggests that to a competent technical expert of the late third century it was a fairly new one, and that the only viable alternative was the use of dividers. Since scaling up measurements with dividers from a drawing at, say, 1 : 16 or 1 : 32 would be both tedious and inaccurate, it is unlikely that the use of scale drawings or models was widespread before the third century.

The problem of design seems therefore to have exercised Greek architects over a considerable period. The first monumental architects found no pre-existing system which suited the demands of Greek temple architecture. The system which they evolved no doubt borrowed elements from outside Greece, but the gradual development of it was in response to the needs of Greek architecture and the changing organization of public construction. The classic Greek system of rules of proportion, detailed written specification, and full-sized specimens probably reached its greatest sophistication in the fourth century. Thereafter it no doubt continued in use, but the much wider range of Hellenistic architecture, helped perhaps by renewed exposure to the methods of Egyptian architecture, led to the development of the system of accurately drawn plan, elevation, and perspective rendering which is recorded by Vitruvius, and which, with some additions and modifications, has served architects until the twentieth century.

4

The problem of scale

The scale of a building was presumably something decided by those who commissioned it, since it was upon the size that the cost would largely depend. For the architect the system of proportional rules on which Greek temple design was based had the advantage of allowing him to follow the same rules for buildings of different sizes—within certain limits. The main load carried by the architrave of a Greek temple is the weight of the entablature, including the architrave itself. Doubling the scale of a colonnade will mean doubling the length of the architrave as well as its height and thickness, so that its weight will be eight times greater; so too will the weight of the frieze and cornice which it carries. The strength of the architrave, however, is dependent rather on its cross-section, which will be only four times greater.[1] Thus as the scale of the colonnade increases, the load on the architrave will increase more rapidly than its strength, and for a given set of proportional rules there is a maximum size beyond which disaster will follow. The limiting factor in the other direction is one of access rather than structure; for as the scale of a colonnade is reduced, the space between the columns will get smaller, as well as the columns themselves.[2]

If asked to build a particularly large temple, the simplest thing an architect could do was to make it very long, for that involved no increase in the roof span. Long, thin temples were therefore the reaction in premonumental architecture to a demand for impressive size (cf. figs. 4, 5), and even in the sixth century there were a number of temples with the normal six columns on the fronts, but sixteen or more along the flanks.[3] This was not regarded as a really satisfactory solution, however, probably because it prevented the development of a harmonious relation of building length to width. It also failed to increase the size and grandeur of the front façade, and although the façade did not have the dominating importance in a Greek temple that it had in a Roman one, the altar of the god normally stood directly in front of the east façade, and it was there that the most important ceremonies were centred.

Both these disadvantages could be avoided if columns were added to the front colonnades as well, so that the width of the temple was also increased. The first temple of Hera ('Basilica'; second half of the sixth century)[4] at Paestum provides a good example of this solution (fig. 24a). The columns

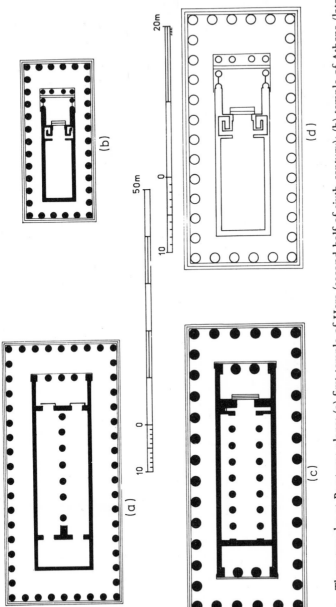

24 Three temples at Paestum: plans: (a) first temple of Hera (second half of sixth century); (b) temple of Athena (late sixth century); (c) second temple of Hera (mid fifth century), all at uniform scale; (d) temple of Athena at 1⅓ scale

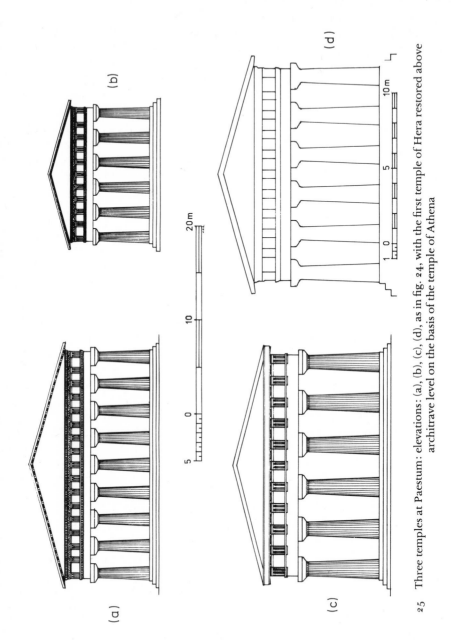

25   Three temples at Paestum: elevations: (a), (b), (c), (d), as in fig. 24, with the first temple of Hera restored above architrave level on the basis of the temple of Athena

are similar in size to those of the small temple of Athena ('Ceres'; late sixth century)[5] nearby (fig. 24b), and the architect has produced a large temple simply by increasing the number of them, using not 6 x 13 large columns but 9 x 18 small ones. It is interesting to see how the architect of the second temple of Hera ('Neptune'; mid fifth century)[6] produced a temple of very similar size in a different way, by increasing the scale of the individual elements rather than their number (6 x 14 columns)[7]; thus its overall proportions are close to those of the temple of Athena (fig. 24c, d; cf. figs. 25c, d, 26c, d.) The smaller, more closely spaced columns of the first temple of Hera allowed smaller architrave blocks to be used, of course, and those would be easier to quarry, transport, and set in place than the larger ones of the second temple; there would be similar economic advantages in other parts of the building. But the aesthetic disadvantages were not wholly avoided, for although the relation of length to width could be regulated by this means, the relation of height to width could not.

In broad terms the height of a Doric column is related to its diameter and spacing rather than to the length of the colonnade in which it stands (fig. 25a, b), so that a façade with many small columns will be lower than one with fewer large ones. Thus the façade of the first temple of Hera with its nine columns looks unpleasantly squat beside that of the later temple with six columns (fig. 25c). This is certainly not because the columns themselves are squatter in the first temple, for in fact they are more slender; nor is it because the first temple has lost its cornice and pediment, for even with those restored its height is only about four-fifths that of its successor, while its width is virtually the same; and a comparatively heavy pediment, related to the façade width not the column height, increases the unpleasant effect.

Any increase in width, however, whether by using many small or few large columns, necessarily increased the problem of roofing the temple. The function of a temple demanded a closed cella with a porch in front (and in the western colonies often a small room at the back of the cella), but once these requirements were met, the architect apparently felt free to arrange the interior of his temple to suit the exterior. In the sixth-century temples of Selinous, which were close in size to the first temple of Hera at Paestum, the side walls of the cella were placed so that they divided the width of the temple into three more or less equal spans;[8] no interior colonnades were used, and the cella side walls were not directly related to the six columns of the façades. The unsureness in handling large spans which is suggested by the use of nine columns in the first temple of Hera at Paestum appears to have affected the woodwork as well. Instead of dividing the width of the temple into three spans, the architect divided it into four, with a single colonnade down the middle of the cella and cella side walls half way between that and the outer flank colonnades (fig. 26a contrast fig. 26b). The decision to use nine columns on the front rather than eight (which would have made the front column spacing closer to that

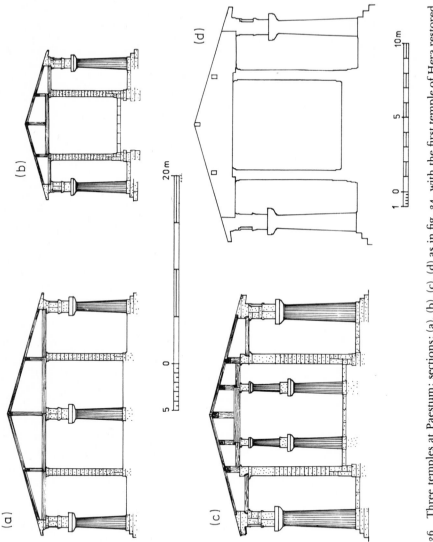

(b)

(d)

(a)

(c)

20m

0

5

1   0   5   10m

26 Three temples at Paestum: sections: (a), (b), (c), (d) as in fig. 24, with the first temple of Hera restored as in fig. 25

on the flanks) may indeed have resulted from the decision to divide the temple roof into four spans. For with nine columns (and so eight intercolumniations) the centre column of each front corresponded to the axial inner colonnade, while the cella walls corresponded to the third column in from the corners; thus five rows of supports ran the full length of the temple. Later architects seem to have felt that this arrangement was misguided, however, for the single inner colonnade interrupted the view down the cella from the door to the cult statue, and in later temples both the axial inner colonnade and the odd number of columns on the fronts are both extremely rare.[9] Normally the cella side walls were aligned on the second column in from the corners, and if that caused difficulties in roofing, two inner colonnades were used, as in the second temple of Hera at Paestum, making five spans in all (fig. 26c).

Both the aesthetic and the structural problems raised by the use of more than six columns on the fronts of a temple were largely avoided in Ionic temples. In fact the earliest unequivocally Ionic temples are already on a colossal scale—45/55 m × 95/110 m—and like many later Ionic temples they have eight-columned fronts (fig. 27a, b). The greater height which was conventionally given to Ionic columns removed the danger of squatness; with six columns along the front the width of the temple of Zeus at Olympia is about $2\frac{2}{3}$ times its column height, whereas, even with ten columns along the front, the width of the Ionic temple of Apollo at Didyma is rather less than $2\frac{2}{3}$ times its column height. In fact Ionic architects commonly preferred eight-columned fronts even in temples which were not particularly large, perhaps to avoid an excessively vertical effect.

Ionic architects also found a way of dealing with the roofing problem in large temples; the cella was surrounded by two colonnades instead of one, so that with eight-columned fronts the cella width corresponded to three outer intercolumniations, just as in a normal Doric temple. In at least two of these temples (the third and fourth temples of Hera at Samos) there were two colonnades within the cella as well (fig. 27a), so that the total width of the building was divided into seven spans rather than five (or four, or three) as in Doric. The roof support system in fact corresponded to the seven spans of the front outer colonnade, and if the spans between the outer columns could be dealt with, so too could the roof spans.

From this close relationship between outer colonnade and cella walls later Ionian architects developed, as we have seen (p. 71), a conception of the temple plan as a more or less regular grid of walls and columns, so that the number of columns on the fronts defines the form of the plan as a whole (figs. 23a, b, 27c). Thus Vitruvius[10] rightly classifies temples with six columns as peripteral (surrounded by a single row of columns), those with eight columns as dipteral (surrounded by two rows of columns) and those with ten columns as hypaethral (with unroofed cella).

To leave the cella unroofed was, of course, the 'ultimate solution' to the roofing problem. It was adopted much less often than was once thought,

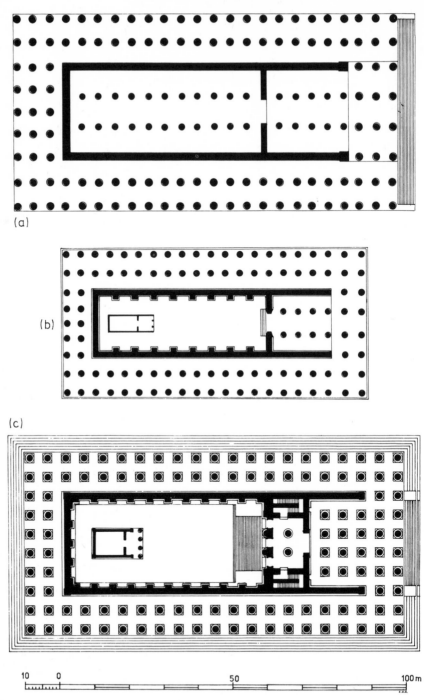

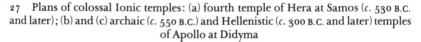

27   Plans of colossal Ionic temples: (a) fourth temple of Hera at Samos (c. 530 B.C.
and later); (b) and (c) archaic (c. 550 B.C.) and Hellenistic (c. 300 B.C. and later) temples
of Apollo at Didyma

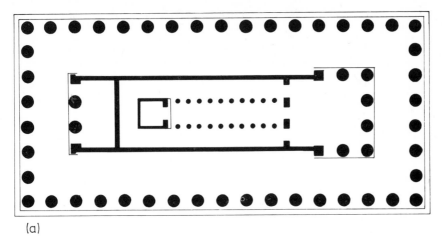

(a)

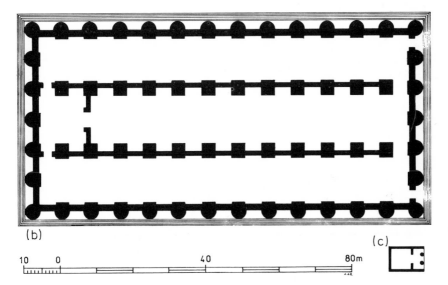

(b)   (c)

10   0   40   80m

28   Colossal Sicilian temples: plans: (a) temple of Apollo ('GT') at Selinous (c.
530–460 B.C.); (b) temple of Zeus Olympios at Akragas (c. 500–460 B.C.); (c) Treasury
of the Athenians at Delphi (c. 510 or 490 B.C.)

and even where a cella was unroofed, it is not always certain that that was
the initial intention. Thus the Olympieion at Athens, one of the examples
quoted by Vitruvius, was unroofed in Vitruvius' time, but a roof was built
later, as had probably always been the intention. The Hellenistic temple of
Apollo at Didyma[11] has ten columns on the fronts, however, and one of the
earliest parts of the scheme to be built was a small Ionic temple within the
'cella' of the colossal one, so that an open cella must have been the
intention from the start. It was the cult which demanded the unroofed cella

at Didyma, for the open 'cella' enclosed the sacred grove of Apollo which stood about the small temple within, and the archaic temple on the site had also had an open 'cella' containing a small temple (compare fig. 27b and c). The Hellenistic temple, however, was a logical revision of its sixth-century predecessor; both temples had two surrounding colonnades, but the archaic temple, like its colossal contemporaries at Samos and Ephesos, had eight-columned fronts, as if to be roofed. Thus the 'cella,' with its side walls aligned on the third column in from the corners, occupied about three-sevenths of the total width; in the later temple, however, with the cella walls still aligned on the third column in from the corners, but with ten columns along the fronts, the 'cella' could occupy about five-ninths of the width, a more spacious setting for Apollo's grove.[12]

The double row of surrounding columns was never executed in a Doric temple,[13] and indeed Doric temples with more than six columns at each end are rare.[14] The Parthenon, with eight-columned ends, will be discussed below (pp. 112–17). More spectacular are the colossal temples of Apollo ('GT') at Selinous and Zeus Olympios at Akragas, both built, presumably, in imitation of the great Ionic temples, but more obviously in a spirit of local rivalry one with the other.[15] The temple of Apollo (c. 530–460 B.C.?) was the first to be started, and apart from its eight-columned fronts, its design and construction were basically conventional; but in the slightly later temple of Zeus at Akragas, both the plan and the method of construction were highly unusual, and seem to have been devised specifically to cope with the colossal scale.

The temple of Zeus (c. 500–460 B.C.?) was made virtually the same length as its rival at Selinous, but about 2·70 m wider; it was also given seven columns at each end instead of eight (fig. 28).[16] Since fewer columns naturally meant larger, taller, more widely spaced columns, the architraves would normally have been longer, taller, thicker, and raised to a greater height (fig 29b);[17] they would also have been subjected to a greater strain. In the light of all this, a fundamental decision was taken to build the temple not just as a gigantic version of a normal temple, like the temple of Apollo at Selinous, with free-standing columns round a walled cella building, but on a quite different plan with half-columns projecting from a continuous screen-wall. Thus the architraves no longer had to be huge beams running from column axis to column axis, but could be built up from smaller blocks; whereas the architraves of the temple of Apollo each consisted of two main blocks weighing about 40 tons (with a low capping course above), those of the temple of Zeus, the total volume of which was more than twice as great, were each made up from 27 blocks, the largest weighing only about 14 tons. Similarly the columns were not built up of drums in the usual way, as was done in the temple of Apollo (with some drums weighing over 50 tons); instead, several comparatively small, wedge-shaped blocks were fitted together to form each course of the half-columns. Since the architraves between the half-columns projected forward from the screen-

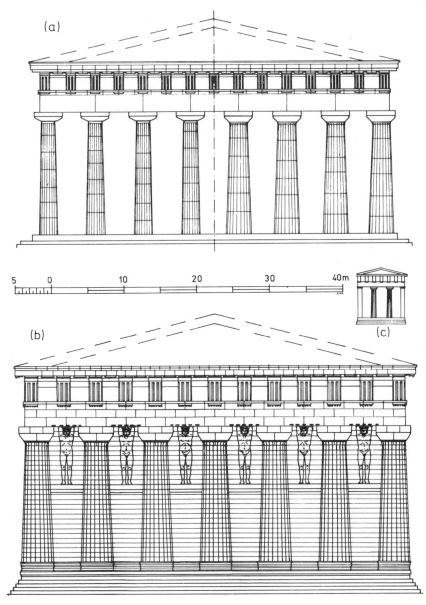

29 Colossal Sicilian temples: elevations: (a), (b), (c) as in fig. 28

wall, and there was a joint between blocks in the centre of each span, some direct support seemed necessary between the columns; giant male figures were therefore placed on a ledge of the screen-wall, carrying the architrave on their upraised forearms, and their efforts were perhaps reinforced by an iron bar about 4·5 m long running from capital to capital in a cutting in the underface of the architrave (cf. also p. 149).

This method of construction solved many of the technical problems associated with colossal scale. The smaller blocks would make quarrying and transport simpler, and so presumably cheaper, and would also avoid the problem of raising massive blocks to a considerable height. The huge architraves of the temple of Apollo at Selinous would have been too heavy for any but a most elaborate type of crane, and they were probably dragged up temporary earth ramps, but even the largest blocks of the temple of Zeus could be lifted by two fairly simple cranes, and almost all of them have U-shaped grooves at each end to take loops of rope which could be attached to cranes.[18]

There is a similar difference between these two great temples in the treatment of the roofing problem. In the temple of Apollo the architect again simply followed the methods of other—smaller—temples at Selinous. He built the cella side walls so as to divide the full temple width into three approximately equal parts (cf. note 8, p. 173); the thickness of the massive outer colonnades reduced the clear span at each side, but the cella was 17·93 m from wall to wall. How the architect intended to roof this great span is a mystery. The other temples at Selinous were roofed without colonnades, and this may have been the original idea in the temple of Apollo, for the pronaos has as great a span as the cella, and could hardly have had inner columns. In the end two small colonnades were built in the cella, but they probably carried a roof which sloped inwards on to an open central area rather than a gabled roof of the normal kind (fig. 30a).[19] When the city of Selinous was destroyed by the Carthaginians in 409 B.C., the temple of Apollo was still incomplete, but the existence of this makeshift inner colonnade and a small shrine at the far end suggests that the idea of finishing the temple as a scaled-up version of a normal Greek temple had already been abandoned as impracticable.

As one might expect, the architect of the rival temple at Akragas produced a more thoughtful solution. Again the width of the temple was divided into three, but instead of walls of normal width, there were two rows of massive pillars, so that the clear spans were substantially reduced. In addition the rows were more effectively placed than the walls at Selinous, for they were aligned on the third column in from the corner of each façade, so that the three aisles were virtually equal, each equivalent to two outer intercolumniations (fig. 30b). Within each row the square pillars were set opposite every half column of the side colonnades, so that there was an unbroken grid of supports centred 8·37 m apart along the length of the building and 16·08 m apart across it. The maximum clear span was about 12·85 m, only about a metre wider than in the perfectly normal temples of Hercules at Akragas and Hera at Selinous, so that a roof of the normal Greek type would probably have been practicable.[20] At any rate the existence of the systematic grid of supports shows that the architect had thought about the problem, and the existence of a gutter with waterspouts,

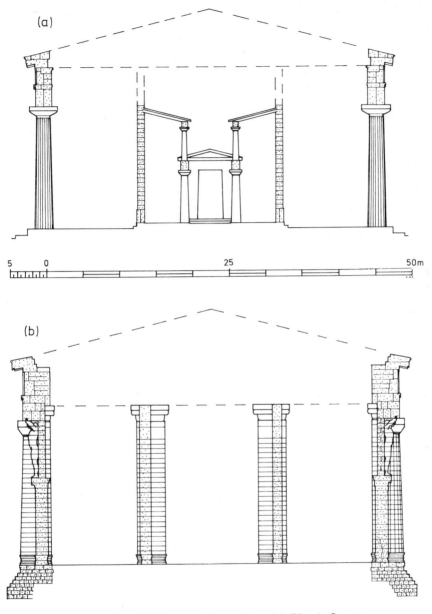

30   Colossal Sicilian temples: sections: (a), (b) as in fig. 28

and (in the Roman period) of pediment sculpture,[21] and so pediments, shows that a normal roof continued to be the intention. Nevertheless, the temple of Zeus Olympios also remained unroofed in the end, for Akragas, like Selinous, was sacked by the Carthaginians in the late fifth century and never regained sufficient prosperity to finish the work off.

In spite of his originality, however—or perhaps because of it—the architect of the temple of Zeus did not really create a successful Greek temple. He dealt admirably with the technical problems raised by the colossal scale, but the unusual method of construction meant that the colonnade existed in theory rather than in effect, and there was no proper cella within. Each row of pillars was joined by a screen wall and the central aisle was given a greater width than the others, partly by making the clear span from pillar to pillar slightly greater, but also by setting the screen walls not along the axis of the pillars but close to their outer edges. There was thus a 'cella' of a sort, but with seven half-columns in each front, there could be no centrally placed door into it, and although the arrangement adopted is uncertain (hence not shown in fig. 29b; cf. fig. 28b), it seems that access to the cella can have been neither impressive nor direct. The scheme as a whole found no imitators.

In the preceding discussion we have concentrated largely on the technical problems raised by exceptionally large temples. The effects of scale were, however, considered even within the normal range of temple size. Vitruvius recommends[22] that the column taper should be reduced and the entablature made heavier as the height of the column was increased; by the Hellenistic period, therefore, at least one school of architectural theorists thought that proportion should vary with scale, and in sculpture that was already normal practice by the fourth century.[23] However, the aim of the variations was not to make the size more obvious, but to ensure that the appearance of ideal proportion was maintained by counteracting the optical distortions which might result from a large scale. It has even been argued that there was no difference in design between a large temple and a smaller one, and that without human figures or lifesize statues nearby it was impossible to tell the size of a temple.[24] This second suggestion is obviously invalid, for there are usually various visual clues to the distance of a temple, and if its distance can be assessed, then so too can its size. There seem also to have been real differences in proportion between temples of the same period and area but different size. Neither of the variations suggested by Vitruvius has yet been recognized in archaic or classical architecture, however, and although other variations in proportion do occur, Vitruvius' explanation does not seem to apply. Thus in Athenian architecture of the fifth century, as the scale of a colonnade was reduced, so the lower diameter of the columns was made proportionately smaller in relation to the intercolumniation, and Dinsmoor[25] has proposed a rule to account for the variation: the clear space between columns was made $1\frac{1}{2}$ Greek feet wider than their lower diameter. At the same time the smaller columns tend to be made more slender, although no rule accounting for that has yet been proposed.

These variations with scale are most regular in Periklean architecture, but both were practised widely by archaic and classical architects. The effect is most clearly seen by comparing the temple of Zeus at Akragas with the

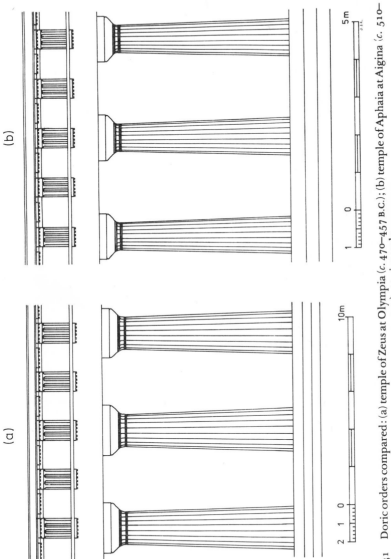

31 Doric orders compared: (a) temple of Zeus at Olympia (*c.* 470–457 B.C.); (b) temple of Aphaia at Aigina (*c.* 510–490 B.C.) at twice scale

Treasury of the Athenians at Delphi (fig. 29b, c; cf. fig. 32).[26] Both were begun at about the same time, but the Treasury of the Athenians has columns about $5\frac{1}{2}$ diameters high and centred nearly 3 diameters apart, while those of the temple of Zeus are about $4\frac{1}{2}$ diameters high and centred only 2 diameters apart. These buildings admittedly belong to different· areas and are entirely different in form and structure as well as scale, but the same effect can be seen by comparing the temples of Aphaia at Aigina (c. 510–490 B.C.)[27] and Zeus at Olympia (c. 470–457 B.C.).[28] In both the height of the columns is twice their axial spacing, but at Aigina, where these dimensions are exactly half the corresponding ones at Olympia, the column diameter is relatively smaller too, so that the columns are more slender and have more clear space between them (fig. 31).

It is hard to form a reliable judgment of the effect of these variations when the two buildings cannot be set side by side at full size, but it seems to be the opposite of that required by Vitruvius. Rather than cancelling it out, the massive columns at Akragas enhance the impression of hugeness, while the slender ones at Delphi bring out the daintiness of the little treasury. More practical considerations may also have operated. Since, as we have seen, stress increases with size, it would be reasonable to make the columns relatively thicker and stronger, and to reduce the clear space between them in large buildings. Similarly, since in a small colonnade the space between the columns may become inconveniently reduced, it would make sense to increase the clear space by making the column diameter proportionately smaller. If at the same time the small columns are made more slender than the large, the relation of column height to column spacing and façade width will remain as far as possible unchanged, and the general proportions of the building will not be spoiled. These changes in proportion certainly do have an aesthetic effect, however, and it would be rash to suppose that architects were unaware of it.

The Treasury of the Athenians (c. 510 or 490 B.C.), at Delphi, occupying about a hundredth of the area of the temple of Zeus at Akragas (fig. 28b, c), brings us to the problems of very small buildings. Just as a temple with the normal surrounding colonnade could not be made infinitely big, so it could not be reduced in scale beyond a certain limit. The smallest such temples are in fact the temple of Nemesis at Rhamnous (9·996 × 21·42 m) and the Metroon at Olympia, about 0·60 m wider and shorter, and in these the space left clear between the columns, in spite of the application of 'Dinsmoor's rule', is less than 1·20 m. In a temple any smaller than these reasonable access could only be maintained by using fewer than six supports in the façade,[29] which meant in effect abandoning the surrounding colonnade. For with only four columns in the façade, a surrounding portico with the usual depth of one intercolumniation would leave the cella ridiculously small.[30] Thus very small temples had columns only in front, or less usually at front and back. The most elaborate ones had four free-standing columns at each end, with a small pronaos in front of the cella, like the Temple by the Ilissos at Athens (c. 450 B.C.). Temples of this type are rare,[31] however, because small temples, being less important, were often set where the back was of little visual significance. In Hellenistic Asia Minor small temples often have four free-standing columns in front,[32] but elsewhere they more usually had just two columns between the extended ends of the cella side walls, like the Treasury of the Athenians. Small treasuries of this form were built by several cities at the great Panhellenic sanctuaries (e.g. fig. 22)—miniature temples in honour of the deity concerned, enhancing his prestige, but also that of the dedicating city.

A façade with four supports would necessarily form a taller, narrower rectangle than a normal six-columned façade using columns of the same proportions—the reverse of the effect produced by a façade with more than six columns. To reduce the column height in compensation would, however, make an already small façade even less impressive, and there is no evidence that the column height was ever reduced in terms of the intercolumniation in such cases. The problem of access between the columns of a small colonnade did exercise the designers of such buildings, however.

The slenderness given to the columns of the Treasury of the Athenians naturally increased the space between them, perhaps by about 0·16 m. But in addition the architect moved the columns further apart than they would normally have been. A normal way of fixing the column spacing in such a case would have been by dividing the width by $3\frac{1}{3}$ (or $3\frac{1}{4}$), giving in this case an intercolumniation of 1·965 m (or 2·02 m), whereas the actual intercolumniation was about one third of the building width, or 2·184 m, so allowing a further 0·16–0·22 m of free space. The triglyph spacing did not follow the column spacing in the usual way, however, for if all the triglyphs and metopes were of uniform size and the axis of a triglyph came over the axis of each column, then the axis of the next triglyph but one would coincide with the edge of the building, giving the façade a half-triglyph at each end, which was unacceptable. That could only be avoided (once the wider central intercolumniation was approved) either by using narrower triglyphs and metopes over the side intercolumniations, or by allowing the triglyph axes to ignore the column axes. Probably because the sculptured metopes had to be prepared in advance, the latter alternative was preferred,[33] and the distance between alternate triglyph axes, normally equivalent to one intercolumniation, was 2·02 m, just what the intercolumniation might have been (fig. 32).

The decision to use the wider intercolumniation was apparently taken after the stylobate was laid. The three northern blocks of the stylobate course (on which the columns stood) are preserved, one of them bearing the mark left on it by the northern column. This shows that the column was set quite near the northern end of the block, not at its centre as would be usual in a careful building like this. If the northern column had been centred on its block and the southern column symmetrically placed, the

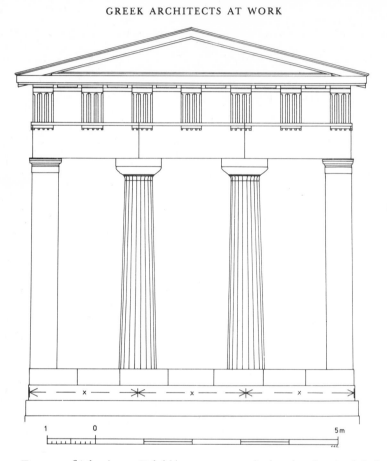

32   Treasury of Athenians at Delphi (*c.* 510 or 490 B.C.): elevation showing jointing

intercolumniation would have been about 1·90 m, so that a closer column spacing was presumably intended at this stage. The jointing of the architrave on the other hand coincides with the column spacing actually adopted.

The architect of the Treasury of the Athenians was apparently stretching exisiting modes to their limit so as to gain space. At Delos the architect of a similar but slightly later building ('Treasury 3') adopted a more radical approach.[34] The central span was enlarged not by displacing the columns in relation to the triglyphs, but by adding an extra triglyph and metope to the frieze; thus there were two metopes (as usual) over the side intercolumniations, but three over the central one. The central intercolumniation could thus be widened from about 2·45 m to 3·18 m, without losing the correspondence between triglyph axis and column axis.

This idea was used again in the pronaos of the Great Temple of Apollo at Delos, and in several other small temples of later date, but it had its greatest popularity in other types of building. There may in fact already have been an extra metope over the central span of the Old Propylaia to the Akropolis at Athens,[35] although the most famous instance is in the later Propylaia of Mnesikles (437–432 B.C.; fig. 33). There the clear space between columns was increased from about 2·06 m to 3·88 m by this means, so that the great procession in honour of Athena could pass freely through the building. In all these cases, however, the three metopes were used only over one span out of three or five, so that there was no major change in the traditional rhythm of the façade. Of greater ultimate importance was the adoption of three-metope spans for a complete colonnade. This occurred first in stoas, for since a stoa carried less architectural prestige than a temple, the expense of large columns was usually avoided. But although stoa columns were usually small, ease of access was essential; not just through one intercolumniation as in a propylon, but along the whole colonnade, for large numbers of people might wish to enter or leave a stoa simultaneously.

The unsuitability of the convention developed for temples is well seen in the sixth-century Stoa Basileios at Athens, one of the earliest Greek civic buildings.[36] It was a small building, only 17·722 m long, but with a façade of eight columns between the end walls. The intercolumniation was 1·9205 m, about the same as in the smallest of the peripteral temples, but in order to deal with the much greater flow of people in and out of a civic building, the lower diameter of the outer columns was made proportionately smaller. It was 0·58 m (compared with 0·714 m in the temple of Nemesis at Rhamnous), so that the clear space was 1·34 m (compared with 1·19 m at Rhamnous). The height of the columns is unfortunately uncertain, so that we do not know whether it was the column or the intercolumnar rectangle

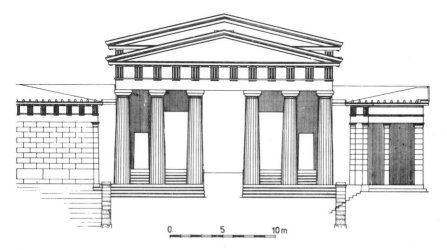

33 Propylaia at Athens (c. 437–432 B.C.): west elevation

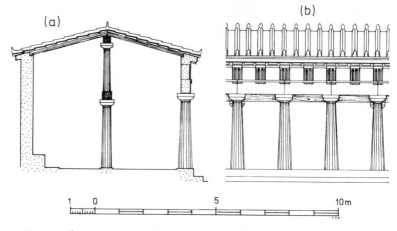

34   Stoa Basileios at Athens (sixth century): (a) hypothetical section; (b) part
elevation

that was given conventional proportions. It is certain, however, that
these columns carried a stone entablature, and since the frieze naturally
had two metopes over each intercolumniation, the width and height of the
triglyphs had to be related to the intercolumniation rather than the
column diameter. The result is a triglyph width about two-thirds of the
lower diameter instead of half, and a frieze height probably greater than
the lower diameter not less. The small columns thus had to carry a
disproportionately heavy entablature (fig. 34b).

Later architects, where they used stone for the columns and entablature
of a stoa, apparently avoided this top-heavy appearance by building on a
rather larger scale, as in the South Stoa at the Argive Heraion (c. 450–425
B.C.; fig. 35b);[37] in this way adequate access was possible without too much
modification of the proportions used in temples. During the last third of
the fifth century, however, Athenian architects seem to have faced the fact
that a stoa was not simply a variant form of temple, and developed a
number of ideas specially applicable to stoas. One of these was the
extensive use of three-metope spans, and the advantages of the system can
be seen by comparing the Stoa Basileios with the Stoa at Brauron in Attica
(c. 430–420 B.C.),[38] which is the earliest building where it was certainly used
over an extensive colonnade (fig. 36). The scale is of course larger at
Brauron, but the difference in proportion is more striking. At Brauron the
clear space between columns was proportionately greater (4 diameters as
against 3⅓ diameters), but the triglyph width was little more than half the
lower diameter and its height less than one diameter. Thus the entablature
was once more related to the lower diameter roughly as it would have been
in a temple on a larger scale using the two-metope system.

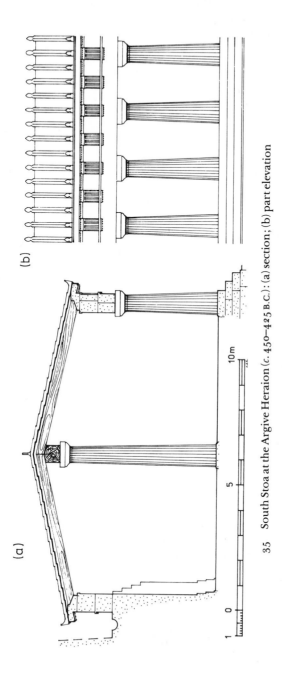

35 South Stoa at the Argive Heraion (c. 450–425 B.C.): (a) section; (b) part elevation

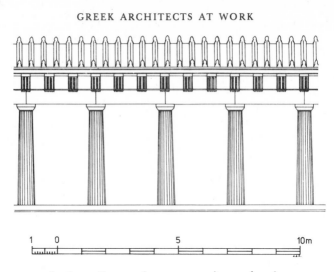

1   0   5   10m

36   Stoa at Brauron (*c.* 430–420 B.C.): part elevation

From the late fifth century onwards, three-metope spans were commonly used in stoas and other porticoes of a similar nature, where there was no question of imitating the overall proportions of a temple. In the Hellenistic period the three-metope system was also common in small non-peripteral temples, but it was rarely used in peripteral ones, for when a peripteral temple was built its order was usually on a large enough scale to make three-metope spans unnecessary.[39] Scale rather than building type seems to have been the governing factor in the adoption of the new system, however, for in the fourth century and even later some architects preferred to build stoas with columns about a metre in diameter, and so continued to use the two-metope system. It was only at the end of the Hellenistic period, during which many more secular buildings than temples were built, that the three-metope system was used with larger orders.

Once the idea of using more than the traditional two metopes to a span had been accepted, there was no reason why architects should limit themselves to three, and during the Hellenistic period we find buildings with four or even five metopes above each intercolumniation (cf. fig. 1). The smaller columns and lighter entablature which this increase allowed would certainly have reduced the cost of construction, but the lighter, more open appearance probably also appealed more to Hellenistic taste. The danger was, however, that the Doric order would lose one of its most important characteristics, the strong visual rhythm of triglyphs and metopes in an immediately perceived relationship to that of the columns and intercolumniations. With four or more triglyphs and metopes to each span, the triglyphs have hardly more importance than the dentils below an Ionic cornice.

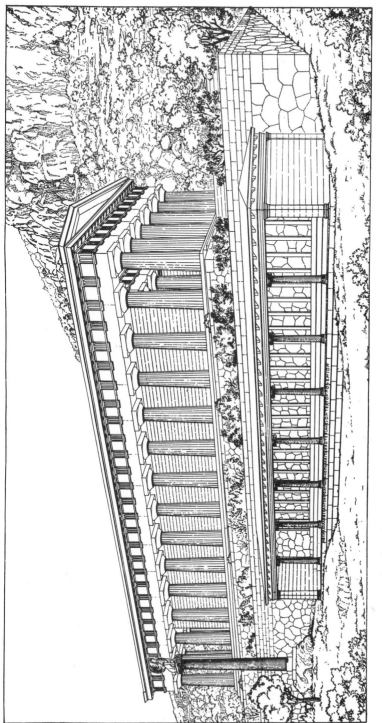

37   Temple of Apollo (*c.* 510 B.C.) and Stoa of the Athenians (*c.* 478–470 B.C.) at Delphi: restored perspective

In an Ionic colonnade it was obviously just as necessary to provide adequate space between the columns as in a Doric one, but the architect working in the Ionic order had no strongly accented frieze to restrict him. Although the columns of Ionic temples were normally fairly closely spaced, the intercolumniations were sometimes increased progressively towards the centre for ease of access or for effect,[40] and in other types of building the columns might be very widely spaced. The Stoa of the Athenians at Delphi (c. 475 B.C.),[41] for instance, which was built to display the spoils of victory, was made as open as possible, with columns only 0·39 m in diameter and 3·31 m high but centred 3·58 m apart (fig. 37). The wide spans and small columns probably necessitated a wooden architrave, but a small Ionic monument at Delos, built in 102–101 B.C. by the half-Hellenized King Mithridates VI of Pontos,[42] had a stone entablature although its columns, only 0·322 m in diameter and 2·90 m high, were centred 2·27 m apart.

In fact the widened column spacing in small buildings rarely caused structural difficulties. Not only were the proportions used in buildings of normal size considerably heavier than was structurally necessary, so that there was scope for increasing the intercolumniation without endangering the structure, but also the reduction in scale would (other things being equal) involve less strain on the architrave, just as an increase in scale involved a greater strain. Various schemes were indeed devised to alleviate the strain on the architrave, especially when the use of three-metope spans was comparatively new (pp. 147, 151, 157), but they were found unnecessary in normal practice.

The preceding discussion has concentrated, perhaps excessively, on the technical problems raised by differences in scale, but those are the most clearly demonstrable and the ones which architects could least avoid considering. Changes introduced for aesthetic reasons, like the variations of proportion suggested by Vitruvius, are much harder to track down, particularly in the Ionic order where, because of the small number of well-preserved temples, variations in proportion arising from differences in scale cannot be clearly distinguished from the variations in proportion which certainly occurred from one place to another and from one period to another. With the Doric order a little more can be done, and there seems enough evidence to show that Greek architects were aware of the aesthetic as well as the technical difficulties raised by changes in scale, and that they reacted to both in a straightforward and sensible way.

5

Form, mass and space

For it was not possible to create the [proper] forms of buildings from the start, without first engaging in experiment, as is clear indeed from ancient buildings, which are extremely unskilful not only in construction, but also in the design of forms for the individual parts. The change to what was required was not the result of a single or random experiment; some of the individual parts of a building, although they were in fact of equal thickness and straight, seemed to be neither of equal thickness nor straight, because our sight is misled in such matters by differences in distance. So by trial and error, by adding to and subtracting from the sizes, by taperings, and by all sorts of experiment, they made them [the parts] in accordance with vision and *apparently* well-shaped; for this was the goal in that art.[1]

These words, written by Philon of Byzantion in the later third century, are the nearest thing we have to the view of a working Greek architect on the history and aims of architecture. For although Philon wrote on mechanics, that was, as we have seen (p. 16), closely related to architecture.

The single-mindedness of this view is in striking contrast to the threefold aim presented by Vitruvius—durability, convenience and beauty.[2] Philon's attention is focused only on satisfying appearance, and only on the solid form of the building and its parts. Although he does not specifically say so, the development considered by Philon must be that of the temple. Yet although formal problems still exercised architects in Philon's time, they were interested also in the creation of spaces, in relating one building to another and to a surrounding space, and in a wide range of new building types. Furthermore, the whole passage is set in the past tense; the development is complete. This view is therefore probably a traditional one, and indeed Philon's argument here requires a readily acceptable analogy rather than a radically original evaluation. Whether Philon is repeating precisely the opinion of some earlier architect is uncertain, but it is the sort of opinion one would expect from a fifth-century architect. Indeed if one leaves out the correction of optical illusions (which was not widespread before the fifth century—see pp. 108–12), the target of regular and satisfying form, and the achievement of it through thoughtful experimentation, could reasonably be ascribed to all Greek architects from the mid-seventh century onwards.

The attainment of real regularity in the temple plan was a slow process, tied up with the problem of design methods (cf. pp. 59–64), but some

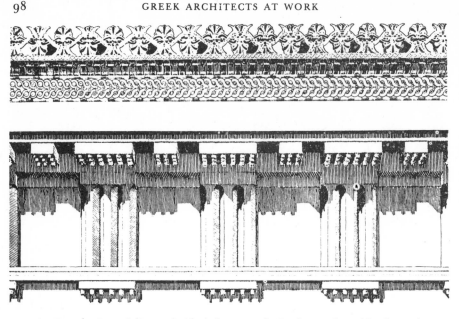

38   Temple C at Selinous (mid sixth century): Doric cornice with alternating
mutules

improvements could be made more easily, for instance in the Doric
cornice. Although during the archaic period (particularly in the western
colonies) a variety of forms was tried, the characteristic Doric cornice had
slab-like mutules projecting above each triglyph and metope. Thus the
rhythm of the colonnade was repeated at double frequency in the frieze and
this frequency was redoubled in the mutules of the cornice. In earlier
cornices, however, the mutules above the metopes were narrower than
those above the triglyphs (fig. 38),[3] so that while the columns and triglyphs
were all uniform, so creating a regular rhythm, the alternating size of the
mutules broke the sequence. By the middle of the sixth century, however,
the metopes were made wide enough to allow *all* the mutules to have the
same width (fig. 71a), equal to that of the triglyphs, without seriously
reducing the intervening spaces (*viae*). The gain in regularity must have
been approved, for by the end of the century cornices with alternating
mutules were no longer being made.

The achievement of regularity can be assessed objectively; the pursuit of
satisfying form is more subjective. The general aims can be identified with
some confidence. A satisfactory balance was sought between verticals and
horizontals, between loads and supports, and between the various
rectangles which constitute a temple in plan and elevation. At the same
time forms were developed so as to articulate clearly the component parts,
and to express effectively the transition from one shape to another. Most
people seem to feel that the experimentation was successful, that the later

buildings are more harmonious and satisfying than the earlier—at least up to a certain period. There may be argument over when the most satisfying results were achieved, but by the Hellenistic period the individual elements were certainly carved with less care and precision than in the fifth century, and to most people's taste also with less sense of expressive form.

Why was the process of experimentation continued beyond the optimum? To some extent there is probably a negative explanation. With the changing aims of architecture the precise form of the details became less important, and the new forms were often cheaper and easier to produce; thus the more slender columns and lighter entablature of Hellenistic Doric, which seem less dignified than their predecessors, would require less stone, and so be cheaper. But such negative explanations are not wholly satisfactory. The Ionic entablature in fact became heavier, through the inclusion of both a frieze and dentils, which had previously been alternatives, and Vitruvius attributes the preference for more slender columns to a positive change in taste.[4] There were probably also strong aesthetic preferences for many other developments in form or proportion which seem to us for the worse. The influence of Ionic on Doric and vice versa was probably an important factor, and may account for both the changes mentioned above. Similarly the mouldings and elaborations added to the Doric order in Hellenistic Ionia[5] were presumably added because the traditional forms were too austere for Ionian taste.

When we move from general to specific changes, however, explanation is much harder. Why, for instance, did Mnesikles add, or at least countenance the addition of, a new moulding on the bed of the Doric cornice of the Propylaia (fig. 39c, contrast fig. 39a)? In general it may be regarded as an Ionic feature, a symptom of the interaction between Doric and Ionic in Athens at that time (cf. fig. 39b); but why that feature in that place, when the (equally Ionic) wall-base moulding used in the Hephaisteion was not used in the Propylaia? Why did later architects accept the principle of a bed moulding, but not the precise way in which

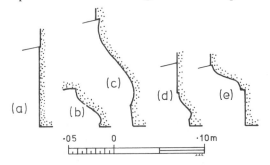

39   Doric cornice bed mouldings: (a) temple of Aphaia at Aigina (without mould-ing; c. 510–490 B.C.); (b) temple of Nike at Athens (Ionic; c. 425 B.C.); (c) Propylaia at Athens (c. 437–432 B.C.); (d) Stoa of Zeus at Athens (c. 430–420 B.C.); (e) temple of Athena at Delphi (c. 370 B.C.)

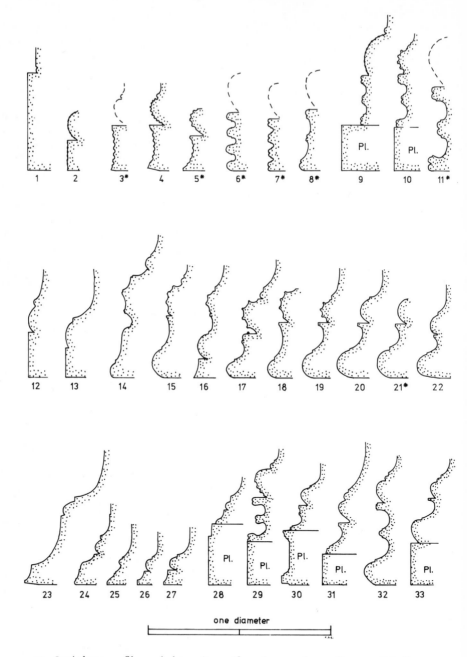

one diameter

40   Ionic base profiles scaled to suit a uniform lower column diameter (* indicates diameter estimated, Pl. indicates square plinth): 1 Naxian Column, Delphi, *c.* 570 B.C.; 2 third temple of Hera at Samos, *c.* 560 B.C.; 3 fourth temple of Hera at Samos, *c.* 530 B.C.; 4 the same, Hellenistic phase; 5 Delos, early fifth century; 6, 7 Managros, Chios, second half of sixth century; 8 Athens, Akropolis, sixth century; 9 archaic

Mnesikles had used it (cf. fig. 39d, e)? Why was the cornice bed moulding accepted almost universally while the wall base moulding was not? The answers to all these questions presumably depend on contemporary taste, but in the absence of ancient comments on such points, it is impossible to discuss confidently the reasoning involved. Similar difficulties unfortunately affect our understanding of almost all detailed changes to, and experiments with, the forms of Greek architecture. The evolution of form is so important, however, not only to our own appreciation of Greek architecture, but also (as the passage from Philon indicates) to the Greeks themselves, that it may be worthwhile to examine the evolution of two particular elements, the Ionic base and the Doric capital. This will not show why changes took place, but it may indicate how they took place.

Ionic columns stood on more or less elaborately profiled bases, and a selection of surviving profiles is shown in figure 40. In brief, the development of the profile was as follows.[6] The idea of a profiled column base was probably influenced by the architecture of the Levant, although simple conical or disc bases had been used in premonumental Greek architecture.[7] In the sixth century the base normally consisted of a convex element (torus) above a disc of similar height; both might be more or less elaborately carved, usually with horizontal fluting or ridges (fig. 40. 2, 8, 9, etc.). The disc tends to be given an increasingly concave profile, and the decoration to be more deeply worked, but there is so much variation that only the Ephesian base, where the disc is cut vigorously back into a double hollow, stands out from the whole group as a clear-cut type (fig. 40. 9–11). This base was copied virtually unchanged in a number of archaic buildings in Ionia, and it became the established form in Asia Minor until the third or second century (fig. 40. 29); it is still presented by Vitruvius[8] as a viable alternative to the Attic type from which almost all Roman and post-Roman bases derive.

Several variants of the torus and disc base are known from sixth-century Athens (fig. 40. 8), but in the fifth century Athenian architects tried adding a

temple of Artemis at Ephesos, c. 560 B.C.; 10 archaic temple of Artemis, Magnesia, sixth century; 11 Klazomenian Treasury at Delphi, c. 540 B.C.; 12 temple of Athena at Paestum, c. 510 B.C.; 13 Stoa I at Kalauria, c. 420 B.C.; 14 Stoa of the Athenians at Delphi, c. 475 B.C.; 15 temple by the Ilissos at Athens, c. 450 B.C.; 16 Propylaia at Athens, 437–432 B.C.; 17 Agora columns, Athens, c. 450–430 B.C.; 18 temple of Nike at Athens, c. 425 B.C.; 19, 20 north and east porches of the Erechtheion at Athens, c. 420–415 B.C.; 21 West Stoa of the Asklepieion at Athens, fourth century; 22 Tholos at Epidauros, c. 350–330 B.C.; 23, 24 temple of Apollo at Bassai, c. 430–400 B.C.; 25 Abaton at Epidauros, c. 350 B.C.; 26 temple of Athena at Tegea, c. 360 B.C.; 27 temple of Zeus at Nemea, 340–320 B.C.; 28 Stoa IV at Kalauria, late fourth century; 29 temple of Athena at Priene, c. 350–330 B.C.; 30 Leonidaion at Olympia, late fourth century; 31 Philippeion at Olympia, c. 330–320 B.C.; 32 temple of Apollo at Chryse, late Hellenistic; 33 temple of Artemis at Magnesia, second century second convex element below the now strongly concave disc (*scotia*), and the fully developed Attic form finally appeared in the Erechtheion (fig. 40. 19, 20; *c*. 420–415 B.C.).[9] Bases of a very different profile at Bassai (fig. 40. 23, 24) led to another series of experimental forms in the Peloponnese during the fourth century, and one type, torus above cavetto (fig. 40. 26–7) had some popularity.[10] However, the Erechtheion base was accepted at once as standard in Attica, and by the early third century it was accepted also in the Peloponnese. Architects in Asia Minor, where a stable type already existed, were naturally slower to adopt the new Attic type, but from the third century onwards it appeared there, too,[11] and during the second it became the dominant type, to reign almost unchallenged thereafter.

From this brief review it can be seen that the development was neither uniform nor steady. The Attic base which eventually became dominant was accepted in some areas more readily than in others, and that was not just a case of a new idea percolating slowly from the centre to 'the provinces' in a generally unitary development, for the Peloponnesian base began at the same time as the Attic and never reached some areas. The various base profiles cannot in fact be arranged in a simple logical progression, but constitute more or less distinct types adopted in particular periods and places. The process of experimentation was similarly restricted in time and space—the sixth century everywhere, except where the Ephesian base was adopted; the mid fifth century in Athens; and the fourth century in the Peloponnese. The second of these periods is perhaps the most interesting, partly because it produced the most successful base profile, partly because most of the buildings involved are closely and reliably dated, so that the process can be seen with unusual clarity.

The addition of a second, larger torus makes a more effective transition from the broad expanse of the stylobate to the narrow column, and the new form is both easier to carve and lighter in appearance than the Ephesian base. The tripartite division, which occurs elsewhere in the Ionic order (for instance in the architrave, in the echinus, volute member and abacus of the capital, etc.), may also have been felt especially appropriate, for the Ephesian base too was given a third element by many architects, a square plinth below the disc.[12] Initially the plinth was regarded as an alternative to the lower torus (fig. 40. 30–2), but both were combined by Hermogenes and many other later architects (fig. 40. 33), who similarly combined both frieze and dentils in the same order. The base from the Temple by the Ilissos,[13] the earliest of the Attic type (fig. 40. 15; *c*. 450 B.C.), might not have seemed out of place by itself among the manifold experimental forms of the archaic period, and there is no point in looking for specific antecedents. What sets it apart is the fact that it was recognized as a particularly promising experiment, worth taking up and modifying. The process of modification may at first sight seem a smooth, logical, almost inevitable evolution, but a close examination belies that. The base from the Ilissos temple is closer to the final form than any intervening form is,

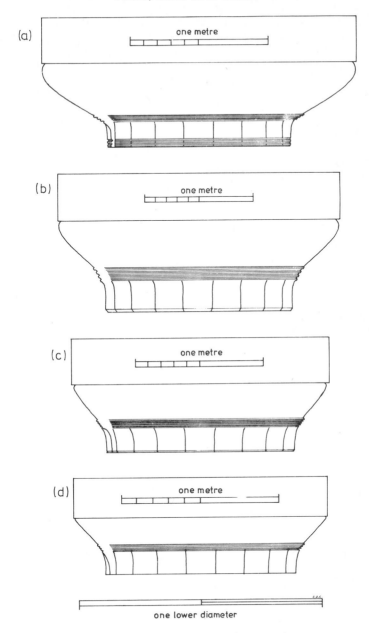

41   Doric capital profiles scaled to suit a uniform lower diameter: (a) temple of
Apollo at Corinth, *c.* 540 B.C.; (b) temple of Zeus at Olympia, *c.* 470–460 B.C.; (c)
Parthenon at Athens, *c.* 447–440 B.C.; (d) temple of Athena at Tegea, *c.* 360 B.C.

while the base with the lowest bottom torus (that of the temple of Athena
Nike, fig. 40. 18) is not the earliest but probably the latest (c. 425 B.C.) before
the Erechtheion. In between these, the bases from the Agora[14] and from
the Propylaia (437–432 B.C.) differ in having a fourth element, unique in
each case (fig. 40. 16–17). The experimentation was thus as fitful and
irregular as in the archaic period, but was bounded by much narrower
limits. Nor did all architects choose to remain within those limits; the
bases from the temple of Apollo at Bassai (fig. 40. 23–4) are roughly
contemporary, but experiment in quite a different direction; yet
Pausanias says the temple was designed by Iktinos,[15] the architect of the
Parthenon, who must have been aware at least of the Ilissos Temple bases.
Thus the whole process was far from inevitable, and it is generally easier to
understand the gradual acceptance of the norm than its initial creation.

  The development of the Doric capital profile is at once less complex and
less clear than that of the Ionic base. All Doric capitals of whatever date
consist of an abacus square in plan above an echinus circular in plan; at its
lower end the echinus runs into the neck of the column shaft which is
almost always cut in the same piece of stone, and at the junction of echinus
and neck there are small, projecting rings, the annulets (fig. 41). The shape
and number of the annulets vary in a most irregular way, not only with the
date and region, but also with the size and importance of the capital, and
probably with the whim of the designer as well, while the shape of the
abacus remains unchanged throughout (except for the addition of a small

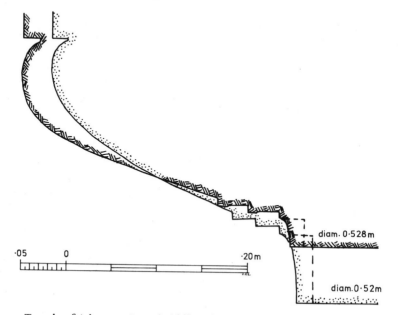

diam. 0·528 m

·05   0   ·20 m

diam. 0·52 m

42   Temple of Athena at Assos (middle to late sixth century): two echinus profiles
compared

crown moulding on some late capitals). Thus the clearest changes in design affect the proportions of each element to the others and the curved profile of the echinus. Early capitals spread widely, with the echinus like a round, bulging cushion (fig. 41a), while late capitals are more compact, with the echinus almost (or quite) in the form of a truncated cone (fig. 41d). Between the two ends of this development, which occupied about three hundred years, various intermediate forms were used, each one less bulging and more cone-like than its predecessors. Thus there are not the clear-cut changes of form we saw in the Ionic base, and the process appears different in kind, a gradual and continuous evolution.

It is probable that no two sets of Doric capitals have precisely the same proportions and echinus profile, and indeed even within a careful building like the temple of Zeus at Olympia the capital profiles are not quite identical. Much more noticeable variations occur in some temples of the sixth century (fig. 42), and such variations within a single set of capitals must derive from imperfect copying of the design, rather than from stylistic evolution.[16] Variations in proportion from one building to another are much more to be expected, even when their architects were aiming at the same design, for any approximation in calculations or rounding out of dimensions would produce them; and if echinus profiles were drawn freehand, they could never be repeated precisely from one series of capitals to another. This effect can be clearly demonstrated even within one building, where more than one series of capitals was required. Thus figure 43 shows four capital profiles from the temple of Aphaia at Aigina, belonging to the outer colonnade, the pronaos, and the two tiers of columns supporting the cella roof. Each set was a different size, so that they could not all follow the same *paradeigma*, but they are here drawn at different scales so as to give them all a uniform abacus height. This shows that the heights of the other elements differ in relation to the abacus height, and the echinus profiles vary both in their general slope and in the curve where they run into the abacus. The general similarity of all four profiles is obvious, however, and there is no reason to believe that the differences represent different architectural intentions.

The problem is therefore to know when the differences between various sets of capitals are simply fortuitous variations about a single ideal design, and when there is an intentional change in the design. Although very few capitals are precisely dated on external grounds, their approximate dates, in terms of about fifty years, are not in much doubt, and from that it appears that the echinus profile underwent at least three definite changes. From about 530 B.C. the bulging echinus of early capitals (fig. 41a) began to be replaced by a stiffer, more conical shape, but still with a pronounced curve at the shoulder (fig. 41b); in mid-fifth-century Attica the curve at the shoulder became smaller (fig. 41c); and in the fourth century it was so far reduced that the echinus was virtually a truncated cone, marked off from the abacus by a more or less emphatic groove (fig. 41d). Most Doric

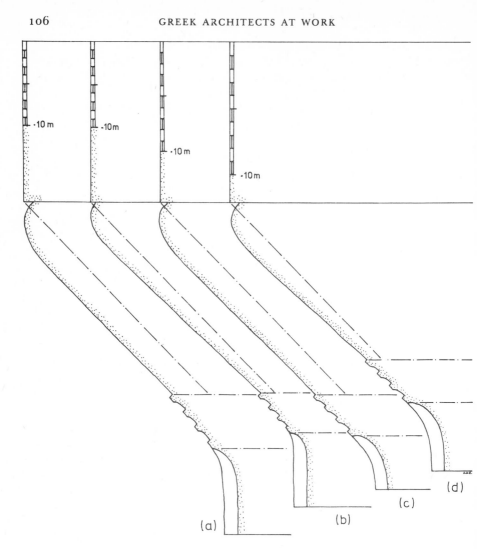

43   Temple of Aphaia at Aigina (c. 510–490 B.C.): capital profiles scaled to give a
uniform abacus height: (a) outer colonnade; (b) pronaos; (c) lower inner colonnade;
(d) upper inner colonnade

capitals from the sixth to the fourth centuries can be assigned at once by eye
to one of these groups, and there are remarkably few which suggest a
gradual transition. These changes did not occur simultaneously over the
whole Greek world; Sicily and south Italy were slow to adopt them,[17] and
the fifth-century Attic profile was little used outside Attica.

   The uniformity of Doric capital designs over considerable areas and
periods is really more striking than the variations, and was probably made
possible by the specification of each new design as a set of proportional

rules (cf. pp. 64–5). The major changes in echinus profile must have involved changes in the rules, and other differences in proportion probably also involve different rules, and therefore different architectural intentions. The rules used have not yet been identified but, given the comparatively crude Greek systems of numeral, and especially fractional, notation, the development of design was probably in a limited number of discrete stages, each one expressible in quite simple proportional terms.[18] Thus the appearance of continuous evolution is probably an illusion, and the development of the Doric capital was not so very different from that of the Ionic base. Major changes only took place at particular times and places, and they were not adopted universally or immediately. The changes were in proportion rather than form, but probably just as distinct to the architects involved. The most experimental period was probably again the archaic period, although the field for experiment was narrower than with the Ionic base. However, there is a striking difference in the apparently unanimous agreement on the direction of change. Each new design apparently produced a capital which was smaller, tighter, and visually less important, and there is nothing equivalent to the abortive experimentation of the Peloponnesian Ionic base.

The rules of proportion, applied with more or less precision, would determine fixed points in the profile of a capital, to which the curve of the echinus would have to be fitted. Vitruvius of course says nothing about how that was done, for by his time it was simply a question of joining up two points with a straight line. Some half-finished capitals from mid-fifth-century Athens have the echinus roughed out as a truncated cone supporting a low disc (fig. 16).[19] Already by this time, therefore, the profile may have been seen in terms of a bevel and a shoulder, with the precise curve drawn freehand within such a simple linear frame, and although in many capitals of the preceding group the echinus has an unbroken curve from neck to shoulder, in many others the middle part is straight for a substantial distance. Of course, it has also been suggested that, in Athenian capitals at least, the echinus profile was designed as a precise mathematical curve, a hyperbola, for instance.[20] The mathematical properties of conic sections (including the hyperbola) were first investigated by Menaichmos in the mid fourth century,[21] but there is no reason why the curves themselves should not have been known and used much earlier, as convenient and satisfying for particular purposes. To demonstrate that, however, it is not sufficient to show that some existing profiles approximate closely to hyperbolic curves (as they do); there must also have been a simple method allowing the architect ignorant of the mathematical properties of such curves to construct an appropriate one from a given upper diameter to a given (approximately at least) abacus width, points which might vary considerably in their relationship to each other from building to building.[22] That has not yet been done, and since some hyperbolic curves make very effective echinus profiles, they may have been unwittingly hit upon by an architect drawing freehand a curve which satisfied his eye.

This pragmatic interpretation of Doric capital profiles draws some support from perhaps the most sophisticated aspect of Greek temple design, the small, unexpected variations from the vertical, the horizontal or the rectilinear, which are known as refinements. For although there is argument about their purpose, it is generally agreed that they had an empirical rather than a theoretical justification; they were meant to improve the actual appearance of the building. The nature and history of these refinements are set out in the standard handbooks on Greek architecture, and need not be described at length here.[23] The most important are these: the horizontal lines of the stylobate and entablature curve slightly upwards in the middle; the columns tilt inwards and taper in a gradual curve, not in a straight line; and the corner columns are slightly thicker than the others. All these are shown in exaggerated form in figure 44. The use of such refinements reached its climax in Periklean Athens, and the Parthenon, on which no expense was spared, displayed all these features and more. No later building matched it, but the refinements must have got themselves a firm place in architectural literature, for Vitruvius sets out all those mentioned above.

Vitruvius is in no doubt about the purpose of these variations from the expected regularity. He gives no reason for the curving taper (entasis) or

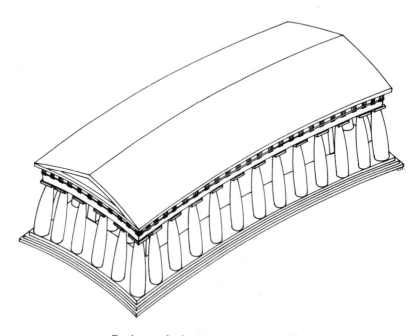

44   Doric temple showing exaggerated refinements

tilting of the columns, but explains the curvature of the stylobate, the enlargement of the angle columns, and also an outward tilting of the entablature and various modifications of proportion according to scale (cf. pp. 86–8), as intended to correct optical illusions which would make a truly regular temple look irregular.[24] The existence of some of these illusions has been denied, and certainly one can argue at length about the actual effect of the refinements,[25] but for an understanding of Greek architects' ideas the question is not what the refinements do, but what they were intended to do. Here the words of Vitruvius are far more valuable than the judgments of modern critics, for although he was writing some four centuries after the heyday of refinements, he formed part of a continuous literary tradition which included the work of Iktinos on the Parthenon. The fact that refinements had been used rarely and elaborated not at all in the intervening period makes it all the more likely that the explanations he gives are derived directly or indirectly from the architects of the fifth century, for whom refinements were important. The theory of vision underlying Vitruvius' explanations—that vision depends on rays emanating from the eyes to objects seen, rather than on light reflected from the objects to the eyes—underlies Euclid's *Optics* (c. 300 B.C.), was maintained by Archytas (early fourth century), and was already used by Empedokles (mid fifth century).[26] Further, although Vitruvius gives the fullest account of particular refinements, Philon must surely be thinking of refinements when he talks of empirical corrections to prevent things which 'were in fact of equal thickness and straight' appearing not to be so.[27] This takes the Vitruvian explanation back to the third century, and precisely the same view was expressed by a later Greek writer on applied mathematics, perhaps Heron of Alexandria.[28]

Contemporary literary support has also been claimed for another explanation of the refinements, that they were intended to save a temple from a mechanical, lifeless appearance, and to create a slight and desirable tension between what the eye saw and what the mind recognized as the underlying form. The fifth-century sculptor Polykleitos, who was deeply concerned with questions of proportion, said 'perfection lies in many numbers [i.e. rules of proportion] *para mikron*'.[29] *Para mikron* is taken to mean 'except for a little,' that is, one must deviate slightly from the rules.[30] However Philon of Byzantion, who quoted the remark, thought it meant 'down to the last little detail', that is, everything must be done according to the rules; and even if the first interpretation is correct, it does not indicate why deviation is necessary—perhaps to correct optical illusions rather than to create a tension between eye and mind. Archaeological support for this interpretation of the refinements is rather stronger, however. The stylobate of the Parthenon is set out with extreme accuracy, parallel sides differing from each other by less than one part in 5000, but the columns are placed on it with much less precision, some intercolumniations varying from the mean by as much as one part in 250. Such avoidable variations in column spacing must, at the very least, have been intentionally tolerated,[31] and since they could correct no optical illusion, they must have been intended to relax slightly the stiffness of complete regularity; if so, then other variations from regularity may well have had the same intention. In spite of this, however, it seems preferable to retain Vitruvius' optical illusion theory wherever possible.

Where Vitruvius gives no explanation, of course, there is more freedom to dispute that theory. Vitruvius tells us that the entablature should be inclined outwards to prevent it seeming to lean inwards; could people who thought that also believe that the columns beneath would seem to lean outwards unless they were inclined inwards? In the fifth century architects were less sure than Vitruvius of the need to tilt the entablature outwards, and sometimes it was tilted inwards, like the columns. In any case the opposite tilting of columns and entablature might not seem as illogical according to Greek optical theory as it seems to us.[32] Nevertheless, many people would prefer to regard the inward inclination of the columns, like the tapering of the columns, as a device to increase the apparent stability and restfulness of the building, and that is not precisely the correction of an optical illusion.

Although Vitruvius does not explain entasis (curving taper), Heron (?)[33] says that it too was a compensation, to counter the apparent concavity of a straight-tapering column. The earliest instances of entasis are very pronounced, however; in the first temple of Hera at Paestum it is five times as great as in the Parthenon, and immediately perceptible. It is hard to imagine the architect thinking this just compensated for an optical illusion, and one cannot argue that it was simply a misjudgment, for the same pronounced entasis occurs in the rather later temple of Athena in the same city.[34] Thus the original purpose may have been to give life and resilience to the column, making it seem to react to the load placed on it. With the much slighter entasis used in the Periklean period, the optical illusion theory is more tenable, and it is quite possible that the architectural intention had changed. If so, it changed again, for in the Roman period the entasis is again inclined to be noticeable.

The pronounced curve in the early instances of entasis makes Pennethorne's theory of an Egyptian origin not unreasonable.[35] Greek architects did not, of course, copy the Egyptian fashion, which makes the column actually bulge out before turning inwards, while the Greek column simply tapers more gradually at the bottom than at the top; but the idea of giving resilience to a column by curving its profile could have been inspired by the Egyptian practice. However, the whole principle of refinements, as modifications of formal rules to take account of subjective perception, is alien to the spirit of Egyptian art, which normally represents each thing and each part as it is known to be, rather than as it would actually appear; for instance in a profile face the eye is always shown as if seen from the front. Since it is precisely in the representation of things as they appear rather than as they are known to be, that Greek art showed itself most independent of earlier cultures, it is likely the idea of architectural refinements was a Greek one.

The use of refinements has been associated with the development of linear perspective in practice and theory, which Vitruvius attributes to fifth-century Athens.[36] However, the refinements are related to the principles of perspective only in the general sense that both concern the complex relationship of reality and appearance, and other parts of this field, such as foreshortening, had been explored by Greek painters and sculptors in the later sixth century. It is not surprising, therefore, that the use of refinements begins much earlier than perspective—indeed before actual regularity of design had been achieved. Entasis, as we have seen, occurs in the first temple of Hera at Paestum (sixth century, perhaps well back in it), and the temple of Apollo at Corinth (c. 540 B.C.)[37] had a curved stylobate. The late-sixth-century temple of Aphaia at Aigina provides the earliest instances of tilted columns and enlarged corner columns.[38] Until the Periklean period, however, these refinements seem to have been used sporadically; for about a generation they were intensively developed, and then once more used intermittently. Present evidence suggests that the development of the idea was entirely the work of Doric architects; although they occur in some post-fifth-century Ionic buildings, refinements were never adopted wholeheartedly by Ionian architects, entasis being the only one widely used in later architecture.

One reason for the brief popularity of the refinements was probably the cost of them, which later patrons did not think justified by the improved appearance. Modern building practice, where many elements are fabricated off the site and all have to fit into a detailed preliminary design, may lead one to overestimate the additional expense and trouble, however. Even in a Greek temple without refinements each block was normally dressed only as it was required, and was specially cut to fit its own particular position; shapes and sizes were not precisely standardized. And although the curves and inclinations would require the masonry to be accurate and careful (which Greek temple masonry was in any case), Bundgaard has pointed out that they can be specified more easily in words than by drawings and set out without complicated instruments by the painstaking use of simple equipment.[39]

An example will show the sort of procedure. In the Parthenon the capitals of the outer colonnade carry an architrave which forms a broken curve; each capital therefore has to provide a correctly angled bed for each of the two architrave ends which rest on it. The angle between these beds is not constant from capital to capital, and since neither the length of the architrave blocks nor the intercolumniation is precisely uniform, tremendously accurate calculations, drawings, and instruments would be required to prefabricate each capital with the necessary precision. Once the capitals were in place, however, the beds could be easily and accurately

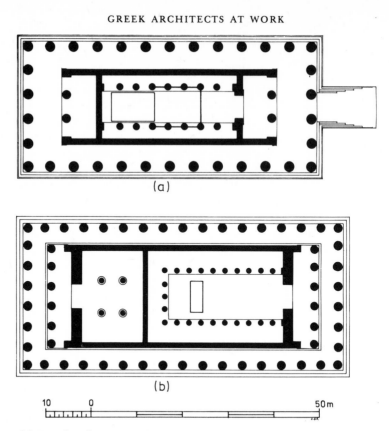

(a)

(b)

10   0   50m

45   (a) Temple of Zeus at Olympia (*c.* 470–457 B.C.); (b) Parthenon at Athens
(*c.* 447–432 B.C.); plans at a uniform scale

formed by laying a straight wooden beam from capital to capital with the
length of the appropriate architrave block marked on it, and then dressing
the relevant areas on each capital until they made contact with the beam
throughout. Indeed a check of this sort would probably be made even if the
architrave was horizontal, so as to ensure that adjacent capital tops were in
precisely the same plane. In some cases the extra work would have been
more than in this example, and it was certainly quicker and easier to omit
all refinements; but basically the work required was more of the same kind
which was normally lavished on a Greek temple, rather than something
exceptional and mysterious.

The refinements deserve treatment at length because they constitute one
of the most interesting and original ideas in Greek architecture, and they
also illustrate its combination of extreme visual sophistication with
technical simplicity, a mixture of qualities the reverse of that commonly
found today.

The Parthenon (447–432 B.C.) with its painstakingly developed forms and
proportions, and its copious use of refinements; marks in some ways the

culmination of Greek architectural development up to that time; as Philon would say, 'by adding to and subtracting from the sizes, by taperings and all sorts of experiment', a building 'suited to the vision and apparently well-shaped' had been produced. In other ways, however, it marks a change in direction. The wealth of sculpture on the outside is itself a departure from traditional Doric simplicity, and it is coupled with an intermingling of Ionic with Doric which was to have a permanent effect on Greek architecture. A less spectacular but perhaps more important change of direction is marked by the interior of the Parthenon.

The extent of the change is shown by comparing the Parthenon with the temple of Zeus at Olympia (*c.* 470–457 B.C.),[40] the most prestigious mainland temple of the previous half century, and begun only about twenty years before the Parthenon (figs. 45–7). The Parthenon is about

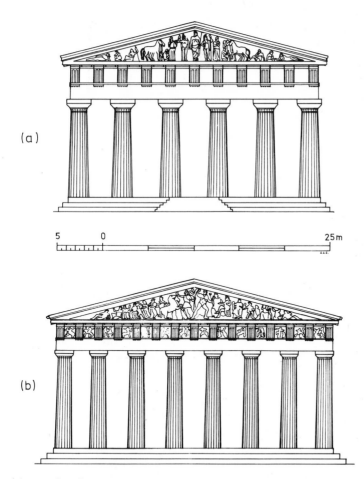

46 (a) Temple of Zeus at Olympia (*c.* 470–457 B.C.); (b) Parthenon at Athens (*c.* 447–432 B.C.); elevations at a uniform scale

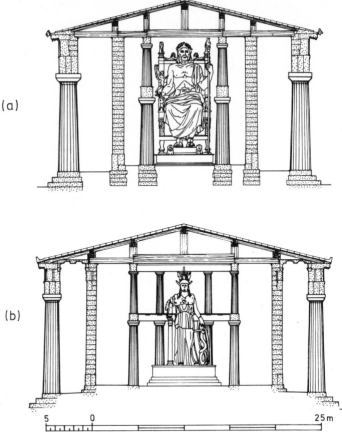

47   (a) Temple of Zeus at Olympia (*c.* 470–457 B.C.); (b) Parthenon at Athens
(*c.* 447–432 B.C.); sections at a uniform scale

three metres wider and five metres longer than the temple of Zeus, but its columns are so similar in height as to suggest that a comparison was intended. The design of the temple of Zeus is fully mature, but with no surprises. The fronts have six columns as usual, and the outer faces of the cella walls are aligned on the axes of the columns one in from each corner; thus the external width of the cella is roughly three-fifths of the temple width.[41] The inner columns are arranged in two rows leaving a central corridor 6·35 m wide, into which Pheidias just managed to squeeze his colossal statue of Zeus (fig. 47a). In the Parthenon the fronts have eight columns, so that with the outer faces of the cella side walls again aligned roughly on the axes of the columns one in from each corner, the external width of the cella is about five-sevenths of the temple width,[42] and the space between the inner colonnades is 9·82 m, within which Pheidias' scarcely less colossal statue of Athena is not at all cramped (fig. 47b). In addition the internal columns are not simply arranged in two straight rows, but return behind the statue, providing a more sophisticated background than the blank wall at Olympia.

This last change may seem of minor significance, but it was the first development in the interior design of Doric temples for over 150 years; the formula used in the temple of Zeus certainly occurs in the first temple of Apollo at Kyrene;[43] almost certainly in the temple of Hera at Olympia (*c.* 600 B.C.). The only known alternative, where inner columns were required, was to use a central single colonnade (cf. fig. 26a), but that spoiled the view of the cult statue, and was rarely used after *c.* 600 B.C. The gain in cella width by using eight-columned fronts is almost as unexpected in a building of this size, for we have seen that temples with more than six columns on the

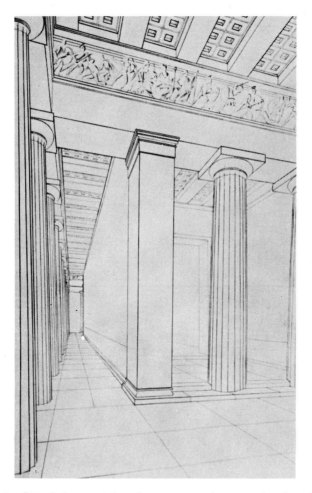

48   Temple of Hephaistos at Athens (*c.* 450–445 B.C.): perspective view of space in
front of pronaos

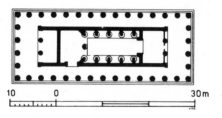

49   Temple of Apollo at Bassai (*c.* 430–400 B.C.): plan

50   Temple of Apollo at Bassai (*c.* 430–400 B.C.): restored perspective of cella

fronts are rare, and no previous architect had used the additional columns to gain a more spacious cella.[44] In order to avoid difficulties with the overall proportions (cf. p. 77), Iktinos significantly raised the column height, not only in terms of the lower diameter, but more strikingly in terms of the intercolumniation.[45] Apparently, therefore, he not only thought about the interior design, but even modified the exterior to allow the spaciousness required within. It is no surprise to learn that Pheidias, the sculptor of the cult statue, was general overseer of all Perikles' public works.[46]

This interest in spaces was not unique to Iktinos. The Hephaisteion architect, besides repeating Iktinos' formula, had a special trick of continuing the pronaos entablature across to the outer colonnade on either side, so that instead of the usual box-within-a-cage effect of a Greek temple, a visitor looking up at the sculptured pronaos frieze would be aware of a substantial space in front of the pronaos, clearly set off from the porticoes on the other three sides (fig. 48).[47] In the temple of Apollo at Bassai (c. 430–400 B.C.), which may also be by Iktinos,[48] the cella was again given a horseshoe colonnade (figs. 49, 50), but this time the columns were frankly non-functional, being half-columns attached to short spur walls, and instead of the normal two storeys of columns, there was a single storey, made possible by the replacement of the normal Doric order by more slender Ionic columns (Corinthian across the end; cf. pp. 127–8). A sculptured frieze running above these columns emphasized the importance of the cella interior, while the exterior of the temple is uninteresting.

The unusual arrangement of the cella at Bassai had a strong influence on Peloponnesian architects, who during the next century and a half often adopted the idea of a colonnade close to or touching the cella walls, not for structural reasons, but so as to make the cella seem richer and more spacious. Of the important Ionic temples of the fourth century and Hellenistic period, however, only that at Didyma (fig. 27c) had anything as elaborate within, and at Didyma of course the 'cella' was an open court (see pp. 81–2);[49] the other cellas either had no columns or columns placed where they could effectively support the roof (fig. 23). It is not this, but the Peloponnesian treatment, which requires explanation of course, for the cult centre was normally the altar outside the temple, rather than the statue within. The unusual cella design at Bassai has been explained as the result of the special demands of the cult, but it seems more likely that its continuation in the Peloponnese was an architectural fashion rather than the result of a widespread but short-lived change in cult practice.

Even in buildings where the interior was functionally important, there was little development of interior design. To some extent architects were hampered by structural difficulties, but even in the spacious Council Chamber at Miletos (c. 170 B.C.; fig. 51),[50] the interior is decorated only with shallow pilasters, while the exterior has half-columns, shields in relief, and other enrichment. In fact Greek architects mainly showed their interest in

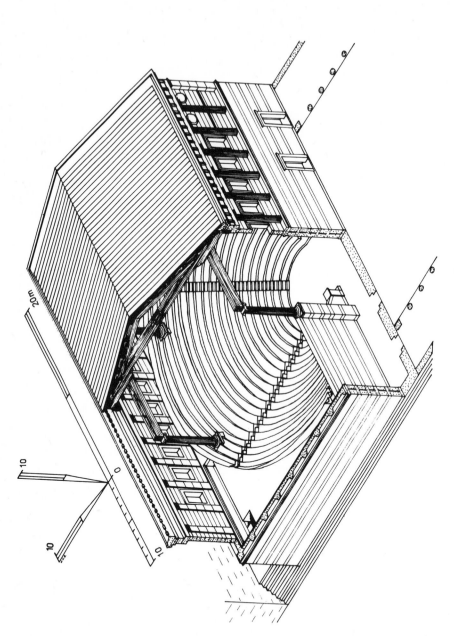

51   Council Chamber at Miletos (c. 170 B.C.): cut-away isometric

manipulating space not inside buildings, but outside. The first clear
example is again a Periklean building. When the Parthenon was virtually
complete, work began on a new monumental entrance to the Akropolis,
designed by the architect Mnesikles.[51] No other work by him is certainly
known, although he has been connected with the Erechtheion and the Stoa
of Zeus in the Athenian agora; but the Propylaia (437–432 B.C.) is one of the
most ingenious, unusual, and successful of Greek buildings. It occupied
the same site as its predecessor (broken lines in fig. 52), and included the
same elements—a main gate-building through which passed the
ceremonial way for the procession in honour of Athena, a chamber
north-west of it intended, according to a recent suggestion,[52] for ritual
dining, and to the south-west a less clearly defined space, unroofed in the
earlier building, leading to the sanctuary of Athena Nike. In addition to
these main elements, Mnesikles also intended to include two rooms to the
north-east and south-east; these rooms were never completed, for work on
the Propylaia stopped prematurely, but Mnesikles had already made some
preparation for them.

If Mnesikles had simply followed the previous arrangement of these
elements, he would no doubt have produced an elegant and sophisticated
building, but nothing more. What he did, however, was to tie the separate
elements into a unified complex. He turned the central building through

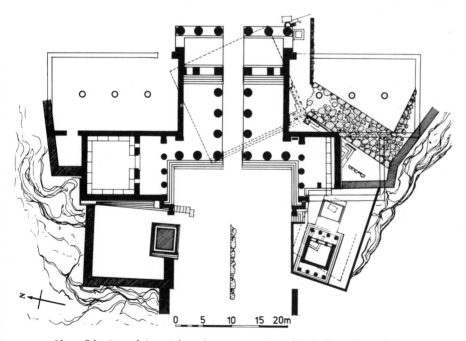

52   Plan of the Propylaia at Athens (437–432 B.C.): outline indicates intended north-
east wing and suggested intention for south-east and south-west wings; broken lines
indicate earlier Propylaia (c. 520–510 B.C.)

23° so that its axis coincided with that of the approach ramp, which he widened from about 11 m to about 21 m; he turned the dining-room (whose walls in the second century A.D. were hung with pictures, so that it is known as the Pinakotheke, or picture gallery) slightly in the opposite direction so that its façade was at right angles to that of the main building; and directly opposite the Pinakotheke he built a matching façade, even though the room on that side was quite small, and the façade projected out beyond it, with nothing behind. Thus the visitor approaching the Akropolis was drawn into a formally organized space, with the lofty façade of the gate-building dominating the minor façades on either side.

There has been much discussion of a supposed 'original plan' intended by Mnesikles (e.g. outline in fig. 52);[53] it was to have been completely symmetrical, with the south-west and south-east wings matching those to the north, but it was scotched by the conservative priesthoods of Athena Nike to the south-west and Artemis to the south-east, on whose sanctuaries it would have encroached. Greek buildings are, of course, normally symmetrical but they also normally form simple units, like the temple and the stoa; a symmetrical complex like the 'original plan' would be as odd in the fifth century as the building actually erected. There is in fact no evidence for the symmetrical scheme, which in many versions runs slightly over the newly completed south wall of the Akropolis, and no purpose has been suggested for the 'intended' south-west room. It is clear that by the time construction had begun, at least, no such room was proposed, for to extend the east wall of the south-west wing, it would have been necessary to remove the roof and dismantle half the east and south walls, so as to bond the new work into the old.

A person approaching the Akropolis is unaware of the asymmetry and the misfit between the south-west wing and its façade. The plan actually built is therefore a more skilful solution of the design problems than the 'original plan', for it allows space and access to the neighbouring sanctuaries, and provides all the necessary accommodation in a simpler and more economical way, while at the same time it does not diminish the architectural effect of the entrance court. The fact that this effect is achieved despite the asymmetry of the south-west and north-west wings, and not simply through an unthinking pursuit of complete symmetry, shows that Mnesikles was specifically interested in this space; it was at least as important to his whole design as the cella of the Parthenon to that of Iktinos. Although some other buildings of the same period show a similar interest in formally defining an exterior space, there was no real precedent to help Mnesikles organize the disparate elements of his plan, and the credit for his success belongs to him.

To a large extent each element of the Propylaia was still conceived separately, but the whole design is held firmly together by the continuous platform on which the central gate-building and the two west wings stood. This was not easy, however, for the façade of the central building, the *raison d'être* of the scheme, was on a large scale, its six columns being about one-third higher than those of the wings (cf. fig. 33), while the scale of the stylobate and its steps in a Doric building is usually related to the size of the columns; how could the same ·stylobate and steps serve columns so different in size? Mnesikles was equal to that problem. He built four steps instead of the usual three, so that all four would suit the large columns of the central building, while the three top ones would suit the smaller columns of the wings (plate 8). All four steps were carried round beneath the three façades; but below the wings the bottom step was built of dark stone instead of marble, so that it could be accepted by the eye to emphasize the unity of the three elements, or rejected to allow for the difference in scale.

There are many ingenious features in the Propylaia, some discussed in Chapter 7, others necessarily passed over.[54] Mnesikles had set himself a difficult problem, however, and although the complex is well held together at the base, the junction of the west wings to the central building at entablature level is inorganic. The separate roofs given to the various

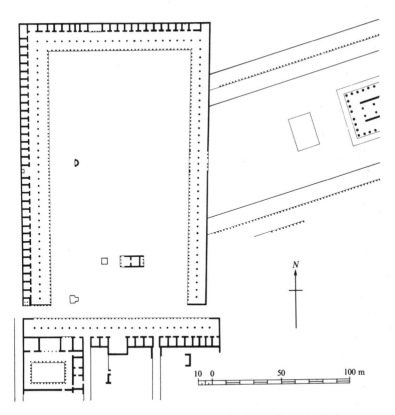

53   Agora at Magnesia on the Maeander (second century): plan

elements also emphasize their individual form (fig. 33), so that the solid masses compete with the space they define. In the slightly later Stoa at Brauron a rather larger rectangular space was surrounded by three uniform colonnades (never fully executed), and as a result the space is more firmly framed and the building about it less important. It was this simplified definition of regular space by uniform porticoes which was at first more popular, and architects often used a colonnaded court to give coherence to complex buildings. Thus in the palaistra which had to provide facilities for mental and physical education, for washing and for storage, the exercise court was defined by a frame of regular porticoes, off which the various rooms required could open.

In mainland Greece architects continued for a long time to visualize their buildings as separate solid entities, even when they took care to relate one to another. In Ionia the space was often more important, and there the characteristic agora of the Hellenistic period was a rectangular space framed on three sides by L-shaped or Π-shaped stoas, with a straight stoa on the fourth side.[55] The way these stoas flex round corners and merge into each other, as buildings never did in archaic or classical architecture, emphasizes the importance of the court rather than the mass of the buildings, or even the space beneath their roofs.

In spite of its regularity there is normally no emphasis on the axis of symmetry of the Ionian agora.[56] It is the space, not some building in or near it, that is the focus of attention. There was indeed a growing tendency to play down the importance of neighbouring buildings by screening them behind a colonnaded façade, so that from within the court there was nothing to break the uniformity of the frame. Thus in the agora at Magnesia on the Maeander (second century; fig. 53) the south stoa conceals behind its façade not only shops but also the prytaneion (city offices) and two streets entering the agora from the south.[57]

In the agora no single building was functionally dominant; in a sanctuary the temple was a natural focus of attention, and in the late Hellenistic period its importance was often formally expressed in visual terms by placing it on the axis of symmetry of a rectangular colonnaded court, with the entrance to the sanctuary at the other end of the axis. The upper terrace of the sanctuary of Asklepios at Kos (second century)[58] shows clearly how the mass of the temple, the surrounding space, the secondary porticoes, and the spectator were all brought into an easily perceived relationship (plate 9). This is very much a repetition of Mnesikles' scheme, with a major element axially approached and minor elements setting it off on either side, but the architect at Kos defines the space more smoothly by running the portico behind the temple, and avoids the difficult junction of large and small orders. A gap of two centuries or more separates these Hellenistic axial sanctuaries from the Propylaia, and different types of building are involved, so that a direct influence is unlikely. It is possible that such symmetrical sanctuaries were developed first for the cults of the

Ptolemaic kings of Egypt, translating into Greek terms ideas long current in the absolutist architecture of the pharaohs. If so, the idea was adopted eagerly by Hellenistic architects; it was widely used in sanctuaries from the second century on, and also in other situations. Thus the Council Chamber at Miletos (c. 170 B.C.) was approached through a colonnaded court with a formal entrance at the opposite end of the axis (fig. 69e).

This was not just a case of a single repeated formula, however. At Lindos on Rhodes[59] effective use was made of a monumental staircase passing up through the centre of successive porticoes (early and late third century) to reach the temple of Athena (late fourth century) on the highest point of the akropolis, and at Pergamon the manipulation of spaces and buildings was carried out on an even larger scale, but with a looser symmetry as the site demanded, and no emphatic axis.[60] The layout of the akropolis there resembles a huge fan, with the theatre at its centre (plate 10). A long terrace lined with stoas forms a horizontal base line at the foot of the theatre, and above it a series of elements radiates out from the theatre—the upper agora, the sanctuary of Zeus with its triumphal altar, the sanctuary of Athena with its temple, and another enclosure later occupied by a temple to the deified Trajan. Except for this last all the elements in their present form date from the reign of Eumenes II (197–159 B.C.), and their combined effect can hardly be accidental. Although not as regular as some of the complexes previously mentioned, each element is clearly defined, so that in the near view each forms a coherent composition of solid building and open space, while from a distance they together constitute one of the most dramatic cityscapes of antiquity.

The preceding paragraphs will show how Hellenistic architects thought not so much in terms of individual buildings, as archaic and classical architects had done, but rather in terms of larger units—the agora, the sanctuary, or even the whole city. In designing on this scale they were naturally less interested in perfection of detail, and more directly involved in the handling of space, and in the balance and relationship of the mass of buildings to the space about them. In pursuing these interests they developed some of the ideas which were later taken up in Roman architecture, but in spite of their interest in space, and not only because they were hampered by technical difficulties, they never showed the interest Roman architects had in designing impressive interiors; for them the important space was outside.

6

Some later problems with the orders

By the third quarter of the fifth century, after some two hundred years of experience, architects had overcome the major problems associated with the normal Doric temple. The forms and proportions had been refined, and appropriate subjective adjustments could be made to taste; the colonnades on fronts and flanks could be equally spaced, with the angle intercolumniation adjusted to allow a virtually regular frieze; an appropriate pronaos order could usually be designed to fit the given height and width, and a satisfactory formula had been found for the colonnades in the cella.

The temple of Athena at Priene, the first Ionic temple that can be called canonical in the same way as, say, the temple of Zeus at Olympia, is a century later, built in the third quarter of the fourth century. One reason for the delay must be the difficult economic and political situation of the Ionian cities, for after a disastrous attempt at independence in the early fifth century, they were under either Athenian or Persian domination until liberated by Alexander the Great in 334 B.C.; no well-preserved temple is known from this area during the period c. 500–350 B.C.[1] However, surviving remains from the archaic period suggest that the Ionians were less concerned than the mainland Greeks with the development of a rigidly defined order (as indicated by the different histories of the Doric capital and Ionic base). A slightly different Ionic canon had been developed in Athens rather earlier than at Priene, however, and it is fair to say that by the end of the fifth century both orders had reached a stage where they fulfilled almost perfectly the purpose for which they had been created, the articulation of the exterior of a temple. This did not mean that development ceased, of course, for tastes and conditions changed, and architects like Hermogenes were still intent on creating the perfect temple in the second century; but since the basic types of temple remained unchanged, the problems involved were straightforward.

From an early date, however, the Greeks had applied these same orders to different types of building, and as the range of monumental architecture widened from the fifth century onwards, the practice continued. Stoas, palaistras, theatres, meeting-halls, houses, tombs, and even fortifications—everything that had ambitions to be considered as architecture was given a dressing of Doric or Ionic (or later, Corinthian). Sometimes the transition from temple to secular building was effortless, but more often the requirements of the new situation made some sort of adjustment necessary, and this process of transference stimulated many of the formal innovations of later Greek architecture.

The stoa was one of the first building types after the temple to be given a monumental treatment, and we have seen (pp. 91–4) how the differences in scale and function led to the adoption of three metope spans in stoas; that is, intercolumniations with three metopes above each instead of two as in temples. Similarly the convention that had been devised for the inner colonnades of Doric temples also proved unsuitable for stoas.[2] The colonnades in a temple cella were conventionally arranged in two storeys separated by an intermediate architrave (cf. fig. 26c, 47). A person entering the cella would look along the length of the architrave, which would thus not break up the interior space; and there would be no position from which he could directly compare the inner colonnades with those of the exterior or the pronaos. In a stoa, however, the intermediate architrave would be seen crosswise, and from outside the building the inner colonnade would be visible behind the outer; thus differences in scale or proportion, such as the much wider spacing of the inner colonnade (which carried wooden beams rather than a stone entablature), could immediately be perceived.

There is no absolute proof that a two-storeyed inner colonnade was in fact used for a stoa or comparable building, although such an arrangement has been argued for the sixth-century Stoa Basileios at Athens (cf. fig. 34).[3] But what else could an architect do? The problem is not easily solved, for since the inner colonnade needs to reach a higher level than the outer one, a single storey of columns would naturally be larger; yet architects practically never made their inner columns more massive than the outer ones, apparently considering it inappropriate. Within a purely Doric framework, therefore, the only alternative to a two-storeyed arrangement was to break the conventional rules relating column height to diameter, and make the inner columns abnormally slender. Thus the architect of the South Stoa at the Argive Heraion (c. 450–425 B.C.) gave the inner and outer colonnades the same lower diameter and capital, but while the outer columns have normal proportions (height = 4·7 diameters), the inner ones, being 2·21 m taller, have a height equal to 7·3 diameters (fig. 35a).[4] It seems likely that a similar solution was adopted in a number of earlier buildings, too.

The most widely accepted solution involved a combination of Ionic with Doric, however; for since Ionic columns were conventionally more slender than Doric ones, Ionic inner columns behind Doric outer ones could reach up to the roof timbers without appearing unduly massive, and without doing violence to the conventions of either order (fig. 54). Not surprisingly,

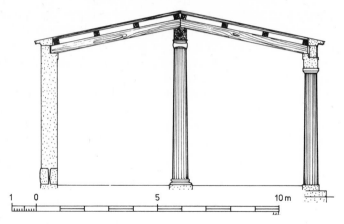

54   Stoa at the Amphiaraion, Oropos (c. 370–360 B.C.): cross-section

this solution was developed in Athens, where Dorian and Ionian fashions most often met, and it was apparently known there by c. 465–460 B.C., for Ionic and Doric fragments of suitable size and style have been attributed to the famous Stoa Poikile, from which Stoic philosophers later took their name.[5] Thus when Iktinos used Ionic columns in the rear room of the Parthenon, he was drawing ideas for a temple from stoa design, a reversal of the usual trend.[6] The use of an Ionic inner colonnade behind a Doric outer one was not restricted to stoas; it became conventional in all sorts of secular portico, and was continued even when changes in the relative proportions of the two orders had removed almost all its practical advantage (fig. 61a). The convention was whole-heartedly accepted for such buildings in Ionia, too, although temples there continued to be designed in Ionic.[7] Thus the choice of order no longer depended on geography as it had done—Ionic east of the Aegaean and Doric west—but on context, convention and taste.

Nothing is known about the upper parts of the Ionic order inside the Parthenon, but when the architect of the temple of Apollo at Bassai (allegedly Iktinos again) decided to use a single Ionic order in the cella, he found that the new context raised new problems.[8] An ordinary Ionic capital had two main faces each with a pair of spiral volutes, and two end faces each looking like a roll of cloth tied up tightly at the centre, more loosely at the ends (fig. 71b). The main faces were set parallel to the line of the architrave, so that they were fully displayed in the normal view of an Ionic temple, while the end faces were much less visible. Since in a stoa the inner architrave ran across the building, the main faces were fully displayed there, too. At Bassai, however, the 'columns' were just half-columns terminating short spur walls, and the architrave ran parallel to the visitor's line of sight (cf. figs. 49, 50); thus if normal Ionic capitals had been used, the visitor would have seen only a row of half end faces, with the main faces strongly foreshortened. To avoid that the architect took up an idea already used in the capitals at the corners of a temple. There two main faces were juxtaposed, with the volute at the corner turned outwards at 45° (fig. 55c).

At Bassai, however, the half-capitals had one whole and two half main faces, so that two volutes were canted outwards; and whereas each main face of a corner capital was normal but for its canted volute (for it had to match others in the same colonnade), at Bassai the whole design was modified. With two canted volutes the face parallel to the architrave became concave in plan (fig. 55a); if the top line joining its two volutes had been almost straight, as in other capitals (fig. 55d), it would have appeared to sag when seen from below. It was therefore given a full rising curve to counter that effect (fig. 55b); at the same time the volutes were drawn together to reduce the concavity in plan, and were tilted outwards to reduce the effect of foreshortening. The result was a highly unusual capital, which, like the bases of the same columns, was never copied precisely, but which strongly influenced the ideas of Peloponnesian architects in the fourth century.[9] From it was developed an Ionic capital with a more normal-looking volute face on each of its four sides, and this also had considerable popularity in Hellenistic Italy.

Besides the problem of the new viewpoint, the internal angle raised

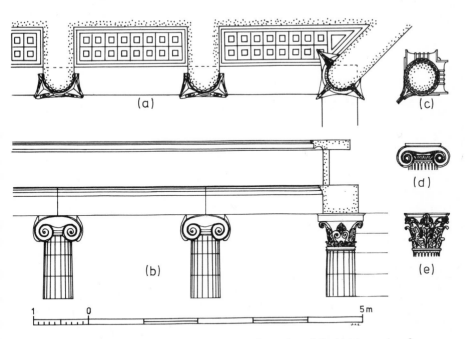

55   Temple of Apollo at Bassai (*c.* 430–400 B.C.): Ionic and Corinthian orders from cella: (a) plan looking up; (b) elevation; (c), (d) Ionic angle capital (plan looking up) and normal capital (elevation) from the Temple by the Ilissos at Athens (*c.* 450 B.C.); (e) normal Corinthian capital (Roman)

difficulties for the architect at Bassai. There was virtually no precedent for such an angle in an Ionic colonnade,[10] and the type of capital devised for a normal external corner was quite unsuitable for an internal, or re-entrant, angle. The architect might simply have modified his normal design to suit the diagonal spur walls at the angles, so that each capital presented two full volute faces towards the visitor, but perhaps he felt that it would be unacceptable to have two such main faces with neither of them parallel to the line of the architrave. At any rate it appears that he used capitals of a quite different form at the angles, our earliest surviving examples of the Corinthian capital (figs. 50, 55a, b right). For in addition to the fairly well-preserved capital found, drawn, and destroyed in the nineteenth century, which belonged to the free-standing column in the middle of the south side of the cella, sufficient small fragments were found to show that there was at least one other Corinthian capital, and if one, then obviously two for symmetry's sake.[11]

The Corinthian capital in its developed form consists of an inverted bell crowned by an abacus with four concave sides. The lower part of the bell is shrouded in a double ring of acanthus leaves, out of which rise two calices on each side of the capital; from each calix two tendrils curl upwards in opposite directions, so that two meet below a flower at the centre of each face and two (from adjacent faces) appear to support each angle of the abacus (fig. 55e). In comparison with this form the Bassai capitals seem a little crude;[12] the acanthus leaves are small and low, the tendrils flat and less plant-like; much more of the bell is bare, and the abacus is rather heavy. Nevertheless, all the elements are present, and there is no difficulty in calling them Corinthian capitals.

Vitruvius attributes the invention of the Corinthian capital to the sculptor Kallimachos, who got the idea from seeing at the tomb of a young girl a basket of offerings which had been weighted down with a tile and around which an acanthus plant had grown up.[13] The date is appropriate, for Kallimachos flourished in the latter part of the fifth century and seems to have had architectural connections.[14] However, the story is really more relevant to the developed form of Corinthian capital than to early examples like those at Bassai, and, more important, it suggests no reason for the invention. It seems unthinkable that a Greek architect should introduce a new capital into monumental architecture simply because he was 'attracted by the nature and novelty of the shape'.[15] At Bassai there *was* a reason for adopting a new form, for since the Corinthian capital has four identical faces, it can be used equally well at external or internal angles; and as we have seen, the architect at Bassai was quite ready to innovate.

At Bassai the Corinthian capital was clearly just a variant form used in an otherwise purely Ionic order, and it only gradually achieved full autonomy. It was again Peloponnesian architects who first took up the idea suggested at Bassai. They improved the design, but reserved the Corinthian capital for interior use, whether or not an internal angle was involved.

7   Wall painting from the Villa at Boscoreale (*c.* 50 B.C.) showing an architectural perspective. New York, Metropolitan Museum of Art, Rogers Fund 1903

8   Propylaia at Athens (*c.* 437–432 B.C.): view of west façade and Pinakotheke
from the south

Gradually the new capital was accepted in other parts of the Greek world, and its design further developed, until by the second century it had reached a stable form—perhaps the most elegant transition from the circle of a column to the rectilinear forms of the entablature above—and had been accepted as suitable for major temples.[16] Roman architects of the late first century B.C. developed a special cornice for use above Corinthian capitals (cf. p. 139), so that then one can talk reasonably of a Corinthian order, but in Greek architecture only the capital was Corinthian, and that was still accepted by Vitruvius.[17]

As interest increased in defining architectural space, it is not surprising that the problem of re-entrant angles occurred more frequently from the fifth century onwards, and since, as we have seen, the space was usually out of doors, and defined by porticoes, it was normally a Doric colonnade which had to turn such angles. The Doric capital, with four identical sides, is just as satisfactory at a re-entrant angle as the Corinthian capital, but the Doric frieze is less convenient. The problem is similar to that arising at external angles, for which an empirical solution had long been worked out

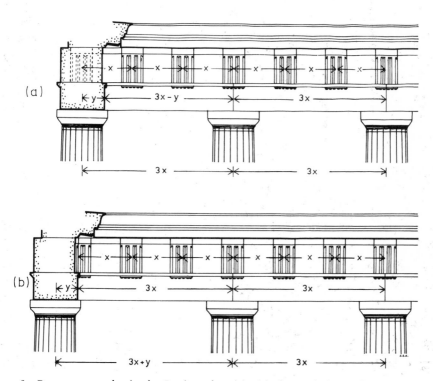

56   Re-entrant angles in the Doric order: (a) with the angle intercolumniation unchanged; (b) with the angle intercolumniation extended to allow two half-triglyphs to meet in the frieze

(cf. pp. 60–4 and figs. 18, 20a). At a re-entrant angle the thickness of the
returning frieze will naturally block the position where the triglyph over
the angle column would otherwise have come, and part of the adjacent
metope as well (fig. 56a).[18] If no adjustment is made, therefore, two
metopes of reduced width will meet at the angle, and that arrangement was
actually used where the angle was visually unimportant. Normally,
however, a stronger accent was preferred at the angle of the frieze, just as it
was at an external angle. The usual arrangement was to have two half-
triglyphs meeting at the angle of the frieze, which meant either extending
the angle intercolumniation by an amount y equal to half the architrave
thickness from front to back (fig. 56b), or by compressing the triglyphs and
metopes by the same amount—or by a combination of both.

The use of two half-triglyphs at the angle is first attested in the Stoa at
Brauron (430–420 B.C.). By using the traditional formula for angle
contraction, but with three metope spans, the architect actually obtained
some increase in the angle intercolumniations; it was not nearly enough,
however, and the metopes near the angles had to be fiercely contracted (fig.
20b).[19] It would have been impossible to crown such an irregular frieze
with a normal Doric cornice, and so the architect used the simpler form
without mutules. The designer of the Peristyle Building in the Agora at
Athens (c. 350–310 B.C.) was apparently determined to avoid this sort of
difficulty, and so instead of making the stylobate $13\frac{1}{3}$ intercolumniations
long for 14 columns (the formula used at Brauron), he made it $13\frac{2}{3}$

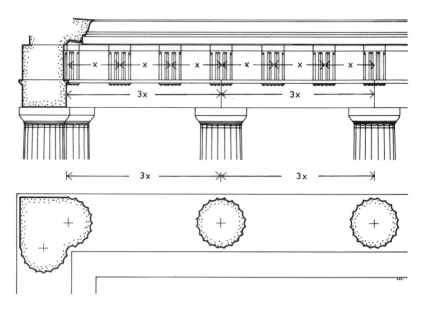

57   Re-entrant angle in the Doric order with heart-shaped pier at the angle: (a)
elevation; (b) plan

intercolumniations long.[20] That, however, was excessive; the angle intercolumniation was extended by 0·49 m, rather than about 0·375 m, as required, so that the triglyphs and metopes near the angle must have been extended, too, unless (which is unlikely) two whole triglyphs met at the angle. A more satisfactory formula, used in several peristylar courts, was to take not the overall stylobate length, as in the above examples, but the stylobate length from front edge to front edge and divide that into equal intercolumniations.[21] Since the columns stood on the axis of the stylobate, not its front edge, the angle intercolumniation was automatically increased by half the stylobate width (from front to back), and although that was slightly more than the increase theoretically required (for the stylobate was always slightly wider from back to front than the architrave), the discrepancy, when spread over three triglyphs and metopes, was negligible.

In the Stoa at Brauron the columns at the angles were slightly thicker than the others—probably an automatic repetition of a feature devised for external angles, since there was no optical justification for such enlargement at a re-entrant angle. Elsewhere in mainland Greece the angle column was usually quite normal, but in Asia Minor architects favoured a special heart-shaped pier, formed by attaching half-columns to adjacent faces of a square pillar.[22] This first occurs in the Stoa by the Harbour at Miletos (late fourth century), the earliest of the Ionian L-shaped stoas (fig. 57), and was accepted and used widely throughout Asia Minor and North Africa.

Since the angle column carries a larger roof-load than the others, it might be thought that the new form had a real or imagined structural justification. However, the roof-load is less than that carried by the inner columns of a two-aisled stoa, which were never reinforced, and since all early examples of the heart-shaped pier occur in Doric porticoes, a formal explanation is more likely. It could well be felt that any extension of the angle intercolumniation, as required by the Doric frieze, looked weak and unsatisfactory at such a critical point; the heart-shaped pier provided a visually stronger form for the corner, and at the same time it reduced to normal the clear space in the extended angle intercolumniation and aligned a half-column directly below each half-triglyph, both matters which Ionian architects seem to have considered important.[23] Although the prime motive for the invention derives from the Doric order, however, the heart-shaped pier eventually became so popular that it was used also in Ionic colonnades (where it allowed a more effective capital for the re-entrant angle than a circular column could) and even in Corinthian ones.

Although the circular column was always by far the most popular type of support in Greek architecture, there were some situations in which it was not convenient. A column is necessarily the same width from side to side as from front to back; it is therefore not satisfactory where a support must look comparatively narrow but must nevertheless be fairly deep from front to back, either to respond to a wall of given thickness or to carry a major beam. The Hellenistic theatre presents such a situation. It had a stage about 2·5 to 3·5 m high, its front edge carried on a series of fairly widely spaced supports between which painted panels of scenery were fixed—the *proskenion* (fig. 1).[24] The restricted height meant that columns could not be more than about 0·25 to 0·35 m in diameter, yet they had to provide support for an entablature with a substantial span carrying the permanent weatherproof stage. Usually, therefore, the supports were not columns but half-columns attached to a rectangular pillar (cf. fig. 58b), with the total depth of the pier usually one and a half times its width or more. Thus although the height of the entablature had to suit the diameter of the half-columns, its depth from front to back could be substantially increased. At the same time it was more convenient to fit the scenery between the flat sides of such piers than between circular columns.

This was not the earliest type of support to fulfill the same general requirements, however. In the second half of the fifth century several Athenian buildings employed narrow rectangular pillars (see fig. 58a),[25] rather like free-standing *antae* (the slightly thickened wall-endings used, for example, at each side of a pronaos). Pillars may have been used by Kallikrates in the Temple by the Ilissos (*c.* 450 B.C.),[26] but the earliest certain instance is in the south-west wing of the Propylaia (cf. fig. 52). Mnesikles may have chosen this form so as to impede access to the sanctuary of Athena Nike as little as possible; on the other hand even if he had used a column, the space on either side would still have been greater than in the single intercolumniation leading into the south-west wing from the central building, so he may rather have felt that a conventional column would have been out of place beneath the unconventional entablature which he

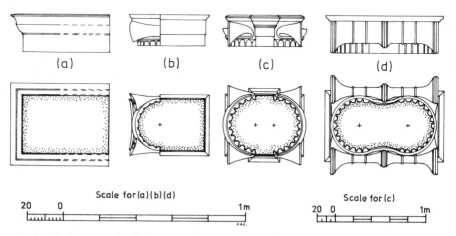

Scale for (a)(b)(d)   Scale for (c)

58 Various types of pier capital: side elevations and plans looking up: (a) rectangular pillar; (b) attached half-column; (c) double half-column; (d) Pergamene double half-column

adopted—architrave with continuous regula and frieze without triglyphs (fig. 33). In the other buildings the pillars seem to have been used so as to keep as wide as possible the free space between supports which, because of the small scale, were closer together than usual.

Some architects, however, apparently felt that the simple rectangular pillar was not sufficiently decorative and lacked the traditional associations of the column. They therefore combined the practical advantages of the pillar with the formal advantages of the column by using a half-column attached to a smaller rectangular pillar.[27] This form, the attached half-column, first occurs in the early fourth century, and it seems to have been another idea developed by Peloponnesian architects, who at that time were experimenting in various ways with the orders as symbolic and decorative rather than functional forms. By the time it became fashionable to present plays on the high *proskenion* stage, the attached half-column was a familiar form in many parts of Greece and in a wide range of circumstances where a small scale had to be combined with adequate strength, so that it was a natural choice for this new situation.

Seen from the back, of course, the attached half-column is no more imposing than the simple rectangular pillar, and it is perhaps a mark of increasing interest in interior space that a third form was developed where the rectangular pillar is reduced to a narrow strip with a half-column attached to the back as well as the front (fig. 58c).[28] This form, the double half-column, appeared first in Macedonian architecture at the end of the fourth century. It also spread widely, and was used in the same situations as the attached half-column, although, being more complex, it was presumably more expensive. It is interesting that even when reduced to a narrow strip, the pillar was still treated as a separate element, projecting slightly beyond the two half-columns, and given its own characteristic capital. It is only in the late Hellenistic period, and (characteristically) in Asia Minor, that the distinction was dropped and the whole double half-column was treated as a continuous form (fig. 58d).

One particular problem which involved the use of all three types of pier was the design of multi-storeyed façades.[29] Greek architecture was essentially one-storeyed, and the orders, whether Doric, Ionic or Corinthian, were developed for single-storeyed buildings. Thus the cornice, the crowning member of any order, embodies the eaves of the sloping roof, and therefore has no logical place beneath a second order. One way out of this difficulty was to treat the lower storey as a closed basement, as in the Mausoleion at Halikarnassos (c. 355–350 B.C.) or (with less logic) the Council Chamber at Miletos (c. 170 B.C.; fig. 51), so that it seemed to form a solid platform for the colonnade above. That was not always practicable, however; a colonnade might be required in the lower storey as well, as in a two-storeyed stoa; and in that case the obvious precedent to follow was the two-storeyed colonnade of a Doric temple cella. The principle of design here was approximately continuous tapering

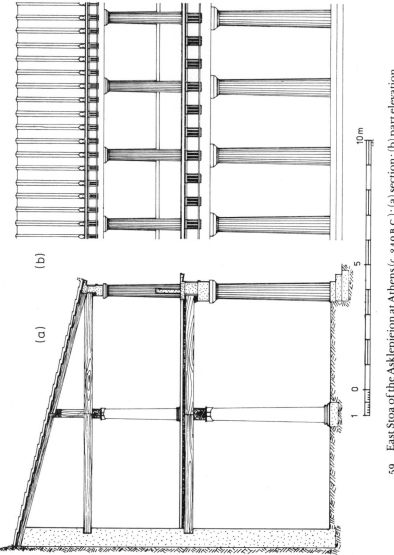

(a)

(b)

10 m

5

0

1

59   East Stoa of the Asklepieion at Athens (c. 340 B.C.): (a) section; (b) part elevation

from the lower column shaft through the capital and architrave to the upper column shaft. Thus the lower diameter of the upper columns was slightly less than the upper diameter of the lower columns, making the upper storey considerably smaller than the lower. Both storeys consisted of circular columns, of course, and in a small temple the upper columns might be no more than 0·50 m in diameter, but since the spans and loads were correspondingly small, no particular difficulty arose.

It is not surprising that the earliest two-storeyed stoa, the East Stoa in the Asklepieion at Athens (c. 340 B.C.), followed this precedent with as little change as possible (fig. 59); both storeys had normal Doric colonnades, the upper one approximately continuing the taper of the lower.[30] Some change was necessary, however. In a temple no upper floor was intended, so that only an architrave was needed between the two colonnades, and only an architrave ran above the upper columns to carry the roof cross-beams. In the stoa a full entablature was needed: in the lower storey to allow space for the thick clay floor of the upper portico and the planks and heavy beams to support it, and in the upper storey to mask the cross-beams and rafters of the roof. In the Doric order, of course, that meant two triglyph friezes, which somehow had to fit the same intercolumniation, but columns of quite different sizes. In the East Stoa the lower order had three metopes to each span, while the upper had five. Since the ratio between the two orders was not consistently 5 : 3, there were numerous differences in proportion between them, most noticeably and inevitably in the proportion of column height to intercolumniation, and since the two colonnades were no longer seen strongly foreshortened, as in a temple cella, such differences would be much more noticeable.

Presumably for reasons such as these few later architects used two Doric colonnades in such façades,[31] although they continued to accept that the upper storey should be considerably smaller than the one that carried it.[32] The next step was taken in temple architecture; in the temple of Zeus at Nemea (c. 340–320 B.C.)[33] a row of free-standing Corinthian columns ran round the inside of the cella, but they did not quite reach the required ceiling height; a small Ionic order was therefore placed above, and since the lower diameter appropriate to their height was only about 0·35 m attached half-columns were used instead of ordinary ones. This idea was taken over in the Stoa at Perachora (c. 300 B.C.; fig. 60);[34] Ionic attached half-columns even smaller than the principle of continuous taper would demand (diameter=about 0·31 m) were placed above ordinary Doric columns. With supports of this form, the upper storey could be made light and delicate, and it was easier to seat the parapet necessary for safety's sake against them than against circular columns. At the same time, the use of different orders, Doric below and Ionic above, made the inevitable differences in scale and proportion less disturbing. This alternation of orders, like the similar alternation in inner and outer colonnades, was accepted very widely, and it could, of course, be applied equally to the

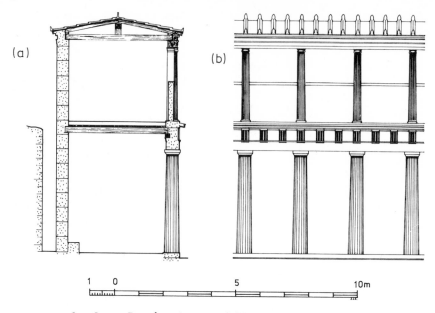

60   Stoa at Perachora (*c.* 300 B.C.): (a) section; (b) part elevation

decoration of façades with non-functional half-columns. In some
Macedonian houses of similar date attached half-columns were also used
in the upper storey,[35] but the two local schools of architecture which seem
to have specialized in two-storeyed porticoes both favoured other forms of
support.

At Delos a number of public buildings of the Hellenistic period, and
several houses, had two-storeyed porticoes. A few used ordinary Doric
columns in both storeys, but most architects preferred for the upper storey
the simple rectangular pillars (fig. 58a) used in Athenian buildings of the
later fifth century. Delos was for much of its history under Athenian
domination, but the Athenians apparently made no striking use of pillars
in the meantime, and the source of the form was probably the fifth-century
Athenian temple of Apollo on Delos itself; the characteristic Delian use of
pillars in upper storeys seems to be original.[36] Functionally, of course, there
is nothing to choose between the pillar and the attached half-column,[37] but
the pillar lacks the inorganic break of the latter, and also makes angles,
both external and re-entrant, easier to handle. The difficulties of a second
triglyph frieze were avoided by giving the pillars of the upper storey an
Ionic entablature.

The other local school was at Pergamon, where the steep slopes of the
citadel (cf. plate 10) meant that in order to gain a flat site of any size massive
terracing was necessary, and on the uphill side of such a terrace a two-
storeyed stoa would mask the cut face of the hill, with the upper portico

conveniently accessible from the high ground behind. Such stoas therefore seem to have been regarded as a Pergamene speciality, and the two stoas donated to the Athenians by Eumenes II and Attalos II were both of this type, even though the site of the Stoa of Attalos has no steep slope behind. The architect of the first of these Pergamene stoas, in the sanctuary of Athena at Pergamon (c. 180 B.C.),[38] ignored the lessons of earlier experience; he used circular columns in the upper storey although it was not easy to seat the parapet against them, and although he made the upper order Ionic, he gave it a triglyph frieze (a typical Hellenistic mixture of the orders), and consequently made trouble for himself where the façade turned a re-entrant angle.

One new problem he dealt with in a more successful way, however, and that was in the choice of an order for the inner colonnade of the upper storey. This problem had not really arisen in the East Stoa in the Athenian Asklepieion, for there both outer colonnades were Doric; it was already conventional, as we have seen, to put an Ionic inner colonnade behind a Doric outer one, and this convention was certainly followed in the lower storey, presumably also in the upper one. However, if the outer colonnade of the upper storey was Ionic, as at Pergamon, some third order was required for the inner colonnade, so as to avoid putting two colonnades of the same order but with different sizes and proportions where they could be directly compared. Doric, of course, would have been too massive for an inner colonnade; one might have expected Corinthian, but instead the architect resuscitated a type of capital with rounded overhanging leaves, which had had some popularity in the sixth century, particularly in the area south of Pergamon.[39] This palm capital (for it was a descendant, however remote, of the much more naturalistic Egyptian palm capital) had not been used for some 350 years, so that its re-use here was a piece of antiquarian scholarship for which there are many parallels in Hellenistic sculpture and literature, but few in architecture.

The two Pergamene stoas in Athens[40] also adopted the palm capital for their upper inner columns (fig. 61; in Hellenistic architecture it was used only in that situation, although later, with the addition of a ring of acanthus leaves, it enjoyed a modest popularity in others); but in other respects their architect avoided the difficulties of the stoa at Pergamon. It was easy enough to omit the triglyph frieze from the upper Ionic order, but the change in the form of the upper colonnade was more thoughtful. The circular columns were replaced not by attached half-columns, but by double half-columns, so that the interior of the stoa was not neglected. They did not follow the normal form, however, with the central strip projecting beyond the half-columns; instead the 'half-columns' were slightly more than half a column, and the central strip was set back to give the whole pier a waisted section which played down its composite character; at the same time the end faces of the Ionic capitals were drawn out to run the full depth of the pier (fig. 58d). This form lacked the

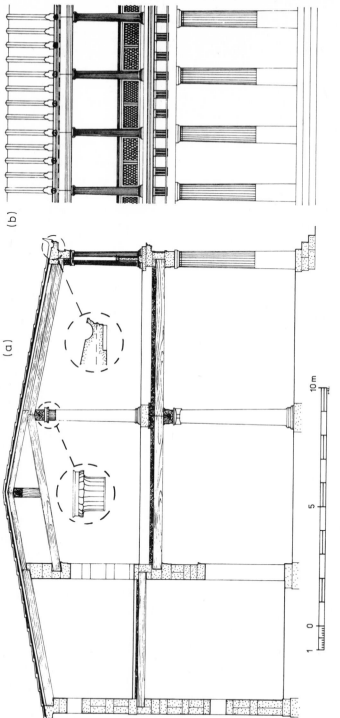

(b)

(a)

10 m

5

0

61 Stoa of Attalos at Athens (c. 150 B.C.): (a) section (details of upper inner capital and upper outer cornice enlarged three times); (b) part elevation

intellectual clarity of the earlier double half-column, but was visually more restful.

There is one further problem which is always raised by a multi-storeyed façade using the Greek orders. The cornice of the upper order is also the crown of the whole building. How can it suit the height of the façade as a whole and also the height of its own order which is just a part of that façade? There is no evidence that earlier architects had considered this problem, but the architect of the Stoas of Eumenes and Attalos apparently *was* aware of it, for that is the natural explanation of the special cornice which he gave to their upper orders. It is reminiscent of a Doric cornice, with mutule-like slabs repeated along its under face, but they are more widely spaced and project further than Doric mutules. The cornice proper is very low, in keeping with the order to which it belongs, but it projects much further than usual, about as far in terms of the whole façade as the lower cornice projects in terms of the lower order, and the special form prevents its identification solely with the upper order.

It is ironical that although this type of cornice was apparently devised for a very special purpose, it was taken up and developed without regard to that purpose; for with its mutule-like slabs elaborated into S-shaped modillions, it was adopted by the Romans as the standard type of cornice above a Corinthian colonnade.[41] Other features, for instance Corinthian capitals, seem to have had a similar history; they were devised to solve a problem, but once accepted, they were further developed and used without regard to that problem. The modification and improvement of established forms was for Greek architects a natural activity. The initial step, however, the creation of a new form or convention, seems to have needed a more specific stimulus. The new types of secular building and the new ideas of space and planning provided that stimulus fairly regularly in the Hellenistic period, and although that period is sometimes regarded as one of decadence, it left Roman, and later Renaissance, architects with a richer and more flexible system of orders than they would have derived from fifth-century Greece.

7

Aspects of structure and technique

After the tremendous changes in building technique associated with the development of monumental architecture in Greece during the second half of the seventh century, the rate of technical development decreased rapidly, and most of the procedures devised or adopted in the first century of monumental building were found satisfactory for the next millenium. The basic system remained a post-and-lintel structure executed in large, carefully dressed stone blocks. This structural conservatism is probably inherent in the Greek conception of architecture as concerned primarily with external form rather than internal space. The conventional forms of the Greek temple were basically established at an early date, and its function—it was primarily a symbol of the sanctuary and a shelter for the god's statue—remained unchanged from start to finish. Changes in structure, although they might make a temple cheaper, could not make it more efficient. There was, for instance, no scope for arched construction in a temple, even though the principle of the arch was known at least from the fifth century; arches in the exterior would interfere with the established image of a temple, while a vault across the cella, where the simple post-and-lintel system might perhaps have been restrictive, would generate lateral thrusts which could hardly be absorbed without visible buttressing. Since the prestige of temple building was so great, even in the Hellenistic period,[1] that its forms were as far as possible transferred to all other building types, the structural system associated with those forms was naturally transferred as well.

There were, however, some experiments, and some more general developments, and before condemning Greek architects for their technical unoriginality, we should explore the range of their ideas in this field. The actual quarrying of stone, the first stage in monumental building, was probably not the direct responsibility of the architect, although he certainly controlled the quality of the blocks delivered, and would probably approve the quarries from which the stone was to be taken.[2] We hear of no stories illustrating the ingenuity of architects in solving special problems of quarrying, however, and there seems in fact to have been comparatively little development in technique until the Roman period, when the increasing use of hard stones such as granite, and the growing demand for thin stone veneers led to the development of new methods.[3] In matters of masonry technique the architects were also responsible for quality, but it is uncertain how far they actually initiated changes in this field. Certainly there were developments, some of them fairly readily understood—the return to a largely two-skinned wall-construction, for instance, in the Hellenistic period, which was probably for economic reasons—but others harder to explain, like the adoption of H-shaped clamps for joining blocks together in the late sixth century. Such matters are not nowadays considered the meat of architecture, however, and since no general principles of interest appear to be involved, there is no need to go into them in detail.[4]

In matters of transport architects did exercise their ingenuity, however, both in getting large blocks from the quarry to the site, and in getting them from the ground to the required level in the building. For horizontal transport it is likely that four-wheeled waggons drawn by oxen were always the normal means.[5] With really heavy blocks, however, the axles of a normal waggon would be subjected to impossible strains, while the four wheels would tend to impose very high pressures on the road surface. A waggon with six or eight wheels might avoid these disadvantages although the difficulty of steering such a vehicle, and of spreading the load effectively over all the axles on any but a perfect road surface, would be hard to overcome, and sledges were sometimes used.[6] Some special vehicle seems to have been used at Eleusis in the fourth century, but its form is unknown;[7] it is simply called a *dittē skeuē*, a 'double contraption', and the load it carried, two capitals weighing about $5\frac{1}{2}$ tons each, was not exceptional. More details are given in descriptions of ancient siege machinery, and these probably indicate the sort of methods used in stone transport. Thus the siege tower built by the Athenian architect Epimachos for Demetrios Poliorketes at the siege of Rhodes (305 B.C.) was about 75 feet (24 m) square, 150 feet (48 m) tall and weighed about 120 tons; it moved on eight wheels about 12 feet (4 m) in diameter and 6 feet (2 m) wide, and it could be steered.[8] Hegetor's armoured battering ram, running on eight wheels about $6\frac{3}{4}$ feet (2 m) high and 3 feet (1 m) wide, weighed about 160 tons and was handled by 100 men.[9] The use of large, wide wheels to reduce the road loading is also likely in heavy stone transporters, for it harmonizes with what Vitruvius tells about the methods used in Ephesos in the sixth century.[10]

The temple of Artemis at Ephesos (*c.* 560 B.C.) was one of the first colossal Greek temples, and its column drums and architraves were probably among the largest blocks handled up to that time. Chersiphron, the architect, was worried that waggons would either break or get bogged down, and so he had the idea of fitting pivots in the centre of each end of the column drums and setting them in wooden frames, so that they could be drawn along like colossal rollers. This avoided both dangers, for the strain on the bearings from the pull of the oxen would be much less than

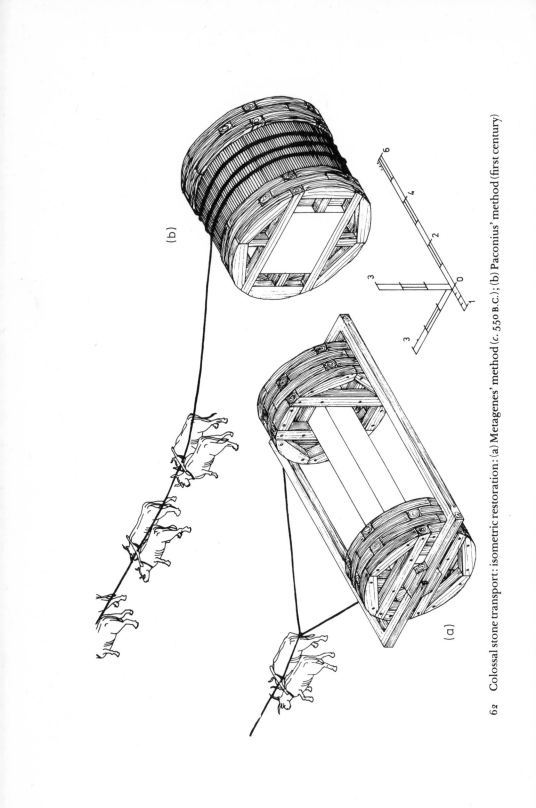

62 Colossal stone transport: isometric restoration: (a) Metagenes' method (c. 550 B.C.); (b) Paconius' method (first century)

the weight of the stone, and the load on the road surface would be spread over a wide area. The method was presumably successful, for it was modified by Metagenes, Chersiphron's son and colleague, for the delivery of the architrave blocks. Since they were of course square in section, he built wooden wheels 12 feet (about 4 m) in diameter round each end of the blocks so that they too could roll along like the column drums (fig. 62a). The same method was probably also used for transporting the architrave blocks for Temple F (c. 530 B.C.) and the temple of Apollo (GT) (c. 530–460 B.C.) at Selinous,[11] and perhaps also for the column drums of the temple of Apollo. Since Chersiphron and Metagenes wrote a book about their work at Ephesos[12] (from which Vitruvius' information probably comes), the architects at Selinous, who in the temple of Apollo were obviously trying to rival the size of the Ionian temples (cf. p. 82), may have learnt both the size they had to match and the appropriate methods to use through this book, rather than by direct contact with Ionian architects.

It was probably also through reading of Metagenes' method that one Paconius, a near-contemporary of Vitruvius, was inspired to try to reintroduce and improve on it.[13] In order to move a block 12 × 4 × 3 feet (about 4 × 1·25 × 1 m), he built wheels 15 feet (about 5 m) in diameter round each end of it, joined them together with numerous wooden beams to form a sort of giant cotton-reel, and then instead of harnessing the pull to pivots in the centre of this roller, he wound a rope several times round its circumference and attached his oxen to that (fig. 62b). Thus he gained a mechanical advantage of 1 : 2, but with a length of only four metres and a diameter of five, the device proved impossible to steer and Paconius spent so much time trying to keep it on the road that he went bankrupt before reaching his goal. Even if he had overcome this difficulty, however, Paconius' method would have been no improvement on Metagenes', for the most difficult stage in moving a heavy load is to get it started; Paconius would have had to stop to rewind the rope after moving the load only half a rope's length, so that he would have had to repeat the effort of acceleration over and over again. Paconius was perhaps a theorist, and if so, he was not the only one to find unexpected difficulties in practice; a writer on mechanics called Kallistratos undertook to transport stone for the fourth-century (presumably) temple of Artemis at Ephesos, but although his 'triangle' (no details are given) worked beautifully as a model, it was useless at full scale.[14]

In spite of their place in the literature, the methods of Chersiphron and Metagenes were probably not widely used. Vitruvius says they were only possible because the quarries were fairly near the building site (11 km at Ephesos, 13 km at Selinous), and obviously the longer the distance, the greater was the risk of damage to the stone. Metagenes' architraves, up to 8·75 m long and weighing up to 40 tons, were supported only at each end, and would be particularly vulnerable to a bump. At Selinous the wheels were built up about a quarter of the way in from each end of the block, so supporting it much more effectively. A more serious disadvantage may have been the width of the road required, greater than the length of the longest block to be transported, and this would almost certainly have to be specially built.[15] For a site in a city these methods were obviously out of the question; both at Ephesos and at Selinous the temples concerned are just outside the city.

Pliny tells us that Chersiphron also devised an ingenious way of getting the architrave blocks of the temple of Artemis into position.[16] He built a ramp of sandbags, and the blocks were hauled up it and then lowered gradually into place by emptying the sandbags at the bottom. As we have seen (p. 48), the ramp was the method of lifting large stones used by the Egyptians and Assyrians, from whom the Greeks probably learnt many of the techniques of monumental architecture, and many blocks used in sixth-century Greek buildings are so heavy that they could not be lifted by a simple crane; the use of a ramp was probably fairly normal at the time.[17] Pliny of course lived about 600 years after Chersiphron, and could not easily know what was normal in the archaic period. It is significant, however, that the main problem for Chersiphron (as Pliny tells the story) was not lifting the blocks but setting them in place; Chersiphron's originality may have lain not in the ramp, but in the use of sandbags instead of loose earth.

It is not absolutely certain that cranes were unknown to early Greek architects, but there is good evidence that they came rapidly into prominence from *c.* 515 B.C. onwards; and from about that time building methods were to some extent adapted to avoid weights beyond the capacity of a fairly simple crane. Surprisingly, no name is recorded as the 'inventor' of the compound pulley system and winch on which this method of lifting depends, but it certainly allowed monumental architecture to fit more comfortably into Greek society and economy, for it meant that all the necessary operations could be carried out by a comparatively small, professional workforce.[18] The ramp on the other hand requires a large workforce for a shorter time; this would be readily available to an Egyptian pharaoh or an Assyrian king, but although it could probably have been raised during the early days of Greek architecture, when temple building was a new and exciting activity in which all citizens were personally involved,[19] it was not a normal feature of the Greek city-state.

During the fifth and early fourth centuries few Greek buildings were on a colossal scale, and the blocks which they required remained within the lifting capacity of fairly simple cranes. Further development would not have been necessary until the new generation of colossal Ionic temples, begun from the mid fourth century onwards, had reached the stage where architraves or door lintels had to be set in place. The first to reach this stage was probably the new temple of Artemis at Ephesos, begun in the third quarter of the fourth century, but nothing is known of weights or methods. The accounts for the temple of Apollo at Didyma (begun *c.* 300 B.C.) record

9　*Above* Sanctuary of Asklepios at Kos: restored elevation (upper terrace, second century)

10　*Below* Akropolis of Pergamon (mainly *c.* 200–150 B.C.): view of model in the Berlin Museums as if from the south-west

11 Relief from the Monument of the Haterii at Rome showing a heavy crane in
operation (*c.* 100 A.D.)

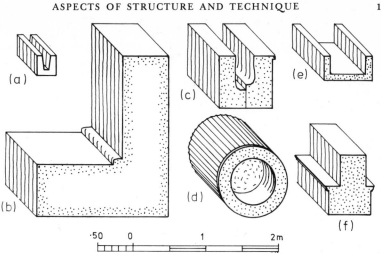

63 Hollowed and extended beams: sections with oblique projection: (a) lintel of
Temple A at Prinias (*c.* 630 B.C.); (b) architrave of temple of Apollo at Syracuse (early
sixth century); (c) architrave of Athenian Treasury at Delphi (*c.* 510 or 490 B.C.); (d)
column drum from Naxian Column at Delphi (*c.* 570 B.C.); (e) ceiling beam from
temple of Apollo at Bassai (*c.* 430–400 B.C.); (f) cross-beam from temple of Zeus at
Stratos (*c.* 320 B.C.)

that the lintel was set in place in 182/1 B.C., and required two cranes; one
was the normal crane with a two-beam jib which had been used for erecting
the columns, the other a specially constructed one with four legs.[20]

It is unfortunate that the Greeks classified their cranes by the number of
their legs, for although that may give some indication of the maximum
load, it does not show how the load was raised. Vitruvius gives two ways in
which the lifting power of a crane may be increased.[21] One is the two-stage
winch, in which a large drum is mounted on the axle round which the
lifting rope is wound, and a second rope is wound round the drum and
taken to a second winch; men turning the second winch will wind in the
rope round the drum, so forcing it to revolve and wind in the lifting rope;
this could increase the mechanical advantage (and so theoretically the
maximum load) at least five times. The alternative is to increase the power
input by mounting a tread-wheel on the main winch axle, which allows
more men to exert their strength more effectively than a simple winch (cf.
plate 11). There is no evidence for the date of either of these developments,
and it is not known whether they occurred first in architecture or some
other field. It is worth noting, however, that in the period around 300 B.C.
there were rapid developments in siege machinery, a field closely related to
architecture, and the power of a catapult is limited by the power of the
winch which tensions it.[22]

Unnecessarily heavy blocks were obviously more awkward, not only to
lift, but also to quarry and transport, so that we find several attempts to

lighten blocks by hollowing them out. The earliest is the lintel of Temple A at Prinias (*c.* 630 B.C.), which was hollowed out on top to form a U-shaped beam, lighter for transport and lifting (fig. 63a).[23] The architrave of the temple of Apollo at Syracuse (early sixth century) and the lintel of the temple of Dionysos at Naxos (late sixth century) were cut down to an L-shaped section (fig. 63b).[24] Since in both cases the beams must have been filled out to their original rectangular section in order to carry the parts above, there was no structural advantage, for the beams would be weakened rather than strengthened; thus the purpose must have been to lighten them for lifting or transport. In the temple of Apollo, where the columns are (unnecessarily) monolithic and the stylobate consists of huge blocks running from column axis to column axis and including the second step as well as the stylobate itself, lifting must have been the major consideration, but at Naxos, where the door jambs have the same L-shaped section, economies in transport must also have been important.

The tendency to hollow out blocks in these and similar ways is more common in the archaic period, and at Delphi, where building stone was often imported by sea from a considerable distance and the site lies at about 550 m above sea level, there was obviously a specially good reason for the numerous instances of the practice (fig. 66c, d).[25] However, it was not restricted to the archaic period, and we find U-shaped marble ceiling beams (fig. 63e) in the temple of Apollo at Bassai (*c.* 430–400 B.C). The weight of the blocks before they were hollowed out, about 2·4 tons, would have presented no difficulty in lifting and there is no structural advantage, for the stone removed reduced the weight and the strength of the beams about equally, leaving the maximum strain almost unchanged.[26] While the main structure of the temple is local limestone, however, the ceiling beams are said to be of Parian marble; they would have to be transported more than 400 km by sea, then hauled some 22 km overland to a height of about 1130 m. The cost of this expensive operation could be substantially reduced by hollowing out the ceiling beams at the quarry, and so reducing their weight by about half.

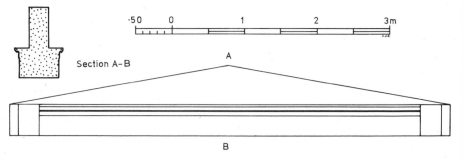

64   Hieron at Samothrace (late fourth century); section and elevation of pronaos ceiling beam

The fact that beams were lightened in this way suggests that some Greek architects realized that the stone was often substantially understressed, and that their beams were dimensioned primarily on aesthetic grounds. For it is never the visible front and lower faces which are cut away, and with the U-section beams the rear face is also unmodified. Thus these beams are not really comparable with modern steel beams, although those may have similar sections. The section of a steel beam is calculated to give the maximum strength for the minimum amount of steel, while with the Greek stone beams no material is saved by giving them an L- or U-shaped section, for the material cut away is useless chips; nor does there appear to be any significant gain in strength.[27] Thus from a structural point of view the work of hollowing out is wasted, and its purpose must be to facilitate handling.

The opposite of cutting out invisible parts of a beam to save weight is adding stone into a beam where it will be invisible, so as to increase the strength, and this too was sometimes done. The most impressive instance is in the Hieron at Samothrace (late fourth century; a temple in form, but used for initiation ceremonies), where the ceiling beams of the pronaos carried a coffered marble ceiling across a span of about 6·15 m.[28] The visible part of each beam is 0·564 m wide and 0·41 m high, but the coffer slabs rest only on the outer parts of the top, and between them rises up a rib of marble which would be invisible from below. This rib, about 0·28 m thick, is about 0·50 m high in the centre of the span, but tapers away to nothing at each end (fig. 64). The triangular shape of the rib at Samothrace is unique, but in several other temples, ceiling beams carrying heavy loads have an invisible rib of constant height to give them extra strength (fig. 63f). In some cases the rib is only a few centimetres high, and may just be the remains of the mantle of stone normally allowed by the quarrymen all round a block, and here left unworked because it came between the beds for the coffer slabs. In other cases, however, the rib is much higher, and clearly an intentional reinforcement of the beam.[29]

The existence of these ribs suggests an awareness that the strength of a beam lies more in its height than in its breadth; that is a difficult proposition to test, however, for it is clear that the shape of the visible beams in a Greek temple depended more on visual than structural considerations, and there was no possibility of strengthening these beams by increasing their breadth except by altering the desired appearance. Similarly one might take as evidence in favour of such an awareness the fact that where three-metope spans were used instead of the two-metope spans normal in temples (cf. pp. 91–4), it was sometimes thought advisable to cut both the architrave and frieze for each span out of a single block, which thus constituted a beam higher than it was broad;[30] but again there was no possibility of increasing the breadth of the beam in such cases, and one could use the popularity of rectangular piers, attached half-columns and double half-columns (cf. pp. 131–3) as an argument on the other side. For

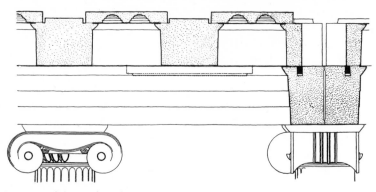

65   Propylaia at Athens (c. 437–432 B.C.): Ionic architrave showing inset iron beam

these forms of support allowed the beams above them to be increased in breadth rather than height. Rather more positive evidence comes from changes in the construction of architraves. Some early architraves consisted of two courses, a roughly square main beam, with a low course carrying the decorative details (*taenia, regulae* and *guttae*) laid above it;[31] but in later buildings, when the architrave consisted of more than one block, it was always divided in breadth not in height, so that each block was higher than it was broad, and door lintels were built up on the same principle. The true answer should be given by the shape of wooden roof-beams, which, being hidden, should have been dimensioned without regard to appearance. The cuttings for such beams suggest that they were usually roughly square in section (which would mean cutting away as little wood as possible in forming them from a circular log); sometimes they were laid with their height greater than their breadth, but more often with their breadth greater than their height, perhaps because that was judged a more stable position.[32] Certainly the arrangement of roof woodwork provides no strong evidence for a systematic appreciation of this elementary principle, that the height of a beam is more important than its breadth.

   The triangular shape of the stone ribs at Samothrace suggests awareness of another principle: that in a simply supported beam the greatest stress is at the middle. There is even less evidence to suggest that this principle was widely understood, but Mnesikles may have been aware of it. In the west porch of the central building of his Propylaia (437–432 B.C.) two rows of Ionic columns support the marble ceiling, and the ceiling beams are arranged so that one comes over each column and one at the mid-span of each Ionic architrave.[33] Since each beam, with its share of ceiling, weighs over 10 tons, Mnesikles decided to reinforce the Ionic architraves with iron bars let into their top face; but the cuttings for the iron bars stop short about 0·90 m from each end of the architrave (fig. 65). So, if the iron bar worked as intended, the load would not fall on the centre of the architrave, but would be transferred to points just in from the supporting columns;

thus only the vulnerable central part of the architrave was protected, and by stopping the iron bar short of the full length of the architrave, not only its length but also its section could be reduced, making it easier to forge.

Over most of its length the cutting was 0·025 m deeper than at the two ends where the iron bar rested. Thus there was free space beneath the bar, so that as it deflected slightly in taking up its load, the bar would not rest on the marble architrave it was intended to relieve. Clearly, therefore, the iron bar was visualized as a simple beam, like the marble architrave but of vastly superior material. The principle was quite different from the use of steel reinforcement in modern concrete beams, for there was no attempt to exploit the high tensile strength of iron; if that had been the intention, the iron bar should have been set, with its ends firmly anchored, into the under face of the architrave, which has to resist the greatest tension. The lintel of a minor doorway in the Erechtheion at Athens (c. 420–405 B.C.) does have an iron bar in its under face, but since it is still in position and its ends are invisible, one cannot say how it was meant to work.[34] In the gigantic temple of Zeus at Akragas (c. 500–460 B.C.) there are cuttings in the under face of some architrave blocks which may have held similar iron bars running from capital to capital (indicated by broken lines in fig. 29b).[35] The cuttings show that the ends of each bar were not anchored, so that the bars were again regarded as simple beams with their tensile strength unexploited. At Akragas the bars were set in the under face of the architrave probably because they were envisaged as supporting the architrave itself (which was here built up like a wall out of three courses of comparatively small blocks), while in the Propylaia they were in the top face because they were envisaged as supporting the ceiling beams. The interpretation of the cuttings at Akragas has been doubted, because the huge figures between the half columns would have supported the architrave blocks effectively on their upraised elbows, without the iron bars.[36] However, the unprecedented system of building may have led the architect of this temple to take all possible precautions to ensure its stability.

So far we have mainly considered the beam supported at each end, but the Greeks also knew of the cantilever beam, where one end of the beam is built into a wall, the weight of which balances the load at the other end. It was probably used in houses, for instance for overhanging balconies,[37] and is not rare in military architecture; the stairways of the Hellenistic towers at Aghios Petros (Andros) (fig. 66) and Chimarrou (Naxos) consist of blocks of stone cantilevered out from the walls.[38] In sacred and civic buildings the cantilever occurs chiefly in the cornice, which is itself supported as a cantilever, and may also have to carry pedimental sculpture. An interesting elaboration occurs in the Parthenon (447–432 B.C.), where iron bars were built into the wall of the pediment to carry the main pediment statues, so relieving the cornice of their weight.[39] However, the effectiveness of the slabs acting as counterweights is reduced by hollowing them out behind, so that for most of their height they are only about 0·25 m thick. The iron bars

66   Tower at Aghios Petros, Andros (Hellenistic): section

were bent up behind the slabs, so that in order to let the statues down they would have to force the slabs forward as well as upward, and that was prevented by clamping the slabs firmly to the rear part of the pediment wall. It would have been simpler, however, not to have hollowed out the pediment slabs at all, and it seems likely that the operation of the cantilevers was not fully worked out beforehand.

Greek architects also used the double cantilever beam, so arranged that the loads on the two arms balance; all weights above then act directly downwards from the centre of the beam. In monumental architecture this device was most commonly used as a means of relieving the strain on an architrave. The most sophisticated example occurs in the Propylaia at Athens, the central openings of which were exceptionally wide so as to allow the passage of processions.[40] In order to relieve the central architrave of the main east and west façades, Mnesikles arranged the frieze above them in long blocks of triglyph-metope-triglyph-metope-triglyph, with the middle triglyph of each block coming directly over the column on one side of the wide span. The central architrave thus carried only the thin marble slab forming the metope required to mask the joints between the two long frieze blocks. The cornice, being of uniform height, would not affect the balance of the cantilever beams, but the pediment blocks, being naturally higher at the centre than at the ends, would normally be correspondingly heavier, and so would upset the balance. To avoid that, Mnesikles probably hollowed out the back of the centre block so that, although taller, its weight was the same as that of the block on the other end of the cantilever (fig. 67).

This refinement suggests that Mnesikles had a clear understanding of the operation of his cantilever. In the temple of Athena ('Ceres') at Paestum (late sixth century),[41] however, where the frieze also consists of long blocks each balanced over a column, the central pediment block was not hollowed out, and although the blocks behind the frieze (frieze backers) are also long ones, they are not balanced symmetrically over the columns. The architect here was less aware of, or less concerned with, the operation of the cantilever than Mnesikles was; but since the spans were small and the west façade stands virtually complete to this day, that clearly did not matter. There are a few other instances of long cantilevered frieze blocks (and some not cantilevered), but the cantilever principle was more widely used with rather shorter frieze blocks in colonnades with three-metope spans.[42] The frieze was cut in blocks consisting alternately of metope-triglyph-metope and triglyph-metope-triglyph; thus with a block of the former type balanced over each column only half the frieze blocks would bear on the architrave. In addition, the shorter blocks were of a more manageable size, while the amount of jointing required was less than if each element had been cut separately.

Another extension of the cantilever principle is the corbelled opening, where the courses are laid horizontally, but each one projects slightly

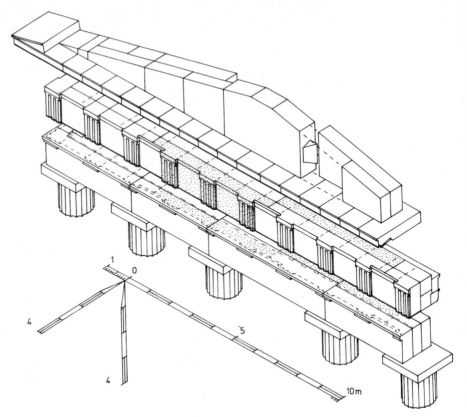

67   Propylaia at Athens, east façade (c. 437–432 B.C.): exploded isometric view
showing cantilevered frieze beams

beyond the one below until the two sides of the opening meet. This
technique can be applied to the roof of a free-standing building, but in that
case the walls must be thick and the clear space is restricted.[43] The chief
advantage of a corbelled roof over a wood-and-tile roof was its durability
in damp conditions; at the same time it could span a wider opening than a
stone lintel without resorting to excessively large blocks. Thus it was most
extensively used in underground tombs and cisterns, and in fortifications
(fig. 66), all situations where its advantages were important and where the
necessary massive supports could easily be provided.[44]

   The Greeks themselves did not normally build elaborate underground
tomb chambers for their dead before the Hellenistic period, but they
certainly knew of corbelling much earlier, for corbelled tombs in a
masonry technique characteristic of Greek masons are found in areas such
as Thessaly, Macedonia, Thrace, Asia Minor and Etruria, where the social
and religious climate was more suitable. Corbelling became more
common in Greek architecture from the late fifth century onwards, largely
because the kind of public works to which it was suited began to be

constructed on a more elaborate scale. Many spans were between three and five metres, with one corbelled dome reaching a diameter of 6·40 m, but there was nothing to approach the corbelled domes of Mycenaean *tholos* tombs which ran up to about 14·40 m in diameter.

The shape given to the under surface of the corbelling varies; sometimes the section is triangular, sometimes it is almost parabolic (although the top is either pointed or cut off flat), sometimes it is semicircular, and quite often corbelling of any type is used only to narrow the span which is bridged by a horizontal beam, presumably to reduce the height of the opening or vault. A section close to parabolic is theoretically the most efficient, and may well have been approximated by experience, while the triangular section corresponds to a simplified conception of corbelling as the projection of each successive course by an equal amount. The semicircular profile is surprising, however, for it is structurally unsatisfactory, and suggests a formal association with the true arch, which in Greece was always semicircular or segmental. This may not be the full explanation, for corbelled vaults with a semicircular section are found in the sixth century,[45] whereas it is uncertain whether the true arch (with radial joints and wedge-shaped voussoirs) was known to the Greeks before the mid fifth century.[46] In such early instances the semicircular section was perhaps chosen because it was easy to appreciate and to set out, and that may apply to later cases, too. Nevertheless it does seem possible that later on there was some confusion between the semicircle as a formal shape and the arch as a structural system.

Both corbelled and arched openings were considered in some way more appropriate than flat-topped openings in certain circumstances, apparently on formal grounds. In fortifications small openings, which could easily have been spanned by stone lintels no bigger than many blocks in the adjacent wall, were sometimes given a triangular top, either truly corbelled or simply cut to shape in the under face of a lintel block;[47] similarly, small or medium-sized gateways were sometimes given a semicircular top, although they were in fact spanned either by two blocks meeting in the middle (each with a quarter circle cut out), which acted as simple corbels, or by a lintel with a semicircle cut out of it, which would weaken it so much that it probably acted in much the same way, rather than as a beam.[48] Such cases suggest that shape was considered more important than jointing. The possibility of some such confusion is also suggested by the fact that the true arch or vault was used in much the same way as corbelling. It occurs in underground tombs and public works, and the spans were also similar; the vaults of tomb chambers usually span 3–5 m, although they run up to 6·48 m. The widest known Greek archway spans only 7·35 m,[49] and the full superiority of the true arch over corbelling was certainly never exploited, for there is nothing to approach the spans achieved with masonry arches by Roman builders, such as the 24·5 m span of the Bridge of Fabricius at Rome (62 B.C.).

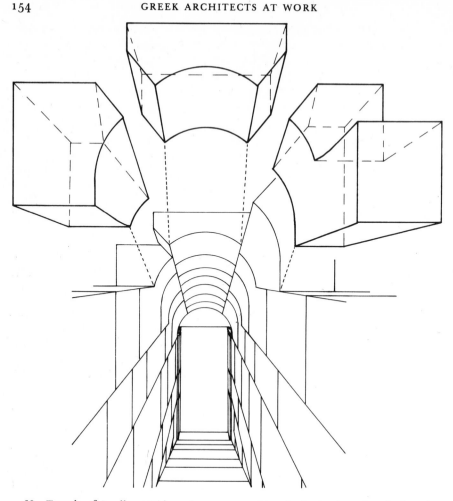

68   Temple of Apollo at Didyma (*c.* 300 B.C. and later): sloping barrel vault above ramp to altar court; perspective view, partly exploded to show shape of vaulting blocks

There is one practical reason why corbelling should be favoured as much as the arch. It was much easier to execute in accurate, dry-laid masonry, for all the blocks could be cut with their two main faces parallel, while in an arch the angles between the faces would have to be carefully calculated and set out. Anything like an intersecting vault would involve blocks with almost all their faces cut to unusual angles, and although such problems were not beyond the powers of Greek builders (cf. the sloping vault in fig. 68), they must still have been problems. Thus there are very few Greek intersecting vaults, and even barrel vaults tend to be constructed as a series of fairly close-set arches, the spaces between which were spanned by flat slabs.[50]

The woodwork of Greek buildings has of course perished, but a good deal can be learnt about its arrangement from the disposition of supports and from the cuttings for beams in surviving stonework.[51] The normal principle involved, as might be expected from the preceding pages, was the simply supported beam. The Greeks certainly knew various complex joints to make a wooden frame, but their structural timbers seem normally to have been laid one above the other, like bricks, without elaborate jointing. That is probably why roof beams were usually laid with their breadth greater than their height.

The side porticoes of a temple were comparatively narrow, so that the fairly small, closely spaced rafters could easily span the distance from outer colonnade to cella wall without intermediate support. Over the cella, however, and in most other types of building, a ridge beam was required to support the inner ends of the rafters, for a low-pitched ridge roof was the form normally used. The ridge beam was carried on an axial colonnade where there was one (as in many stoas; cf. figs. 34, 35), but since there rarely was one in a temple cella, the ridge beam could be given only indirect support, by props from a set of cross-beams running between the inner colonnades or the cella walls. Thus in temples and in other buildings with ridge roofs but no axial colonnade, there had to be three distinct sets of beams: cross-beams supporting ridge beam supporting rafters. Before the end of the fifth century, however, such a complex structure was avoided where possible. Purlins (beams running parallel to the axis of the building) might be used to help support the rafters in the middle of a long span, but they were used only where they themselves could be supported directly from the stonework. Thus purlins do not occur in stoas where there was no such support, while temples usually did have purlins since the cella walls (fig. 26b) and inner colonnades if present (fig. 26c) could give them direct support.[52]

In the Hellenistic period more complex roofs became popular, however.[53] Thus in a typical stoa roof of the fifth century the heavy beam carried by the inner colonnade acted as the ridge beam, and directly on it rested the rafters—fairly thick timbers because they might span up to 6 m, but closely spaced so as to carry the tiles (and battens if used). In a Hellenistic stoa, on the other hand, the beam carried by the inner colonnade did not support the rafters directly. It supported the inner ends of heavier and more widely spaced sloping cross-beams (or principal rafters), above which came purlins and a small ridge beam, and then on top of those the common rafters; thus instead of two series of wooden beams there were four (cf. fig. 54). Although in theory both types of roof need about the same volume of wood, the second is more economical, for only the sloping cross-beams have to span the full aisle width, while the purlins span only about half that distance and the rafters normally less again; thus most of the beams can be quite small in section, and if convenient, short in length.

Since the Greeks were normally prodigal in their use of timber, their

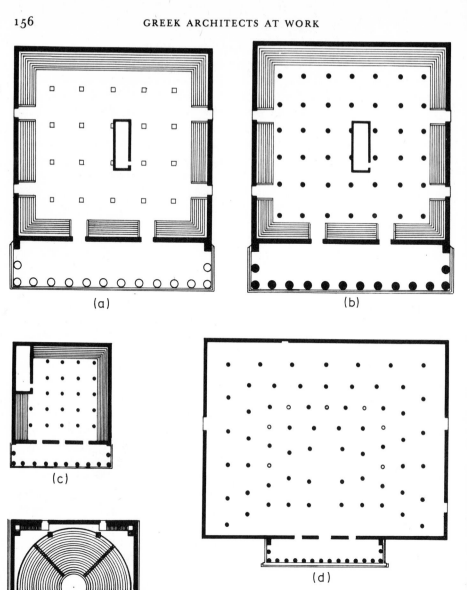

(a)

(b)

(c)

(d)

(e)

(f)

10   0   50m

appreciation of this economy is rather surprising. There is no doubt that the development took place, apparently beginning in the second quarter of the fourth century, but there may also be another reason for it. The cross-beams are widely spaced, and are commonly (although not always) placed one above each outer column. In this way most of the roof load comes down through the purlins and cross-beams on to the columns, and thus lightens the load on the stone outer architrave. As we have seen, Greek architects were sometimes very anxious to reduce the strain on their stone beams,[54] and that may help to explain the popularity of the more complex roof.

The Greeks tended to use very heavy timbers, the main beams in a roof normally being between 0·50 and 0·90 m each way; but because they usually treated them as bearer beams subject to a bending strain, and such beams cannot be built up from several pieces, the spans they achieved were limited. Greek buildings usually provided support for the roof at intervals of 5–7 m, and that may be one reason why the stoa was so popular, for such a long narrow space could be roofed without a complex system of supports. Where a deeper building was required, as in the Hall of the Mysteries at Eleusis (for initiation into the mystéries of the Demeter-Persephone cult), its roof was simply supported on a grid of columns (fig. 69a–c); the view of many a would-be initiate must have been blocked. The only contribution of an original architect like Iktinos was apparently to make the grid as wide as possible (fig. 69b),[55] and the only development of the grid system before the Hellenistic period was to arrange the columns in concentric rectangles but along lines radiating from the centre, as in the great meeting hall of the Arcadians at Megalopolis (c. 360 B.C.; fig. 69d).[56]

During the Hellenistic period several large meeting halls were built with the interior much less obstructed and the roof spans correspondingly greater. In the Council Chamber at Miletos (c. 170 B.C.) the clear spans reached about 16 m (fig. 69e),[57] and although this falls far short of Roman roof spans a century later, which could be over 25 m,[58] it certainly raises the possibility that a more sophisticated roof structure was known. It has in fact been argued that the roofs of such halls were based on the tie-beam truss[59]—that is, a triangular frame of timbers so jointed to one another that the horizontal beam acts in tension tying together the feet of the two rafters (cf. fig. 51). It is easier for a beam to resist tension than bending, so that the horizontal beam need not be as thick as in the bearer beam system normally used by the Greeks; in addition a tie-beam can be made up of two pieces, provided that they are properly jointed. A much larger span is thus possible without any increase in the size of timber used. A knowledge of

69   Plans of meeting halls: (a), (b), (c) Hall of the Mysteries at Eleusis, (a) Iktinos' project (c. 430 B.C.), (b) as executed (late fifth–fourth centuries), (c) later sixth-century predecessor; (d) Thersilion at Megalopolis (c. 360 B.C.); (e) Council Chamber at Miletos (c. 170 B.C.); (f) Arsinoeion at Samothrace (c. 285 B.C.)

this system must explain the vastly increased spans achieved by the Romans,[60] but even in the Hellenistic period Greek buildings normally have supports at the same 5–7 m intervals as in earlier centuries, so that the normal system of roofing was probably (in some cases certainly) the same, too.

In two regions Greek architects seem to have felt themselves less subject to this limitation. In the Greek colonies of Sicily and in the northern Aegaean, especially on Samothrace, spans of 7–12 m are often left undivided, and one might suppose that the truss principle was known, but only in those areas.[61] Both, however, were areas unusually rich in timber, and this, rather than a greater skill in carpentry, is more likely to explain their larger spans. Knowledge seems to have travelled freely in the Greek world, but large timbers, besides being awkward to handle, were an important strategic reserve, for they could be used not only for roofs but for ship-building and siege machinery as well. Even the Council Chamber at Miletos may be explained in this way, for it was built with assistance from Antiochos of Syria, the king who controlled the famous cedar forests of Lebanon; the wide spans may have resulted from the gift of a few spectacularly large timbers, rather than from a knowledge of the truss.[62] However, although the available evidence suggests that the tie-beam truss was neither properly understood nor widely used in any part of the Greek world, there is some evidence that something approaching a truss roof, but not providing all its advantages, may have been tried from time to time.

Circular buildings could not be roofed in the normal Greek way, for since a beam along any diameter of a circle must pass through its centre, there could be only one bearer beam to serve the whole roof.[63] A more natural way to roof a circular building is with a wigwam-like cone of rafters, their inner ends meeting at a central finial and their feet resting on the wall (or colonnade).[64] In a building roofed like this the longest timbers required are the rafters, with a length rather more than half the total span; it is therefore not surprising that the largest clear span known in Greek architecture is in a circular building—16·80 m in the Arsinoeion at Samothrace (c. 285 B.C.; fig. 69f).[65]

The outward thrust generated by such a roof can be reduced by increasing the slope of the rafters. In the Arsinoeion the cornice top is at an angle of 21° (compared to the normal 10° to 15°), and the main rafters may have risen at a much greater angle (fig. 70b); other circular buildings also have steeper roofs than normal.[66] The substantial remaining thrust could be countered by tying each rafter to the one diametrically opposite, but all such tie-beams would necessarily meet in the centre, where very skilful design of the fastenings would be required. It is simpler and more elegant to tie each rafter to its neighbours, so that a firm ring is created. If the span is small, the normal battens for the tiling, assisted by the weight of wall or colonnade, may be sufficient to counter the thrust, but in a large building like the Arsinoeion more specific precautions would be required, and the

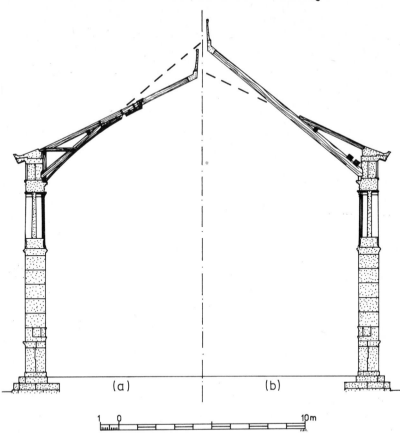

70 Arsinoeion at Samothrace (c. 285 B.C.): section showing roof structure (a) as restored by G. Niemann; (b) with steeper main beams

architect would probably need a conscious understanding of the force he was trying to deal with. Two small circular pavilions in the monumental fountain built by Herodes Attikos at Olympia (A.D. 157–60) provide significant, if late, evidence for an understanding of this type of structure.[67] Their roofs consisted of quite thick triangular marble slabs set against each other to form a cone, and the cornice on which their feet rested has a continuous channel all round, which was probably cut to hold an iron tie-ring. It was thus perhaps in the roofs of circular buildings that the Greeks came nearest to a systematic use of beams in tension, and the structure they used could not easily be adapted to a rectangular building.[68]

This survey of the structural ideas in Greek architecture suggests that most architects were indeed conservative and unadventurous. They failed to make the most of the arch even where they used it, and did not develop a full understanding of the truss roof even though they may have built structures approximating to it. They saw structure almost entirely in terms of simple horizontal beams, but there was little consistent development in their handling of them. Little progress was made towards a theory of structure. Demokritos (c. 460–380 B.C.?) is said to have studied the arch, and Vitruvius gives a discussion of its action which is brief and general,[69] but contrasts markedly with his discussion of post-and-lintel structures which is almost entirely restricted to aesthetic aspects. A full mathematical treatment was hardly to be expected in view of Greek mathematicians' lack of enthusiasm for practical matters, particularly experiment.[70] No mathematical treatment of the lever is known before c. 300 B.C., and the behaviour of a beam under stress is more difficult to treat mathematically. However, one might have expected some general understanding of the action of a beam to have been built up gradually from experience; for instance, an awareness that the under face of a beam is in tension, or that the strain in a beam is greatest in the middle. However, such ideas seem to have been grasped only by a few individuals, like Mnesikles, whose intuition or interest in structure was greater than usual. They do not seem to have passed into the general lore of architecture.

This underdeveloped sense of structure contrasts strikingly with Greek architects' highly developed sense of form. However, the buildings which leave an impression that they might have been improved by greater structural skill are few—among them some colossal temples and a number of meeting halls—and are not of major significance to the Greek achievement. If Greek architects had required more sophisticated structural methods, they would presumably have developed them, just as they apparently did in another technical field, that of design procedure, which was more important to them. Some knowledge of structure and technique was of course necessary to Greek architects, but it was not apparently central to their aims; and it was precisely because they concentrated intensively on a tightly restricted field that they were able to attain such an extraordinarily high level in that chosen field.

Notes

(For abbreviations used see Bibliography, pp. 182–8.)

Chapter 1. Architect, patron and project

1   Orlandos, *Ylika*, 2, fig. 46, MacDonald, *Architecture* 1, pl. 127; contrast plate 5 below (Mesopotamian).
2   Plato, *Polit.* 259e–260a.
3   e.g. Bundgaard, *Mnesicles*, 184–5, Burford, *Epidauros*, 139.
4   cf. also Arist., *Metaph.* 981a30, *Pol.* 1325b23.
5   For a guide to these see R. L. Scranton, *Harvard Library Bulletin* 14 (1960), 159–82.
6   e.g. *IG* 2², 1666.b.67, 1675, 1678.a.6, *IG* 7, 3073.131, 160.
7   Vitr., 10.2.11–12; Diog. Laert., 2.103.
8   Hdt., 3.60; cf. 4.87. Plutarch, *Per.* 27.3 would be an easy anachronism.
9   Vitr., 10, esp. 10.16. cf. also Biton, 44.2, 49.2, 52.1, etc., Philon, *Bel.* 51.13, Strabo 14.1.24 (641).
10 e.g. at Pella, Priene, Delos, Pergamon, etc.
11 Theoph., *Char.* 2.12.
12 Boersma, *Bdg. Policy*, 11–27.
13 Strabo 14.1.22 (641); but at Priene the offer was accepted (*IvPri*, 156).
14 For such donations by the kings of Pergamon see Hansen, *Attalids*², 284–98; donations by other dynasties include stoas at Delos and Priene, a Gymnasium of Ptolemy at Athens, and buildings donated by Philip III and Alexander IV, by Ptolemy II, and by Arsinoe II at Samothrace.
15 *Didyma* 2, no. 479.2–19; *Milet* 1.7, 31–47, nos. 193a, 270.7; Coulton, *Stoas*, fig. 63.2, 86.10.
16 Travlos, *Pict. Dict.*, 506–19, 523–6; Coulton, *Stoas*, 69.
17 e.g. the Thersilion at Megalopolis (Paus., 8.32.1), choragic monuments at Athens, and the cases cited below.
18 Plutarch, *Them.* 22.2; *IG* 1², 54.
19 *Olympia* 2, 83–93; 5, no. 651; note the Ionic outer order with no frieze and bases showing Asiatic influence (fig. 40.30). Vitruvius (7. pr. 14) cites a Leonidas who wrote on proportion, but the name is not uncommon. On the architect's responsibility for details see below pp. 56–7.
20 Vitr., 1.6.4–5.
21 Note the public enthusiasm for Pixodaros, who discovered the marble beds used for the sixth-century temple of Artemis at Ephesos (Vitr., 10.2.15; S. Kasper, *AA* 1975, 223–32).
22 For Athens see Boersma, *Bdg. Policy, passim*.
23 e.g. Paus., 2.9.6, 6.24.4, 8.30.7, 10.11.5–6 (?) (spoils); Hdt., 3.57.2–4 (mines).

For the financing of fortifications see F. G. Maier, *Griechische Mauerbauinschriften* 2 (1961), 55–66; for stoas see Coulton, *Stoas*, 13–16.

24   Hdt., 2.180; *FDelphes* 3.5, 35–58; cf. Strabo, 14.1.22 (640).

25   Plutarch, *Per.*, 12.1–3. A talent=6000 drachmas: a drachma was a skilled man's daily wage in the late fifth century. The Parthenon may have cost some 450–500 talents (R. S. Stanier, *JHS* 73 (1953), 68–76).

26   There are no hard figures for archaic cities. The capital of the sanctuary of Nemesis at Rhamnous in *c.* 450–440 B.C. (probably just before the temple there was built) was about 9 talents (Meiggs–Lewis, *GHI*, no. 53); the temple should have cost about the same as the temple of Asklepios at Epidauros (23 talents; *IG* 4², 102, Burford, *Epidauros*, 82).

27   By analogy with sixth-century temple costs at Delphi and Akragas (see below p. 22) the cost of temples C, D, FS, GT, ER, A, and O at Selinous would have been somewhere about 1500–2000 talents.

28   e.g. Aeschin., *Ctes.*, 23, 31; *IG* 7, 4263; A. Wilhelm, *JOAI* 11 (1908), 56–61.

29   *IG* 1², 343.90; Plutarch, *Kim.* 13.6.

30   Burford, *Epidauros*, 83, 164–6; cf. the ineffectual law of the Ephesians (Vitr., 10. pr. 1).

31   e.g. the Naopoioi at Delphi and the Hieropoioi at Delos.

32   *SIG*³, 1185.12–14.

33   For Athens see Boersma, *Bdg. Policy*, 5–6; B. D. Merritt, *AJP* 56 (1935), 359–72, li. 21–5.

34   e.g. at Delos in the third century, and cf. *IG* 1², 76.11; on city architects see below p. 29.

35   B. D. Merritt, *AJP* 56 (1935), 359–72, li. 21–5; Meiggs–Lewis, *GHI* no. 44.

36   *IG* 1², 88.5–8; *IG* 2², 244.1–10; Arist., *Ath. Pol.* 49.3.

37   *IG* 1², 372–4.

38   Burford, *Epidauros*, 110–12.

39   *Didyma* 2, nos. 26–7, 38–44; so also some work at Delos.

40   Burford, *Epidauros*, 112–18.

41   *IG* 4², 102.45–7, 279–80.

42   Hdt., 2.180. The contract must have been let before 526 B.C. because it preceded the fund raising to which Amasis of Egypt (d. 526 B.C.) made a contribution.

43   Hdt., 5.62.2, cf. Arist., *Ath. Pol.* 19.4, Philochoros, *FrGrHist* III B, 328 F 115. These sources suggest that the Alkmaionids got access to the money and became active at Delphi only after their defeat at Leipsydrion (*c.* 512 B.C.), but the family was also in exile after *c.* 546 B.C. (Hdt., 1.64.3), at an appropriate time for the contract to be let, and there was a tradition that Megakles took it up then (Schol. on Dem., *Mid.*, 561.16). Since the collection of funds followed the contract and may have taken some time, and since in the meantime the Alkmaionids had returned to Athens, it would not be surprising if work at Delphi had progressed little before Leipsydrion; cf. H. Pomtow, *RhMus* 51 (1896), 329–44, 52 (1897), 106–22. For contrary views see M. Homolle, *BCH* 26 (1902), 597–627, P. de la Coste Messelière, *BCH* 70 (1946), 271–87. For the parts made of marble see *FDelphes, Temple*, 98–107, 110–11.

44   Polyainos, 5.1.1.

45   Polyainos, 6.51 (doubted by some as too similar to 5.1.1, but a good trick is worth repeating and the temple concerned is of appropriate date); on class see Arist., *Pol.* 1310b, cf. J. A. de Waele, *Acragas* 1 (1971), 103–4, 109–10.

46 Boersma, *Bdg. Policy*, 7–8.

47 Burford, *Epidauros*, 112–13.

48 M. Lacroix, *RevPhil* NS 38 (1914), 303–30.

49 Before the Roman period perhaps only at Kastabos (J. M. Cook, W. H. Plommer, *The Sanctuary of Hemithea at Kastabos* (1966), 59) and *IG* 5.1, 690, and when the architect was donor (see above p. 18). Architects did not 'make' buildings in the sense that sculptors made statues, and were perhaps proud of it. There is a *mason's* signature from Thasos (*IG* 12 (8), 390; A. Burford, *Craftsmen in Greek and Roman Society* (1972), pl. 72).

50 e.g. Phaneas: *IG* 11 (2), 161.A.44–9, 162.A.48, 165.13–14, 20, 24–5, 175A.b.13, 199.C.41–5, 203.A.60.

51 Sixth century: Boupalos (Paus., 4.30.6), Rhoikos (Hdt., 3.60, Paus., 10.38.3), Theodoros (Vitr., 7. pr. 12, Plato, *Ion* 533b, Diod. Sic., 1.98.5–9), and perhaps Bathykles (Paus., 3.18.9–19.2). Fourth century: Pytheos (Vitr., 7. pr. 12, Pliny, *NII*, 36.31), Satyros (Vitr., 7. pr. 12, *SIG³*, 225), Skopas (Paus. 8.45.5, etc.), and perhaps a younger Polykleitos (Paus., 2.27.5, 6.6.2).

52 Trophonios and Agamedes (*Hom. Hym. Apo.* 294–9, Paus., 10.5.13). Whether real persons to whom legendary status became attached or legendary figures associated with a real project, they still indicate high status for early monumental architects. The signature on the stylobate of the temple of Apollo at Syracuse might be adduced here, but its date and meaning are too uncertain (L. H. Jeffery, *Local Scripts of Archaic Greece* (1961), 265).

53 Hdt., 1.74, 75, 170; cf. Arist., *Pol.* 1259a9–18. Richter, *Kouroi³*, 53.

54 Richter, *Kouroi³*, 2–3; Diels-Kranz⁶, 11.A.11. Arist., *Ath. Pol.* 11.1, Plutarch, *Sol.* 26.1; cf. also H. Hoffmann, *AJA* 57 (1953), 189–95.

55 Vitr., 7. pr. 12. The ancient sources confuse the sixth-century temple of Artemis with its successor, identical in size, site, and plan. Chersiphron's methods connect him clearly with the sixth-century temple (Pliny, *NH*, 36.21; 96–7).

56 For Thales see n. 54 above; Anaximandros (d. *c.* 546 B.C.) is said to have invented the set-square, the sundial, and the map; on Hekataios see A. Lesky, *History of Greek Literature* (1966), 220–1.

57 e.g. Vitr., 10.2.11–12, Pliny, *NH*, 36.21, 96–7.

58 Pliny, *NH*, 7.56, 198; 36.19, 90; H. Johannes, *AM* 62 (1937), 15–17.

59 See n. 57.

60 Pliny, *NH*, 36.21, 95–7; 36.56, 179.

61 Vitr., 4.3.1, 1.1.12.

62 Vitr., 4.3.1, 3.3.8–9.

63 Xen., *Mem.* 4.2.8–10.

64 Cicero, *De Orat.* 1.62, Val. Max., 8.12.2. Philon also wrote on the project (Vitr., 7. pr. 12); the book is lost but Philon's specification survives (see n. 3.13).

65 On Philon see n. 64, on Pytheos, n. 61. For a reflection of Pytheos' claim (or a similar one) in Sosipater see Kock, *ComAttFrag*, 3.314.

66 Vitr., 1.1; cf. MacDonald, *Architecture* 1, 137–8; Pappos, *Opera* 3, 1022–4 (quoting Heron of Alexandria); G. Downey, *Byzantion* 18 (1946–8), 99–118.

67 Vitr., 6. pr. 6.

68 Metagenes, son of Chersiphron (Vitr. 10.2.12); Damon and Agathokles, sons of Agasikrates, grandsons of Agathon (*SIG³*, 494); see also Diog. Laert., 2.125, Vitr., 6. pr. 4, 6, and perhaps also Paus., 6.19.8 (architects?).

69   Plutarch, *Per.* 13.5, calls Kallikrates the *ergolabos*, but may be varying his
      phraseology for effect. The *ergolabos* organized the execution of a work, but
      sometimes on behalf of another man who was strictly speaking the
      contractor; a distinction is clearly drawn in Polyainos, 6.51, but in other cases
      no distinction is possible (e.g. *ID*, 365.24). Demetrios, slave (servus=ἱερός?) of
      Diana at Ephesos (Vitr., 7. pr. 16) need not imply low status (C. Picard,
      Ephèse et Claros (1922), 134–5).

70   He shared in a trierarchy (*IG* 2², 1622.694); see J. K. Davies, *Athenian Propertied
      Families* (1971), 555–6; compare Kleisthenes 'of good birth *but* poor and an
      architect'. (Diog. Laert., 2.125).

71   Vitr., 4.3.1; and above p. 18, and perhaps also Sostratos of Knidos, 'friend
      of kings' (in spite of P. M. Fraser, *Ptolemaic Alexandria* (1972), 19–20).

72   Compare the 5 obols a day paid to members of the Council, 3 obols a day to
      men chosen to supervise wall construction (*IG* 2², 244.28–31), and a doctor
      giving his services free (*IG* 2², 483.17). The underarchitect's wage, however,
      seems to have been based on the contract price of the work he supervised (*IG*
      2², 1678.13–15).

73   See below pp. 56–7, and J. J. Coulton, *JHS* 95 (1975), 20.

74   The main exceptions are: Theodoros of Samos at Sparta (Paus., 3.12.10);
      Bathykles of Magnesia at Sparta (Paus., 3.18.9—mainly sculpture);
      Chersiphron and Metagenes of Knossos at Ephesos (Vitr., 7. pr. 16);
      Eupalinos of Megara at Samos (Hdt., 3.60.3); Iktinos of Athens (?) at Bassai
      (Paus., 8.41.5; cf. n.76); Hippodamos of Miletos at Piraeus and Thourioi
      (Arist., *Pol.*, 1267b22, Hesychios *s.v.* Hippodamos—an urbanist rather than
      an architect); Theodoros of Phokaia (or Phokis?) at Delphi (Vitr., 7. pr. 12);
      Skopas of Paros at Tegea (Paus., 8.45.9); Satyros of Paros (?) at Halikarnassos
      (Vitr., 7. pr. 12); Kallias of Arados at Rhodes (Vitr., 10.16.3); and several
      Hellenistic architects working under royal patronage. Architects seem to have
      travelled less than sculptors, perhaps because a knowledge of local sources of
      labour and materials was more important.

75   Iktinos, Kallikrates, Koroibos (*SEG* 10, 24; 25, 15) and the Hephaisteion
      Architect (cf. n.3.38) from *c.* 450 B.C., Mnesikles from *c.* 440 B.C. R. Carpenter,
      The Architects of the Parthenon (1970), equates the Hephaisteion Architect with
      Kallikrates, for whom he also proposes a Kimonian Parthenon; both
      propositions are doubtful.

76   Paus., 8.41.9. The attribution has been much debated; cf. U. Pannuti, *Atti 8ᵃ*,
      16 (1971–2), 233–8. The problem raises many questions of principle, for
      instance, the responsibility of the architect for detailed design (cf. below pp.
      56–7). A certain answer is impossible at the moment and in the meantime
      Pausanias' statement should be allowed to stand.

77   *IG* 1², 372–4; Caskey, *Erechtheum*, 277–422.

78   *IG* 1², 374.256.

79   *IG* 2², 1672.A.11; *FDelphes* 3.5, 19.40, 19.88, 23.II.22; M. Lacroix, *RevPhil* 38
      (1914), 303–30. But cf. Burford, *Epidauros*, 139–45.

80   e.g. at Selinous (Koldewey–Puchstein, 123–4), Sardis (G. Gruben, *AM* 76
      (1961), 155–96, esp. 170–5), Didyma (Akurgal, *Ruins²*, 227–31).

81   *IG* 4², 102.9, 31, 54, 104, 112; cf. Burford, *Epidauros*, 141–2.

82   The Erechtheion was perhaps designed by Kallikrates (I. M. Shear, *Hesperia* 32
      (1963), 408–24), who was working by 450 B.C. and so could well have died by

409/8 B.C.. Spintharos of Corinth, designer of the fourth-century temple of Apollo (Paus., 10.5.13), may well have left Delphi when work was interrupted by the Sacred War in 356 B.C. Plato, *Polit.* 259e–260a suggests that designing architects normally saw their projects through.

83   Vitr., 7. pr. 15–16; cf. also Paus., 6.19.7, 6.19.8 (?), 10.5.13, *IG* 2², 1668 (?), Plutarch, *Per.* 13 (cf. Vitr., 7. pr. 12). A distinction between architect and engineer in the archaic period (R. R. Holloway, *HSCP* 73 (1969), 281–90) does not seem possible.

84   *IG* 2², 1678.7–8, 13; *FDelphes* 3.5, 25.ii.A.13, 90.7; *IG* 7, 30973.160–2; F. J. Mahaffy, *The Flinders Petrie Papyri* (1891–1905) 2, 52.

85   For the Erechtheion see above p. 27; at Delphi three architects worked between 353 and 335 B.C. (*FDelphes* 3.5, 19, 22, 23; for the date G. Daux, *Chronologie Delphique* (1943), 13–14, G. Roux, *RevArch.* 1966, 262–3); at Didyma Kratinos cannot have worked for more than five years (*Didyma* 2, nos. 34, 35, 40); at Delos there were at least three architects between *c.* 314 and 299 B.C. (*IG* 11(2), 142, 144–5, 148).

86   *SIG*³, 494; cf. also *SIG*³, 707, *Samothrace* 2.1, 112–16; J. & L. Robert, *REG* 68 (1955), 244, 163a.10; 69 (1956) 144, 188.

87   'The architect' in *IG* 1², 76.11 (Eleusis, 423/2 B.C.) was probably the architect then supervising the Telesterion, not a permanent official.

88   *IG* 2², 244.6–7, 40–1; but an architect was specially elected for repairs in 307/6 B.C. (*IG* 2², 463.6).

89   Dem., *Cor.* 28; *IG* 2², 456.32–3, 500.33–6; 512.7–8, 792.7–9.

90   *IG* 2², 841.21–3, 842.14–15.

91   Vitr., 10.16.3–8; cf. *SIG*³, 581.97–8.

92   *Milet*, 1.3, no. 37.f.91, 141.49–51, 143.36–7, 144A5, 145.82–3, 146.46–8, 147.62–4, *Milet*, 1.7, no. 270.7–8; *Didyma*, 2, 479.17–19; *SIG*³, 725.6 (Lindos); *SIG*³, 679.17–18, 28–9 (Magnesia on the Macander); cf. *SIG*³, 479.8–9, 483.28–30 (Delphi) and *SIG*³, 736.90–1 (Messene).

93   Strabo, 12.8.11 (575).

94   *CIG*, 4342.d², d³ (addenda, p. 1162).

95   Vitr., 10.16.3–12; *SIG*³, 707.

96   Cicero, *De Off.* 1.151.

Chapter 2. The problem of beginning

1   See Drerup, *Geom. Baukunst*, and also Snodgrass, *Dark Age*, 369–73, 408–13, 421–9.

2   D. Kurtz, J. Boardman, *Greek Burial Customs* (1971), 57–8.

3   Snodgrass, *Dark Age*, 192–4, 394–9.

4   Some Bronze Age buildings (other than tombs and fortifications) may have survived through the difficult days of the early Iron Age right down to the seventh century, but none of the possible instances demonstrates the forms and techniques of a monumental architecture.

5   cf. Homer, *Il.* 5.302–4, 12.445–50.

6   E. Buschor, *AM* 55 (1930), 13–17, E. Buschor, H. Schleif, *AM* 58 (1933), 150–2 on the date see Snodgrass, *Dark Age*, 410–12.

7   For other views see G. Rodenwaldt, *Griechische Tempel* (1941), 12–14, Plommer, *Anc. Class. Arch*, 118–19, V. Scully, *The Earth, the Temple and the Gods*

(1962), 50, R. R. Holloway, *A View of Greek Art* (1973), 47–8.

8   E. Buschor, *AM* 55 (1930), 34–9; E. Buschor, H. Schleif, *AM* 58 (1933), 152–7; on the date see Snodgrass, *Dark Age*, 412.

9   It is not clear how far the regular coursing was due to the use of a well-bedded stone.

10   Both types are known on building models (Drerup, *Geom. Baukunst*, 69–75).

11   Homer, *Od.* 5.261; some large stones at Zagora (Andros) and Tsikalario (Naxos) would require a crowbar.

12   R. V. Nicholls, *BSA* 53–4 (1958–9), 97; cf. J. W. Shaw, *Annuario* 49 (1971), 59–69.

13   Snodgrass, *Dark Age*, 334–5.

14   J. Boardman, *Pre-Classical* (1967), 97–8.

15   Hdt., 2.152–4, cf. Hdt., 4.152.1; there may have been occasional earlier contacts (Boardman, *Overseas*[2], 110–12).

16   Hdt., 2.153, 169, 175–6. For surviving remains from the reign of Amasis see F. Petrie, *Nebesha and Defenneh* (1888), 12–13, A. Piankoff, *RevEg* 1 (1933), 161–79, D. P. Hansen, *JARC* 4 (1965), 32, M. V. Seton Williams, *JEA* 55 (1969), 5–10.

17   Most strikingly at Dair al-Bahri (e.g. plate 4), and Beni Hasan (e.g. J. Capart, *L'Art égyptien* 1, *L'architecture* (1922), pls. 68, 70, 72); but cf. also *ibid.*, pls. 91, 122.

18   J. Vandier, *Manuel d'archéologie égyptienne* 2.2 (1955), 793–817; Plommer, *Anc. Class. Arch.*, fig. 16.

19   Richter, *Kouroi*[3], 2–3, 27–8, Boardman, *Overseas*[2], 142–4; against this view, R. M. Cook, *JHS* 87 (1967), 24–32.

20   e.g. reliefs from Prinias (Crete) (L. Pernier, *Annuario* 1 (1914), 48–63) and Mycenae (G. M. A. Richter, *Korai* (1968), 32), both *c.* 630–620 B.C.

21   Pindar, *Ol.* 13.21–2, Vitr. 4.1.3; Pliny, *NH* 35, 152; *Corinth* 4.1, 5–7.

22   M. C. Roebuck, *Hesperia* 24 (1955), 153–7, H. S. Robinson, *AD* 26 (1971), pt. B1, 96–100; *Isthmia* 1, 3–56; on the date of Isthmia see J. J. Coulton, *JHS* 95 (1975), 271.

23   H. Sulze, *AA* 1936, 14–36; A. J. B. Wace, *Mycenae, an Archaeological History and Guide* (1949), 84–6; *Argive Heraeum* 1, 110–11, P. Amandry, *Hesperia* 21 (1952), 223–6.

24   Note also the ashlar masonry in the early seventh-century walls at Leontinoi (G. Rizza, *BdA* 42 (1957), 62–73; F. E. Winter, *Greek Fortifications* (1971), 128–9).

25   Similar tiles, not independently dated, have been found at Perachora (unpublished) and Delphi (*FDelphes, Terres cuites*, 21–8).

26   At Lerna (J. L. Caskey, *Hesperia* 23 (1954), 25–7) and Tiryns (*Tiryns* 3, 85–6, 92).

27   So A. Åkerstrom, *OpArch* 2 (1941), 164–73; cf. A. D. Keramopoullos, *AD* 3 (1917), 76; I. Threpsiades, *PAE* 1961, 38; but against their interpretation as roof tiles see C. W. Blegen, *AJA* 49 (1945), 35–44. No cover-tiles have been found with the supposed pan-tiles.

28   Boardman, *Overseas*[2], 73, J. N. Coldstream, *Greek Geometric Pottery* (1968), 383.

29   Schist slates are still a local roofing material on the slopes of Mt. Parnon, to the south of the Argolid (J. L. Caskey, *Hesperia* 23 (1954), 26) and their convenience may have inspired the manufacture of artificial tiles in the Early Bronze Age and, independently, in the seventh century. Geometric tiles from

the Ismenion at Thebes (E. D. Van Buren, *Greek Fictile Revetments from the Archaic Period* (1926), 62–3) seem to be mythical (A. D. Keramopoullos, *AD* 3 (1917), 72).

30   G. Soteriades, *AE* 1900, 171–211, G. Kawerau, G. Soteriades, *Antike Denkmäler* 2.5 (1908), 1–8.

31   R. Demangel, *BCH* 71–2 (1947–8), 364–5, fig. 5.

32   An important landmark is the late seventh-century temple of Athena at Smyrna (J. M. Cook, *JHS* 72 (1952), 104–6, E. Akurgal, *Die Kunst Anatoliens* (1961), 182–3, 284–6. Akurgal. *Ruins²*, 119, Wesenberg, *Kapitelle*, 111–14). It had fluted stone columns with carved capitals (or bases) and stone walls; but the walls, although coursed and well finished, were still two-skinned and were not dressed after laying, and the technique is not comparable to that of the early sixth-century Doric temples discussed on pp. 43–5. A fully monumental technique and a developed Ionic order first appeared in the colossal temples of Hera at Samos and Artemis at Ephesos (*c.* 570–550 B.C.). The Ionic order is lighter and more decorative than Doric, and its forms owe less to Egypt, nothing to Mycenae, but a good deal to the Near East.

33   Vitr., 4.2.2–3.

34   Saws were certainly known; p. 32 (stone), and Homer, *Od.* 8.404, 18.196, 19.564 (ivory); but Odysseus did not use a saw for making his raft (Homer, *Od.* 5.234–57), or his bed (Homer, *Od.* 23. 195–221) nor was one found among the tools in the temple at Halieis (*AR* 20 (1973–4), 12).

35   The slender proportions of early stone Doric columns (height=6½–7 diameters) are often used as evidence for their derivation from wooden prototypes. Since the Greeks themselves for centuries made Ionic columns in stone with heights of 9–10 diameters, the argument is weak. As recent vernacular architecture shows, wooden posts are likely to have a height of 10–20 diameters and a spacing of 7–15 diameters, and in spite of the fragile material the Perachora model has posts about 10 diameters high (H. Payne, *Perachora* 1 (1940), 34–50, plates 8–9). If, as is likely, the Greeks made wooden columns with a height of 6½–7 diameters and a spacing of about 4 diameters, they were probably imitating the effect of stone columns in wood, not vice versa.

36   Drerup, *Geom. Baukunst*, 115, 118, 132, argues for an internal development from premonumental architecture, but the features quoted are not sufficiently close or specialized to support the argument.

37   T. J. Dunbabin *et al.*, *Perachora* 2 (1962), 61–2, no. 420, pl. 22; Wesenberg, *Kapitelle*, 51–2, 59–61.

38   So R. M. Cook, *BSA* 46 (1951), 50–2, 65 (1970), 17–19.

39   J. Boardman, *Greek Art* (1964), fig. 10.

40   e.g. Lawrence, *Gk. Arch.³*, fig. 38. For the later history of the capitals see British Museum (F. N. Pryce), *Catalogue of Sculpture* 1.1 (1928), 14–24. On the relation of such capitals to Doric see Wesenberg, *Kapitelle*, 54–62.

41   A. J. B. Wace, *Mycenae, an Archaeological History and Guide* (1949), 36. Most Bronze Age columns were unfluted; where flutes were used, their number was usually greater than the 16 to 24 favoured by sixth-century builders (Graham, *Palaces*, 195–6).

42   Graham, *Palaces*, 146.

43   See *Korkyra* 1, 89. Columns with 20 flutes appear equally early, however.

44   Clarke–Engelbach, 137, 139–40.

45   Vitr., 4.2.2.

46   e.g. J. N. Coldstream, *Greek Geometric Pottery* (1968), pls. 10, 15e–m.

47   G. Contenau, *Manuel d'archéologie orientale* 3 (1931), 1323, fig. 833, W. Andrae, *Farbige Keramik aus Assur* (1923), 12–15, P. Amiet, *Elam* (1966), 508–15, figs. 383–91. There were figure paintings on the ashlar walls of the early temple at Isthmia, but sculpture soon replaced painting as the major art associated with architecture.

48   Its importance is argued by M. L. Bowen, *BSA* 45 (1950), 113–25, but the similarity is not close enough to constitute a complete explanation of the Doric frieze.

49   P. Montet, *Tanis* (1942), 116, fig. 24, P. Montet, *Fouilles de Tanis*, 2, *Les constructions et le tombeau de Psousennès* (1951), 117–19, pls. 82–9. This sarcophagus was noticed by J. G. F. Hind, who will discuss it in a forthcoming article. Other variants on this theme are on painted sarcophagi of the ninth to seventh centuries (*Catalogue général des antiquités égyptiennes du Musée du Caire*, A. Moret, *Sarcophages de l'époque Bubastite à l'époque Saite* (1913), nos. 41.031, 41.038), and fourth-century and Ptolemaic tombs at Kyrene (A. Rowe, *Cyrenaican Expedition of the University of Manchester, 1952* (1956), 19–20, figs. 6, 7). Compare also the use of a triglyph frieze on altars (G. Roux, *BCH* 77 (1953), 116–23).

50   G. Soteriades, *PAE* 1906, 136, K. Rhomaios, *AD* 2 (1916), 186–8, H. Koch, *AM* 39 (1914), 237–55, *RM* 30 (1915), 51–68, E. D. Van Buren, *Greek Fictile Revetments in the Archaic Period* (1926), 64–71.

51   For the history of decorative roof terracottas see Martin, *Manuel* 1, 87–112. Their use may have developed slightly earlier east of the Aegaean.

52   e.g. the monumental vases of the eighth century (n. 2.2) and the even larger relief *pithoi* of the early seventh (J. Schäfer, *Studien zu den griechischen Reliefpithoi* (1957), M. Ervin, *AD* 18 (1963) A. 37–75).

53   See n. 1.54.

54   *Olympia* 2, 27–36; *Korkyra* 1, 15–143.

55   The stone columns vary in form according to the style current when each was set up (cf. fig. 11b). One column of the rear porch was still wooden in about A.D. 170 (Paus., 5.16.1).

56   See Orlandos, *Ylika* and Martin, *Manuel* 1, both concentrating on the fifth and later centuries, for which evidence is fuller.

57   Thresholds, door jambs, and column bases might need to be of a specific size, but the control would not need to be so close as to demand a different system of quarrying.

58   Contrast the walls of the first and second temples of Hera at Samos with those of the two roughly contemporary buildings at Antissa on Lesbos (W. Lamb, *BSA* 32 (1931–2), 42–8); the two earlier buildings would nevertheless have demanded a similar level of skill in masonry, and so would the two later ones.

59   Quarries worked in this way can be associated definitely with sixth-century buildings: Durm, *BGK*³, 94–9, fig. 62, W. Koenigs, *AA* 1972, 381–3, S. Kasper, *AA* 1975, 230–1.

60   Clarke–Engelbach, 12–33.

61   C. Nylander, *AA* 1968, 6–10, C. Nylander, *Ionians in Pasargadae* (1970), 28–30, R. Naumann, *Die Architektur Kleinasiens* (2nd ed., 1971), 38–9, C. H. E.

Haspels, *The Highlands of Phrygia; Sites and Monuments* (1971), 71, pl. 237.

62 Clarke–Engelbach, 34–45, 87–91; A. H. Layard, *Nineveh and Babylon* (1867), 18–28.

63 See n. 7.5.

64 H. Müller-Karpe, *JdI* 77 (1962), 66, Snodgrass, *Dark Age*, 432–3.

65 Homer, *Il.* 12.447–9; but in *Od.* 9.241–2 the Cyclops Polyphemos uses a huge stone as his door: 'Not even twenty-two good four-wheeled waggons [not horses or yokes of oxen] would shift it from the ground'!

66 See n. 7.6 and Orlandos, *Ylika* 2, 89–90, 93, 108, Martin, *Manuel* 1, 164–9.

67 Vitr. 10.2.11–14; cf. below pp. 141–4.

68 Note the difference of about 0·50 m between the two ends of Temple A at Prinias (L. Pernier, *Annuario* 1 (1914), 32, fig. 6).

69 See J. J. Coulton, *BSA* 70 (1975), 90–3.

70 Clarke–Engelbach, 61–2.

71 Orlandos, *Ylika* 2, 135–7, Martin, *Manuel* 1, 188–9. Earliest evidence for its use in Greece is Plato, *Phlb.* 56b; for its use on large surfaces *IG* 2², 1668.10, *IG* 7, 3073.69, 186, and (in medieval Spain) T. F. Glick, *TechCult* 9 (1968), 169–73; cf. also the 20 foot *chorobates* of Vitruvius (8.5.1–2).

72 Orlandos, *Ylika* 2, 176–7, Martin, *Manuel* 1, 193–9.

73 Clarke–Engelbach, 99–109. In *Olympia* 2, 35 and Lawrence, *Gk. Arch.*³, 225, *anathyrosis* is referred to Mycenae or Egypt, but without detailed references. Both Mycenaean and Egyptian masonry sometimes have ashlar blocks with the vertical joints only tight at the outer face, but such blocks do not have a dressed rear face, so do not demonstrate true *anathyrosis*.

74 Orlandos, *Ylika* 2, 176, Martin, *Manuel* 1, 195–6.

75 C. Nylander, *OpAth* 4 (1962), 47, figs. 56–60.

76 On this whole problem see J. J. Coulton, *JHS* 94 (1974), 1–19.

77 Pliny, *NH*, 36.21, 96–7; cf. below p. 144.

78 This is the most reasonable interpretation of Hdt., 2.125.1–4, but cf. Clarke–Engelbach, 94.

79 H. Frankfort, *The Art and Architecture of the Ancient Orient* (1954), 68, 77, 117, 169, 175.

80 Clarke–Engelbach, 78–83.

81 Clarke–Engelbach, 112–13; Orlandos, *Ylika* 2, 179–83, Martin, *Manuel* 1, 241–55, 260. Dovetail clamps had been used in Bronze Age Greece (Graham, *Palaces*, 152, British Museum (F. N. Pryce), *Catalogue of Sculpture* 1.1 (1928), 21, 26), but they were probably reborrowed from Egypt in the seventh century, for there was no continuity of use in Greece.

82 Königliche Museen zu Berlin, *Ausgrabungen in Sendschirli* 2 (1898), 164.

83 Clarke–Engelbach, 192–7, Orlandos, *Ylika* 2, 148–51, Martin, *Manuel* 1, 297–302.

84 Techniques of lifting and handling colossal stones, the simple dovetail clamp, and the finishing process are the most likely to have been learnt directly from Egypt. Among formal borrowings from Egypt may also be mentioned the use of the half-round and cavetto mouldings (L. T. Shoe, *The Profiles of Greek Mouldings* (1936), 5, 130, 145).

Chapter 3. The problem of design

1 Pedimental sculpture would also involve communicating a design; cf. B.

Ashmole, N. Yalouris, *Olympia; the Sculptures of the Temple of Zeus* (1967), 9.

2 A. Parrot, *Tello* (1948), 161, 163, pl. 14b–d.

3 Clarke–Engelbach, 51–6; N. de G. Davies, *AncEgy* 1917, 21–5.

4 H. Carter, A. H. Gardiner, *JEA* 4 (1917), 130–58.

5 F. Petrie, *Ancient Weights and Measures* (1926), 40.

6 Clarke–Engelbach, 46–8; for a schematic ziggurat elevation from Babylon see D. J. Wiseman, *AS* 22 (1972), 141–5.

7 E. Iversen, *Canon and Proportion in Egyptian Art* (1955), *Catalogue général des antiquités égyptiennes du Musée du Caire*, C. C. Edgar, *Sculptors' Studies and Unfinished Works* (1906), *passim*.

8 E. MacKay, *AncEgy* (1916), 170–1.

9 A plan on boards might be wider, but see N. de G. Davies, *JEA* 4 (1917), 194–9.

10 E. Heinrich, U. Seidl, *MDOG* 98 (1967), 24–45, D. J. Wiseman, *AS* 22 (1972), 145–7.

11 A. Petronotis, *Zum Problem der Bauzeichnungen bei den Griechen* (1972), argues convincingly for the use of architectural drawings.

12 See Bundgaard, *Mnesicles*, 97–8.

13 *IG* 2², 1668; recent discussions with translation: Bundgaard, *Mnesicles*, 117–32, Jeppesen, *Paradeigmata*, 69–101.

14 *IG* 2², 1666; recent discussions with translation: Bundgaard, *Mnesicles*, 99–116, Jeppesen, *Paradeigmata*, 109–31. No space was left for insertion of the contractors' names and contract prices as in *IG* 2², 463.

15 e.g. *IG* 2², 1666.b.67, *IG* 7, 3073.131.

16 Heron, *Metr.* 2, p. 126.22; see J. J. Coulton, *AJA* 80 (1976), 302–4.

17 Wood: *FDelphes* 3.5, 20.4–5; *IG* 2², 1627.b.325–6, 1629.c.983, 1631.b.219; *IG* 11(2), 161.A.43, 75–6; *ID*, 1417. A.1.11.32–3. Stucco: *IG* 4², 102.A.250–1. Stucco or clay: *IG* 1², 374.248.

18 *IG* 2², 1678.a.11–13. cf. inadequate miniature capitals from Corinth, M. C. Roebuck, *Hesperia* 24 (1955), 152, pl. 61a.

19 See J. J. Coulton, *BSA* 70 (1975), 91–4.

20 Assos: *Assos*, 71; Athens: G. P. Stevens, *Hesperia* 27 (1958), 174–88; Messene: *Ergon* 1960, 166, 1971, 168.

21 *IG* 1², 374.248; *IG* 4², 102.A.250–1, 102.B.296, 303, 103.90–1; *FDelphes* 3.5, 19.106, 20.4–5.

22 See *Tégée*.

23 Bundgaard, *Mnesicles*, 96–7. Nevertheless, there are Atticisms at Bassai, and much that is original there has closer antecedents in Attica than in the Peloponnese (Roux, *Argolide*, 405–6). On the attribution see n. 1.76.

24 Hdt., 5.62.2 (on which see n. 1.43). *IG* 2², 1668.95 might suggest a scale model of Philon's Arsenal, but the clause is probably a recapitulation of the elements of the design so far specified: the specifications as a whole, and the numerous measurements and single *paradeigma* (for a tackle-chest, line 87) mentioned therein. Further specimens were in fact used (*IG* 2², 1627.b.300, 325).

25 On Hellenistic *paradeigmata* see below pp. 71–2.

26 Burford, *Epidauros*, 114, 118.

27 e.g. J. H. Breasted, *Ancient Records of Egypt* 3 (1906), 212–23; D. D. Luckenbill, *Ancient Records of Assyria and Babylon* (1922, 1968), 321–3.

28 Gen. 6.14–16; the more elaborate description of Solomon's Temple (1 Kings 6, 2 Chron. 3–4) is perhaps also based on specifications.

29 *IG* 2², 1666.48, 55–6, 1668.95–6; cf. *IG* 2², 244.54–6.

30 Vitr., 3.5.

31 The *apergon* in *IG* 2², 1666.47, etc.; see Orlandos, *Ylika* 2, 121, 148, Martin, *Manuel* 1, 191, and the dotted area in fig. 16.

32 Detailed evidence for pp. 59–64 is set out in J. J. Coulton, *BSA* 69 (1974), 63–86.

33 Vitr., 4.3.2; Robertson, *Gk. & Rom. Arch.*, 106–12.

34 There are partial cases earlier; cf. J. J. Coulton, *BSA* 69 (1974), 73.

35 Vitr., 4.3.2.

36 Intercolumniation = 2·82 m ± ; 10⅓ × 2·82 = 29·14; stylobate length = 29·19 m. On this stoa see Bouras, *Brauron*, and on re-entrant angles see below pp. 129–31.

37 The aims were regularity *and* satisfying form (see below p. 97 and n. 5.1); it was pointless to pursue one and neglect the other entirely.

38 cf. W. B. Dinsmoor, *Hesperia* 9 (1940), 47. W. H. Plommer, *BSA* 45 (1950), 66–112. But H. Knell, *AA* 1973, 94–114, separates the Hephaisteion and temple of Ares from the temples at Sounion and Rhamnous.

39 Commensurability was considered important, but how far theory went beyond that broad principle is uncertain; see Pollitt, *Anc. View*, 15–22, 256–8, J. J. Coulton, *BSA* 70 (1975), 66–7, 70; contrast *FDelphes, TrCyr*, 77–104, R. R. Holloway, *A View of Greek Art* (1973), 64–8.

40 Vitr., 4.1.6–8.

41 Philon, *Bel.* 50.30–51.7, quoted below p. 97.

42 J. J. Coulton, *BSA* 70 (1975), 66–74.

43 Note, however, Vitr., 4.1.11, 6.3.3.

44 Pliny, *NH*, 36.56, 179; cf. Vitr. 4.7.2. The rule fits the temples of Athena at Assos and Apollo at Corinth.

45 So apparently in the temples of Aphaia at Aigina and Zeus at Olympia (fig. 31).

46 Vitr., 4.3.3–9.

47 Thus according to Vitruvius' rules, the proportion column height to intercolumniation should be 14 : 7½ in temples (but 2 : 1 in stoas), and in a Doric temple with 6 × 14 columns the proportion stylobate width to length should be 42 : 92½ or 29½ : 67 rather than 1 : 2½.

48 Vitr., 4.3.4 and 3.5.8–9.

49 Vitr., 1.2.4, 4.3.3, uses a Greek word for module (*embates*) which is otherwise unknown in that sense. Hermogenes' rules for eustyle temples were based on a module (Vitr. 3.3.7–8) and artillery had been designed on a modular basis from the third century (Philon, *Bel.* 53.8–9).

50 Vitr., 3.5.

51 W. B. Dinsmoor, *Hesperia, Suppl.* 5 (1941), 30, n. 83; see also Dinsmoor, *AAG*, 170, J. J. Coulton, *JHS* 95 (1975), 15, n. 10. In the Old Parthenon the cella wall base was already partly set although no column had more than two drums in place (B. H. Hill, *AJA* 16 (1912), 535–58; R. Carpenter, *The Architects of the Parthenon* (1970), 46). At Segesta the outer colonnade, entablature and pediments were structurally complete, yet the inner building, although begun (H. Schläger, *RM* 75 (1968), 168–9), cannot have progressed far, for there is no sign of pronaos or opisthodomos orders on the site.

52 On numerals and fractions see J. J. Coulton, *BSA* 70 (1975), 75–85.

53 B. Bergquist, *The Archaic Greek Temenos (Acta Instituti Atheniensis Regni Sueciae* 4°. 13, 1967).

54 Vitr., 1.1.4, 1.2.2.

55 C. Huelsen, *RM* 5 (1890), 46–63; G. Carettoni *et al.*, *La Pianta marmorea di Roma antica* (1960), 207–10; H. W. Dickenson, *Transactions of the Newcomen Society* 27 (1949–51), 73–83.

56 Arist., *Poet.* 1449a18; Vitr., 7. pr. 11; Pollitt, *Anc. View*, 236–47.

57 Diog. Laert., 2.125; much later Heron/Damianos (cf. n. 5.28) associates *skenographia* with architectural design.

58 The 'Second Pompeian Style', probably derived from Hellenistic theatrical scenery; T. B. L. Webster, *Hellenistic Art* (1967), 134.

59 *IvPri*, 207 (=*SIG*³, 1156); 'which' refers to the *hypographe* not the temple.

60 Vitr., 3.2.6, 3.3.8, 4.3.1, 7. pr. 12. The identification is strongly contested by A. v. Gerkan, *Das Altar des Artemistempels in Magnesia am Mäander* (1929), 27–9.

61 e.g. Xen., *Mem.* 3.1.2; Plutarch, *Per.* 13, 31, *Mor.* 498E; *ID*, 365.24, etc.

62 In general *hypographe* means an outline, often as opposed to a finished picture (e.g. Plato, *Prot.* 326d, *Rep.* 6.504d, 8.548d, *Laws*, 5.737d, 11.934c; Arist., *Gen. Anim.* 2.743b24).

63 *ID*, 500.37, 41; cf. T. Homolle, *BCH* 14 (1890), 465, n. 2.

64 cf. the full-size profile of a column for the temple on the Theatre Terrace at Pergamon, set out on its marble floor (*Pergamon* 4, 53, pl. 36; third century A.D.?).

65 Akurgal, *Ruins*², 225–31; so also at Sardis (G. Gruben, *AM* 76 (1961), 155–96).

66 *Magnesia/M*, 39–83.

67 Perhaps implied by Vitr., 1.1.12–13.

68 Vitr., 10.16.3; cf. Philon, *Bel.* 55.12–56.8, where the small scale is emphasized by the adjective *mikros* and the use of a diminutive noun form.

69 *IG* 11 (2), 161.A.75–6, 165.17, 199.B.90, 203.B.95.

70 *IG* 11 (2), 161.A.66–72.

71 So Bundgaard, *Mnesicles*, 219; but these cannot be 'Apollo's doors' of *IG* 11 (2), 203.B.96, for cf. *IG* 11 (2), 199.B.90.

72 That would explain why it was up on scaffolding (*IG* 11 (2), 165.17). The interpretation of *ID*, 1417.A.1.11.32–3 ('*paradeigma* of a wooden naiskos') is hampered by our ignorance of the size of the naiskos.

73 Vitr., 6. pr. 5; for examples, *IG* 2², 244, 6–10 and perhaps Vitr., 2. pr. 1; cf. also Vitr., 10.16.3.

74 Plutarch, *Mor*, 498E. Gellius, 19.10; cf. Greg. Nys., *In Chr. Res.* 3 (ed. Migne, 3, 666D).

75 Philon, *Bel.* 55.12–56.8.

Chapter 4. The problem of scale

1 Strictly speaking, doubling the scale will increase the moment of bending by 2^4, while the moment of resistance increases by 2^3. On the actual functioning of architraves see J. Heyman, *JSAH* 31 (1972), 3–9.

2 cf. Vitr. 3.3.3, where the difficulty is attributed solely to proportion, although scale is necessarily involved.

3 Temple of Hera at Olympia and Older Parthenon at Athens (6 × 16); temples of Apollo and Zeus Olympios at Syracuse, and Temple C at Selinous (6 × 17).

cf. also the long narrow shape of stoas and storehouses.

4   Koldewey–Puchstein, 13–18, Krauss, *Paestum*, 20–33.

5   Koldewey–Puchstein, 18–24, Krauss, *Paestum*, 34–43, Krauss, *Athenatempel*.

6   Koldewey–Puchstein, 24–35, Krauss, *Paestum*, 44–63.

7   First temple: $24 \cdot 51 \times 54 \cdot 27$ m; second temple: $24 \cdot 264 \times 59 \cdot 975$ m. First temple: D (lower column diameter) $= 1 \cdot 442$ m, I (axial intercolumniation) $= 2 \cdot 871/3 \cdot 102$ m; temple of Athena: $D = 1 \cdot 267$ m, $I = 2 \cdot 625$ m; second temple: $D = 2 \cdot 110/2 \cdot 03$ m, $I = 4 \cdot 47/4 \cdot 50$ m.

8

Temple	Overall width	Cella width	Overall width/3
C	26·357 m	c. 8·80 m (int.)	8·795 m
D	28·096 m	9·37 m (ext.)	9·365 m
FS	28·39 m	9·32 m (ov.)	9·46 m
GT	53·31 m	17·93 m (int.)	17·10 m

9   The fifth-century temple of Poseidon at Isthmia had an axial colonnade (*Isthmia* 1, 63), and the temple of Zeus at Akragas had an odd number of front columns (cf. p. 82).

10   Vitr., 3.2.

11   *Didyma* 1, Akurgal, *Ruins*[2], 225–31.

12   Other unusual features of this temple are also explained by its special cult and oracle.

13   The Olympieion at Athens was probably intended as dipteral and Doric (G. Welter, *AM* 47 (1922), 61–71; Dinsmoor, *AAG*, 91), but was actually built, after three centuries' delay, with Corinthian columns.

14   Besides those noted here, the temples of Artemis at Kerkyra, Hera at the mouth of the Silaris, and Zeus at Kyrene.

15   Koldewey–Puchstein, 121–7 and 153–66.

16   Apollo: $50 \cdot 07 \times 110 \cdot 12$ m; Zeus Olympios: $52 \cdot 74 \times 110 \cdot 09$ m.

17   At Selinous the column height was about 16·27 m as given by Koldewey–Puchstein, rather than the 14·69 m given by Dinsmoor, *AAG*, 338; the column height at Akragas is much harder to establish; Koldewey–Puchstein suggest 19·20 m, and Dinsmoor 17·265 m (*AAG*, 338). In figs. 29–30 I have followed Koldewey–Puchstein for both temples.

18   J. J. Coulton, *JHS* 94 (1974), 15.

19   cf. Plommer, *Anc. Class. Arch.* 143–5. If a normal roof had been intended at this stage, there is no reason why larger inner colonnades should not have been built to support it in the same way as in the second temple of Hera at Paestum.

20   See the table in Hodge, *Roofs*, 39.

21   Diod. Sic., 13.82.4.

22   Vitr., 3.3.12–13, 3.5.8–9; cf. 3.5.7.

23   Plato, *Soph.* 235e–6a.

24   R. Carpenter, *The Esthetic Basis of Greek Art* (rev. ed., 1959), 138–9.

25   W. B. Dinsmoor, *Hesperia* 9 (1940), 22; see also J. J. Coulton, *BSA* 68 (1973), 79–80.

26   *FDelphes, TrAth.*

27   *Aegina*, 10–68.

28   *Olympia* 2, 4–27.

29   The temple of the Athenians at Delos has six-columned façades, although it is 0·31 m narrower than the temple of Nemesis at Rhamnous, but it was not

peripteral and the arrangement probably arose from the need to build an impressive temple with a wide cella on a very constricted site. Other temples with this plan probably also adopted it for special reasons of cult or site.

30 The Hellenistic temple at Cape Zephyrion near Alexandria, peripteral with 4 × 5 columns, was probably influenced by similar Egyptian sanctuaries (cf. Plommer, *Anc. Class. Arch.*, fig. 16).

31 e.g. temples of Nike at Athens, Artemis at Eleusis, Athena at Lindos, and Artemis and the Twelve Gods at Delos.

32 e.g. Market Temple, Theatre Temple and Temple of Hera at Pergamon, and temple of Zeus at Priene.

33 Compare the relationship of architrave joints and regulae in the Sikyonian Monopteros at Delphi (P. de la Coste Messelière, *Au Musée de Delphes* (1936), 45, fig. 2). The pronaos intercolumniation of the temple of Aphaia at Aigina was similarly made one third of the cella width, but since the metopes were unsculptured, they were made to vary in width, leaving the triglyphs centred over the columns. Compare also the pronaoi of the temples at Tegea and Nemea (J. J. Coulton, *JHS* 95 (1975), 20–3).

34 Vallois, *AHHD* 1, 114, 2, 216; on the three-metope system see Coulton, *Stoas*, 114–18.

35 Most scholars agree on the extra metope, but their estimates of date range from *c.* 530 to *c.* 465 B.C. Boersma, *Bdg. Policy*, 21, argues well for a date *c.* 520–510 B.C.

36 T. L. Shear, *Hesperia* 40 (1971), 243–55.

37 *Argive Heraeum* 1, 127–40, J. J. Coulton, *BSA* 68 (1973), 65–85.

38 Bouras, *Brauron*.

39 An exception is the temple of Athena at Pergamon, probably third century B.C., where the intercolumniation is 2·37 m and the lower column diameter 0·74 m.

40 e.g. the two temples of Artemis at Ephesos; cf. also Vitr., 3.3.6–7, 4.3.3–7.

41 *FDelphes, Colonne*, 33–121.

42 *Délos* 16, 13–43.

Chapter 5. *Form, mass, and space*

1 Philon, *Bel.* 50.30–51.7. Closely related is Heron, *Def.* 135.13=Damianos, *Optica*, 28–30, on which see n. 28.

2 Vitr., 1.3.2. The six qualities set out in Vitr., 1.2 must represent a Greek view, but its complexity suggests a Hellenistic date, which would be confirmed by the explanations of *proprietas* and *oeconomia*, if they are not due entirely to Vitruvius. On the terms used see Pollitt, *Anc. View*, 164–7, 173–80, 343–7.

3 e.g. in Temple C at Selinous (Dinsmoor, *AAG*, fig. 29).

4 Vitr., 4.1.8.

5 e.g. in the Council Chamber at Miletos (*Milet* 1.2, pl. 8).

6 L. T. Shoe, *The Profiles of Greek Mouldings* (1936), 179–80, L. S. Merritt, *Hesperia* 38 (1969), 186–91, Wesenberg, *Kapitelle*, 116–30.

7 Wesenberg, *Kapitelle*, 127–9.

8 Vitr., 3.5.3.

9 Caskey, *Erechtheum*, pl. 16, 22.

10 Roux, *Argolide*, 336–8, *Nemea*, 31–3.

11 e.g. in the Mausoleum at Belevi (Akurgal, *Ruins²*, 170–1).

12 So already in the archaic temple of Artemis at Ephesos (D. G. Hogarth, *Excavations at Ephesos; the Archaic Artemisia* (1908), *Atlas*, pl. 3–4).

13 A. Rumpf, A. Mallwitz, *AM* 76 (1961), 15–20.

14 H. A. Thompson, *Hesperia* 29 (1960), 353–4; the date is less certain than in the other cases.

15 On the attribution see n. 1.76.

16 Olympia: F. Krauss in *R. Boehringer, eine Freundesgabe* (ed. E. Boehringer, W. Hoffman, 1957), 365–87; Corinth: *Corinth* 1.1, 121, pl. 7; Assos: *Assos*, 159; Athens: T. Wiegand, *Die archaische Porosarchitektur der Akropolis zu Athen* (1904), 21, fig. 23. These do not seem to be variations arising from a long-drawn-out building programme, like those in fig. 3.

17 Note the bulging echinus of the probably late-sixth-century temple of Athena at Paestum (Krauss, *Athenatempel*, pls. 17–18); but few western Greek temples are externally dated.

18 Studies of the Doric capital profile usually assume a smooth development, reasonably enough if the actual stages were small, but perhaps a premature assumption. P. de la Coste Messelière, *BCH* 66–7 (1942–3), 22–67, *BCH* 87 (1963), 639–52; Roux, *Argolide*, 27–9, 410–11; Bouras, *Brauron*, 150–3.

19 W. B. Dinsmoor, *Hesperia, Suppl.* 5 (1941), 122–4; Travlos, *Pict. Dict.*, fig. 111–12.

20 e.g. Penrose, *Principles*, 48–50; Pennethorne, *Anc. Arch.*, 128–32.

21 T. L. Heath, *A History of Greek Mathematics* 2 (1921), 110–11. Some of their properties were assumed by Menaichmos, so that they were presumably known a bit earlier.

22 Pennethorne, *Anc. Arch.*, 119–26, tries to face this problem, but his mathematics seem too complex for pre-Menaichmean architects. Simple ways of setting out parabolic and hyperbolic curves are given by G. P. Stevens, *MAAR* 4 (1924), 121–52, and these could be used for capital profiles if the angle and distance of the point from which the generating lines radiate were decided. See also Caskey, *Erechtheum*, 93–4, Bouras, *Brauron*, 68–9 for parabolic cornice soffits.

23 Robertson, *Gk. & Rom. Arch.*, 115–18, Dinsmoor, *AAG*, 164–9, Plommer, *Anc. Class. Arch.*, 179–81, Lawrence, *Gk. Arch.*[3], 170–5. For the Parthenon, Penrose, *Principles*[2].

24 Vitr., 3.3.11, 3.4.5, 3.5.13; cf. Vitr., 3.3.10–11, 4.4.2, and above n. 4.22. The only surviving specification for a refinement is *IG* 2[2], 1680, 11–14 (enlarged angle capitals for the portico of Philon at Eleusis).

25 Fullest discussion in W. H. Goodyear, *Greek Refinements* (1912), although his curvatures in plan are largely discredited (A. v. Gerkan, *RM* 40 (1925), 167–80, D. Mertens, *RM* 81 (1974), 107 n. 7).

26 Euclid, *Optics*, p.2.7–9; Diels–Kranz[6], 47.A.25; 31.A.90, B.94. cf. Vitr., 3.5.9. Vitr., 6.2.3 notes also the theory that vision results from the emission of images by objects seen.

27 Philon, *Bel.* 51.2–6; cf. above p. 97.

28 Heron, *Def.* 135.13, repeated exactly by Damianos/Heliodoros, *Optics*, p.28–30, and also attributed to Geminus of Rhodes (early first century B.C.). On this passage see Pollitt, *Anc. View*, 96, n.4, and 239–40.

29 Diels–Kranz[6], 40.B.2 = Philon, *Bel.* 50.6.

30 So R. Carpenter, *The Architects of the Parthenon* (1970), 126–8. cf. LSJ s.v.

μικρὸν III.5.C; Pollitt, *Anc. View*, 15 n. 6.

31   Note that there is also a practical reason for setting out the stylobate more accurately; the whole temple design depends on it.

32   Lawrence, *Gk. Arch.*[3], 174. Contrary tilting of columns and entablature would tend to equalize the angle between the colonnade and the visual ray to its base with the angle between the entablature and the visual ray to its base. An alternative explanation based on apparent sizes could be derived from Euclid, *Optics*, Postulate 4.

33   In the passage discussed in n. 28.

34   Entasis in the first temple of Hera = 1/120 of the column height, in the temple of Athena = 1/160, in the Parthenon = 1/600. Some early columns in the temple of Hera at Olympia also have pronounced entasis, e.g. in *Olympia 2*, pl. 21.1, where entasis = 1/140 of column height.

35   Pennethorne, *Anc. Arch.*, 120.

36   Pollitt, *Art. & Exp.*, 54–6; Vitr., 7. pr. 11.

37   *Corinth* 1.1, 119.

38   Dinsmoor, *AAG*, 165, claims enlarged corner columns and inclination of the flank colonnades only; *Aegina*, 27, records inclination on all sides but no enlargement.

39   Bundgaard, *Mnesicles*, 133–41.

40   Parthenon: Penrose, *Principles*[2], 9–57, N. Balanos, *Les Monuments de l'Acropole; relèvement et conservation* (1938), 33–87; temple of Zeus: *Olympia 2*, 4–27, A. Mallwitz, *Olympia und seine Bauten* (1972), 211–34.

41   Cella width over toichobate = 0·592 times temple width over stylobate.

42   Cella width over toichobate = 0·701 times temple width over stylobate.

43   L. Pernier, *Il tempio e l'altare di Apollo a Cirene* (1935), 34.

44   See n. 4.14; except at Kyrene the cella width is less than half the stylobate width.

45   No earlier mainland Doric temple had a column height more than twice the intercolumniation; in the Parthenon it was 2·4 times, in the roughly contemporary Hephaisteion 2·2 times. Whereas Iktinos had a clear reason for increasing the column height, the Hephaisteion Architect did not, and was probably the follower here, as in the design of the cella colonnade.

46   Plutarch, *Per.* 13.4. There is no reason to suppose that this was a normal relationship of architect and sculptor (Burford, *Epidauros*, 154–5).

47   W. H. Plommer, *BSA* 45 (1950), 112.

48   On the attribution see n. 1.76; on the temple see C. R. Cockerell, *The Temples of Jupiter Panhellenius at Aegina and Apollo Epicurius at Bassae near Phigaleia in Arcadia* (1860), 41–59, W. B. Dinsmoor, *MetMusSt* 4 (1933), 204–7, Roux, *Argolide*, 21–56, F. A. Cooper, *AJA* 72 (1968), 103–11, U. Pannuti, *Atti* 8[a], 16 (1971–2), 171–262; on the date, see *AR* 19 (1972–3), 18.

49   See n. 4.11.

50   *Milet* 1.2.

51   R. Bohn, *Die Propyläen der Akropolis zu Athen* (1882), Bundgaard, *Mnesicles*, Travlos, *Pict. Dict.*, 482–93. Early Propylaia: C. H. Weller, *AJA* 8 (1904), 35–70, W. H. Plommer, *JHS* 80 (1960), 146–50.

52   Travlos, *Pict. Dict.*, 482, figs. 618–19.

53   e.g. W. Doerpfeld, *AM* 10 (1885), 38–56 (from which the analysis in the preceding paragraph is drawn, Dinsmoor, *AAG*, 204–5, figs. 75–6).

54   L. T. Shoe, *Hesperia, Suppl.* 8 (1949), 344–50, W. B. Dinsmoor, *AJA* 14 (1910), 143–84; cf. below pp. 148–9, 151.

55   R. E. Wycherley, *JHS* 62 (1942), 21–32.

56   Coulton, *Stoas*, 172–4.

57   *Magnesia/M*, 111–12.

58   R. Herzog, *Kos* 1 (1932), 3–21.

59   *Lindos* 3.1, 155–289, 3.2, 515–20.

60   R. Martin, *L'Urbanisme dans la Grèce antique* (1956), 131–46, Hansen, *Attalids*[2], 245–80.

Chapter 6. Some later problems with the orders

1   The temple of Athena (prob. *c.* 480–470 B.C.) is very ill preserved (*Milet* 1.8, 52–70, 121–3).

2   See Coulton, *Stoas*, 99–101.

3   T. L. Shear, *Hesperia* 40 (1971), 248.

4   J. J. Coulton, *BSA* 68 (1973), 65–77.

5   L. S. Merritt, *Hesperia* 39 (1970), 233–64.

6   For Ionic columns in the Parthenon see Penrose, *Principles*[2], 10. In Ionic temples any inner colonnades seem to have consisted of a single storey of ordinary Ionic columns, but details are entirely lacking; cf. also W. H. Plommer, *BSA* 65 (1970), 186.

7   Vitr., 4.3.1, quoting Pytheos, Arkesios and Hermogenes.

8   For a good analysis of these problems see Roux, *Argolide*, 40; for a bibliography of the temple see n. 5.48. A new study of the temple being prepared by F. A. Cooper may affect the explanation of the Corinthian capital offered here.

9   Roux, *Argolide*, 342–8.

10   The Ionic Stoa of the Naxians at Delos turned such a corner, but the angle capital has not survived.

11   W. B. Dinsmoor, *MetMusSt* 4 (1933), 210–12.

12   G. Roux, *BCH* 77 (1953), 124–38, H. Bauer, *Korinthische Kapitelle des 4 und 3 Jahrhunderts v. Chr.* (*AM Beiheft* 3, 1973), 14–65.

13   Vitr., 4.1.8–10; cf. Roux, *Argolide*, 359–62.

14   G. M. A. Richter, *Sculpture and Sculptors of the Greeks* (4th ed., 1970), 185–6. The Corinthian capitals must antedate the frieze, but the date of neither can be accurately fixed.

15   Vitr., 4.1.10. The form could alternatively have had symbolic significance (Pollitt, *Art & Exp.*, 129–30), although the circumstances of its later use do not particularly suggest that.

16   Roux, *Argolide*, 362–88, H. Bauer, *Korinthische Kapitelle des 4 und 3 Jahrhunderts v. Chr.* (*AM Beiheft* 3, 1973), 81–106.

17   Vitr., 4.1.1–3. Although for Vitruvius the columns are Ionic apart from their capitals, he regards Doric and Ionic entablatures as equally permissible above. East of the Adriatic a Doric entablature above Corinthian columns is very rare.

18   For more detail see J. J. Coulton, *BSA* 61 (1966), 132–46.

19   Bouras, *Brauron*, esp. 56–61, 164–6; cf. above p. 64.

20   J. J. Coulton, *BSA* 61 (1966), 136–7. Stylobate width = 1·055 m, so that angle

intercolumniation + stylobate width/2 = 4·027 m; normal intercolumniation × 1⅓ = 4·008 m. The same formula was perhaps used in the Parthenon cella; for figures see W. Doerpfeld, *AM* 6 (1886), 289–93; west stylobate length = 12·260 m; 12·260/4⅔ = 2·634; normal intercolumniation = 2·625 m. In this case with (notionally) two-metope spans, the extension is insufficient to allow two half-regulae at the angle.

21   e.g. the Heroon at Kalydon according to the plan (E. Dyggve *et al.*, *Heroon von Kalydon* (1934), pl. 3.2); the figures given there fit less well, but there is a discrepancy between plan and figures.

22   J. J. Coulton, *BSA* 61 (1966), 137–40, Büsing, *Halbsäule*, 56–63.

23   cf. the criticisms of Pytheos, Arkesios and Hermogenes, Vitr., 4.3.1–2.

24   M. Bieber, *History of the Greek and Roman Theatre* (2nd ed., 1961), 114–16; A. v. Gerkan, *Das Theater von Priene* (1921), 37–51.

25   They were called *columnae atticae* (Pliny, *NH*, 35.56, 179).

26   I. M. Shear, *Hesperia* 32 (1963), 391.

27   Büsing, *Halbsäule*, 45–51, Coulton, *Stoas*, 125–6.

28   Büsing, *Halbsäule*, 52–6.

29   Coulton, *Stoas*, 105–8, 124–31.

30   G. Allen, L. D. Caskey, *AJA* 15 (1911), 32–43.

31   When the upper columns are Doric, they usually carry an Ionic entablature, e.g. the stoas at Assos (*Assos*, 33–51).

32   Vitr., 5.1.3, 4.

33   *Nemea.*

34   J. J. Coulton, *BSA* 59 (1964), 100–31.

35   Ch. Makaronas, *AD* 16 (1960), 80, pl. 36b; M. Andronikos *et al.*, *Τὸ ἀνάκτορο τῆς Βεργίνας* (1961), pl. 8.2.

36   Vallois, *AHHD* 1, 247–59.

37   Rare but known on Delos (Büsing, *Halbsäule*, 49–50); but even the theatre proskenion at Delos had rectangular pillars.

38   *Pergamon* 2, 28–56.

39   Wesenberg, *Kapitelle*, 43–9, Coulton, *Stoas*, 121.

40   Travlos, *Pict. Dict.*, 505–19, with further references.

41   D. E. Strong, *JRS* 53 (1963), 73–84, Coulton, *Stoas*, 128–9.

Chapter 7. Aspects of structure and technique

1   Hermogenes' claim to fame lay in his temple designs (Vitr., 3.3.8–9), and even Vitruvius devotes more space to temples than to any other type of building.

2   The patron's or commission's views were presumably important too; cf. Dion Chrys., 40.7. Transport costs were high (R. S. Stanier, *JHS* 72 (1953), 70–1, Martin, *Manuel* 1, 172).

3   J. Röder, *AA* 1965, 507–24; but iron wedges were used by the Greeks from the sixth century (W. Koenigs, *AA* 1972, 381–3, S. Kasper, *AA* 1975, 230–1).

4   For a full discussion see Orlandos, *Ylika* or Martin, *Manuel* 1.

5   Diod. Sic., 4.80, *IG* 1², 313.26–7, 116, *IG* 2², 1656.8, 1673.47, *IG* 11 (2), 173.10; cf. also above p. 45; on the use of oxen see A. Burford, *Economic History Review* 13 (1960), 1–18, Burford, *Epidauros*, 184–91.

6   A. H. Nelson, *TechCult* 13 (1972), 391–416; for sledges, *IG* 11 (2), 203.B.97, Heron, *Mech.* 3.1 (Nix-Schmidt p. 294), and cf. Orlandos, *Ylika* 2, 90–1, fig. 37; but the same method of braking could be used with a cart (Heron, *Mech.*

3.9, Nix–Schmidt p. 220), so avoiding the transfer from sledge to cart.

7   *IG* 2², 1673, 72–3.

8   Slightly differing descriptions in Diod. Sic., 20.91.2–8, Vitr., 10.16.4, Ath.,
Mech. W27, Plutarch, *Dem. Pol.* 21.1; cf. Marsden, *Treatises*, 84–5.

9   Vitr., 10.15, Ath., *Mech.* W21–6. Diodoros says that Epimachos' tower needed
3400 men!

10   Vitr., 10.2.11–12. The method has been doubted (Durm, *BKG*³, 100, n. 1,
Orlandos, *Ylika* 2, 96–7) but Paconius (n. 13) was not fictitious, and his
method derives naturally from Metagenes'.

11   Koldewey–Puchstein, 119–20, 125; but the drums of the temple of Apollo
were tapered as they were quarried, so could not roll straight unless one end
was built up.

12   Vitr., 7. pr. 12; see above p. 24.

13   Vitr., 10.2.13–14.

14   Ath., *Mech.* W28–9.

15   Stone transport would require road maintenance in any case; *IG* 1², 363.46,
IG 2², 1673.28, *Didyma* 2, nos. 40, 11–12, 26, 41.22, 27–8, Martin, *Manuel* 1,
166.

16   Pliny, *NH*, 36.21, 96–7.

17   See J. J. Coulton, *JHS* 94 (1974), 1–19 on this whole topic.

18   cf. the way in which most cities of the Delian League preferred to commute
personal service in the League's navy for a money payment which went to
professional Athenian sailors.

19   Note the excitement and response at Ephesos when the shepherd Pixodaros
discovered a marble supply for the sixth-century temple of Artemis (Vitr.,
10.2.15; S. Kasper, *AA* 1975, 231–2).

20   *Didyma* 2, no. 32, 9–17; cf. Heron, *Mech.*, 3.1–5 (Nix-Schmidt, pp. 200–12).

21   Vitr., 10.2.7.

22   Powerful winches would be needed to tension Archimedes' catapults, which
could throw stones weighing up to 10 talents (*c.* 270 kg.) (Plutarch, *Marc.*,
15.4).

23   L. Pernier, *Annuario* 1 (1914), 60–61, cf. 48–53 (frieze).

24   G. Cultrera, *MonAnt* 40 (1951), 821–2; G. Gruben, W. Koenigs, *AA* 1970,
138–40.

25   P. de la Coste Messelière, *Au Musée de Delphes* (1936), 25, 43, fig. 1; G. de Miré,
Delphes, pl. 39; *FDelphes, Colonne*, 8–9; *FDelphes, TrAth*, 34.

26   W. B. Dinsmoor, *AJA* 26 (1922), 154–6; Dinsmoor believed the blocks were
hollowed out to take iron bars from which the marble beams were
suspended; but no sign of an adequate method of suspension has been found.
The ceiling slabs bear on the marble beams not on the notional iron bars, and
Dinsmoor's calculations show that the marble beams would just be strong
enough without reinforcement.

27   R. A. Jewett, *TechCult* 9 (1968), 424.

28   *Samothrace* 3.1 (1967), 110, pl. 77–80; the beams ran parallel to the ridge of the
roof.

29   Low ribs: H. Koch, *Studien zum Theseustempel in Athen* (1955), pl. 50; high ribs:
M. H. McAllister, *Hesperia* 28 (1959), 38–9, *Tégée*, 30–1, pl. 53, *Stratos* 45–6.

30   Coulton, *Stoas*, 145.

31   e.g. Koldewey–Puchstein, 15, 19, 39, 99–100, 108, cf. 125; in Italy the

architrave is square *with* the decorative course, at Selinous it is square *without* it.

32 Hodge, *Roofs*, 92–4. A square beam is only 8 per cent weaker than the strongest rectangular beam that can be cut from a given circular log.

33 W. B. Dinsmoor, *AJA* 26 (1922), 152–4, R. A. Jewett, *TechCult* 9 (1968), 420–2.

34 W. B. Dinsmoor, *AJA* 26 (1922), 151–2, Caskey, *Erechtheum*, 110.

35 W. B. Dinsmoor, *AJA* 26 (1922), 150–1, Koldewey–Puchstein, 163.

36 Durm, *BKG*³, 402–4; cf. also J. Heyman, *JSAH* 31 (1972), 3–9.

37 e.g. Arist., *Ath. Pol.* 50.2.

38 P. Le Bas, E. Laudron, *Voyage archéologique en Grèce et en Asie Mineure* (2nd ed., S. Reinach, 1888), *Archit., Îles de Grèce*, pl. 2; L. Haselberger, *AA* 1972, 431–7.

39 W. B. Dinsmoor, *AJA* 26 (1922), 156–7.

40 W. B. Dinsmoor, *AJA* 14 (1910), 144–51.

41 Krauss, *Athenatempel*, 20–2, pl. 15.

42 Coulton, *Stoas*, 145–6.

43 e.g. T. Wiegand, *AM* 21 (1896), 11–17.

44 Numerous examples illustrated by Orlandos, *Ylika* 2, figs. 273–328; maximum span at Pantikapaion, fig. 292.

45 e.g. at Belevi, S. Kasper, *AA* 1975, 223–32.

46 Seneca, *Ep.* 90.32 (cf. n. 69); Lawrence, *Gk. Arch.*³, 228–9.

47 e.g. Orlandos, *Ylika* 2, figs. 310, 317–18.

48 e.g. Orlandos, *Ylika* 2, figs. 344–51.

49 Maximum tomb span at Leukadia (P. M. Petsas, Ὁ Μακεδονικὸς τάφος τῶν Λευκαδίων (1966)); maximum span at Pergamon (*Pergamon* 2, 80, pls. 10–11). A span of 11 m at Pergamon is suggested by Orlandos, *Ylika* 2, 350, but evidence is lacking (*Pergamon* 3.1, 83–4, pl. 20).

50 *Ergon* 1958, 102, fig. 107; G. E. Bean, *Aegaean Turkey* (1966), pl. 46, 48; Vallois, *AHHD* 1, 264–8.

51 Hodge, *Roofs*; Coulton, *Stoas*, 149–65.

52 On the Parthenon roof see P. M. Mylonas, *AE* 1953–4, pt. 2, 208–14.

53 Coulton, *Stoas*, 155–7.

54 See above pp. 148–51; Coulton, *Stoas*, 144–6.

55 F. Noack, *Eleusis* (1927). The plan attributed to Iktinos involves spans of up to 9.82 m.

56 E. A. Gardner *et al.*, *Excavations at Megalopolis 1890–91* (*JHS Suppl.* 1, 1892), 17–33.

57 *Milet* 1.2; F. Krischen *et al.*, *Antike Rathäuser* (1941), 7–12.

58 e.g. J. Overbeck, A. Mau, *Pompeii* (4th ed., 1884), 172; H. A. Thompson, *Hesperia* 19 (1950), 31–141.

59 F. Krischen *et al.*, *Antike Rathäuser* (1941), 15–16.

60 The roof with *transtra* and *capreoli* specified by Vitruvius (4.2.1) for large spans, and used across the 60-foot span of his basilica at Fanum (5.1.9), was probably a truss roof.

61 Hodge, *Roofs*, 38–44; *Samothrace* 3.1, 198–200; contra, Coulton, *Stoas*, 162–5, 295–6. Diagonal bracing in a siege machine is mentioned once (Biton, 54.4).

62 For a royal gift of timbers to Rhodes, see Polyb., 5.89.6.

63 G. Roux, *BCH* 76 (1952), 466–83; Coulton, *Stoas*, 295–6.

64 cf. Paus., 5.20.9.

65 A. Conze, A. Hauser, G. Niemann, *Archäologische Untersuchungen auf Samothrake*

1 (1875), pl. 55, 57; K. Lehmann-Hartleben, *AJA* 44 (1940), 338.

66 25° in the Monument of Lysikrates, 27° in the Tower of the Winds, 37° in the pavilions of the Nymphaeum of Herodes Attikos at Olympia.

67 *OlyForsch* 1 (1944), 72–4.

68 Roofs based on pairs of rafters set against each other without tie-beams have been proposed for some rectangular buildings (Vallois, *AHHD* 1, 279–80, Roux, *Argolide*, 46–8), but are difficult to accept because of the thrust generated by a low-pitched roof of this kind (cf. P. Bruneau, J. Ducat, *Guide de Délos* (1965), 90). The principle involved was widely known, however, and used (like arches and corbelling) in situations where the resulting thrust could be countered; the pitch is never less than 26½° (1 : 2) (Orlandos, *Ylika* 2, 325–30).

69 Seneca, *Ep.* 90.32 (Seneca's doubts seem unjustified since Demokritos wrote on other technical subjects); Vitr., 6.8.4. Note also the lost work on vaulting by Heron of Alexandria.

70 e.g. Archimedes (Plutarch, *Marc.* 17); for a formula based on a systematic experimental programme (rare, if not unique) see Philon, *Bel.* 50.19–26.

Bibliography

A *Ancient sources*

There is no convenient collection of inscriptions relating to Greek architecture; for a brief guide see R. L. Scranton, in *Harvard Library Bulletin* 14 (1960), 159–82. The abbreviations for epigraphical works are explained in section B of the bibliography.

The most important ancient author for Greek architecture is Vitruvius: there is a good translation of his *Ten Books on Architecture* by M. H. Morgan (1914, reprinted 1960). Other authors refer to architecture only in passing; a Loeb edition (with English translation facing the ancient text) is available for all the works cited (including Vitruvius), except where some other edition is specified below.

The following abbreviations for ancient authors and their works have been used.

Aischin.   Aischines, orator, 389–314 B.C.
  Ctes.   *Against Ctesiphon*

Arist.   Aristotle, philosopher and scientist, 384–322 B.C.
  Ath. Pol.   *Athenaion Politeia (Constitution of Athens)*
  Gen. Anim. *On the Generation of Animals*
  Metaph.   *Metaphysics*
  Poet.   *Poetics*
  Pol.   *Politics*

Asklepiodotos, writer on various subjects, fl. late first century B.C.
        Tactics (Loeb edition with Aeneas Tacticus)

Ath.   Athenaios, writer on mechanics, fl. late first century B.C.
  Mech.   *Mechanics* (ed. R. Schneider, *Abhandlungen der Gesellschaft der Wissenschaften zu Göttingen, Ph.-hist. Kl.* NF 12 (1922))

Biton, artillery engineer, fl. mid third century, B.C.
        Construction of War Engines and Artillery (ed. Marsden, *Treatises*)

Cicero, orator and philosopher, 106–43 B.C.
  De Off.   *De Officiis*
  De Orat.   *De Oratore*

Damianos/Hermodoros, writer on optics, probably third or fourth century A.D.
        Optics (ed. R. Schöne, 1897)

Dem.   Demosthenes, orator, 383–322 B.C.
  Cor.   *On the Crown* (no. 18)
  Mid.   *Against Meidias* (*scholia* in edition by W. Dindorf, vol. 9, 1851)

Diod. Sic.   Diodoros of Sicily, historian, fl. second half of first century B.C.
　　　　　　Historical Library

Diog. Laert.   Diogenes Laertios, philosopher, early third century A.D.
　　　　　　Lives of the Famous Philosophers

Dion Chrys.   Dion Chrysostomos, sophist, A.D. 40–120.
　　　　　　Speeches

Euclid (Eukleides), mathematician, fl. *c.* 300 B.C.
　　　　　　Optics (ed. L. J. Heiberg, H. Menge, 1895)

Gellius   Aulus Gellius, grammarian and scholar, born *c.* A.D. 130.
　　　　　　Attic Nights

Greg. Nys.   Gregory of Nysa, churchman, *c.* A.D. 335–94.
　In Chr. Res.   *In Christi Resurrectionem* (ed. J. P. Migne, *Patrologiae Cursus Completus, Patrologia Graeca* 46 (1863))

Hdt.   Herodotos, historian, *c.* 484–410 B.C.
　　　　　　Histories

Heron of Alexandria, writer on mechanics and applied mathematics, fl. second half of first century A.D.
　Def.　　　　*Definitions*　⎫
　Geom.　　　*Geometrica*　⎪　(ed. W. Schmidt, H. Schöne, J. L. Heiberg,
　Mech.　　　*Mechanics*　⎬　1899–1914)
　Metr.　　　*Metrica*　　　⎭

Hesychios of Alexandria, grammarian, fifth or sixth century A.D.
　　　　　　Lexikon (ed. K. Latte, 1953–).

Homer, epic poet, eighth century B.C.
　Il.　　　　*Iliad*
　Od.　　　　*Odyssey*

Hom. Hym. Apo.   *Homeric Hymn to Apollo*, seventh century B.C.

Pappos, mathematician, fl. late third century A.D.
　　　　　　Opera (ed. F. Hultsch, 1876–8)

Paus.   Pausanias, travel writer, fl. *c.* A.D. 160–80.
　　　　　　Description of Greece

Philochoros, historian of Athens, *c.* 340–261 B.C.
　　　　　　Fragments (ed. F. Jacoby, *Die Fragmente der griechische Historiker* (1923–58) 3, no. 328)

Philon of Byzantion, writer on mechanics, fl. late third century B.C.
　Bel.　　　　*Belopoeia* (ed. Marsden, *Treatises*)

Pindar, lyric poet, *c.* 522–447 B.C.
　Ol.　　　　*Olympian Odes*

Plato, philosopher, 428–347 B.C.
　　　　　　Ion
　　　　　　Laws

Phlb.	*Philebos*
Polit.	*Politikos*
Prot.	*Protagoras*
Rep.	*Republic*
Soph.	*Sophist*

Pliny the Elder, encylopaedist, A.D. 23–79.
  NH   *Natural History*

Plutarch, historian and philosopher, A.D. 46–127.
  Dem. Pol.   *Life of Demetrios Poliorketes*
  Kim.   *Life of Kimon*
  Marc.   *Life of Marcellus*
  Mor.   *Moralia*
  Per.   *Life of Perikles*
  Sol.   *Life of Solon*
  Them.   *Life of Themistokles*

Polyainos, military writer, fl. mid second century A.D.
        Stratagems (ed. E. Wolflinn, 1860)

Polyb.   Polybios, historian, 200–118 B.C.
        Histories

Seneca the Younger, dramatist and philosopher, *c.* 4 B.C.–A.D. 65.
  Ep.   *Epistles to Lucilius*

Strabo, geographer, 64 B.C.–A.D. 19
        Geography

Theophrastos, philosopher, 372–287 B.C.
  Char.   *Characters*

Val. Max.   Valerius Maximus, historian, fl. A.D. 26.
        Memorable Deeds and Words

Vitr.   Vitruvius, architect, fl. second half of first century B.C.
        Ten Books on Architecture (De Architectura)

Xen.   Xenophon, soldier and historian, *c.* 430–350 B.C.
  Mem.   *Memorabilia*

B   *Modern works*

The following general handbooks on Greek architecture will give more information on most of the buildings discussed, with references for further reading and much fuller glossaries.

D. S. Robertson, *Greek and Roman Architecture* (2nd ed., 1943): with a useful glossary of ancient as well as modern technical terms.

W. B. Dinsmoor, *The Architecture of Ancient Greece* (1950): with an excellent classified bibliography up to 1950.

W. H. Plommer, *Ancient and Classical Architecture* (1957): note especially Chapter 5 on the Greek orders.

A. W. Lawrence, *Greek Architecture* (1957, 1967, 1973): the most up-to-date and best illustrated.

More specific references to matters treated in the present work have been given in the notes, using the following abbreviations for periodicals and for frequently cited books.

AA   *Archäologischer Anzeiger*
AD   Ἀρχαιολογικὸν Δελτίον
AE   Ἀρχαιολογικὴ Ἐφημερίς
Aegina   A. Furtwängler, *Aegina, das Heiligtum von Aphaia* (1906)
AJA   *American Journal of Archaeology*
AJP   *American Journal of Philology*
Akurgal, *Ruins*[2]   E. Akurgal, *Ancient Civilisations and Ruins of Turkey* (2nd ed., 1970)
AM   *Mitteilungen des Deutschen Archäologischen Instituts, Athenische Abteilung*
AncEgy   *Ancient Egypt*
Annuario   *Annuario della scuola archeologica di Atene*
AR   *Archaeological Reports* (published with *BSA* and *JHS*)
Argive Heraeum 1   C. Waldstein *et al., The Argive Heraeum* (1902) 1
AS   *Anatolian Studies*
Assos   F. H. Bacon, J. T. Clark, R. Koldewey, *Investigations at Assos 1881–3* (1902–21)
Atti   *Atti della Accademia Nazionale dei Lincei, Memorie: Classe Sci. Mor.-Stor.-Filol.*
BCH   *Bulletin de Correspondence Hellénique*
BdA   *Bollettino d'Arte*
Boardman, *Overseas*[2]   J. Boardman, *The Greeks Overseas* (2nd ed., 1973)
Boersma, *Bdg. Policy*   J. Boersma, *Athenian Building Policy from 561/0 to 405/4 BC* (1970)
Bouras, *Brauron*   Ch. Bouras, Ἡ Ἀναστήλωσις τῆς στοᾶς τῆς Βραυρῶνος (1967)
BSA   *Annual of the British School of Archaeology at Athens*
Bundgaard, *Mnesicles*   J. A. Bundgaard, *Mnesicles, a Greek Architect at Work* (1957)
Burford, *Epidauros*   A. Burford, *Greek Temple Builders at Epidauros* (1969)
Büsing, *Halbsäule*   H. H. Büsing, *Die Griechische Halbsäule* (1970)
Caskey, *Erechtheum*   L. D. Caskey *et al., The Erechtheum* (1927)
Chron.   Book of Chronicles
CIG   A. Boeckh, *Corpus Inscriptionum Graecarum* (1828–77)
Clarke–Engelbach   S. Clarke, R. Engelbach, *Ancient Egyptian Masonry* (1930)
Corinth   *Corinth, Results of Excavations conducted by the American School of Classical Studies at Athens* (1932–)
   1.1, H. N. Fowler *et al., Introduction, Topography, Architecture* (1932)
   4.1, I. T. Hill, L. S. King, *Decorated Architectural Terracottas* (1929)
Coulton, *Stoas*   J. J. Coulton, *The Architectural Development of the Greek Stoa* (1977)
Délos   École française d'Athènes, *Exploration archéologique de Délos* (1909–)
   16, F. Chapouthier, *Le Sanctuaire des dieux de Samothrace* (1935)
Didyma   T. Wiegand, *Didyma*
   1, H. Knackfuss, *Die Baubeschreibung* (1941)
   2, A. Rehm, *Die Inschriften* (1955)
Diels–Kranz[6]   H. Diels, W. Kranz, *Die Fragmente der Vorsokratiker* (6th ed., 1951–2)
Dinsmoor, *AAG*   W. B. Dinsmoor, *The Architecture of Ancient Greece* (1950)
Drerup, *Geom. Baukunst*   H. Drerup, *Griechische Baukunst in geometrischer Zeit* (*Archeologia Homerica* O, 1969)

Durm, *BKG*³   J. Durm, *Die Baukunst der Griechen* (3rd ed., 1910)

Ergon   Ἔργον τῆς ἐν Ἀθήναις Ἀρχαιολογικῆς Ἑταιρείας

FDelphes   École française d'Athènes, *Fouilles de Delphes* (1908–   )
    3.5, E. Bourguet, *Les Comptes du ive siècle* (1932)
    Colonne: P. Amandry, *La Colonne des Naxiens et le portique des Athéniens* (1953)
    Temple: M. F. Courby, *La Terrasse du temple* (1927)
    Terres cuites: C. Leroy, J. Ducat, *Les Terres cuites architecturales et la sculpture en terre-cuite* (1967)
    TrAth: J. Audiat, *Le Trésor des Athéniens* (1933)
    TrCyr: J. Bousquet, *Le Trésor de Cyrène* (1952)
    TrTh: J-P. Michaud, *Le Trésor de Thèbes* (1973)

Gen.   Book of Genesis

Graham, *Palaces*   J. W. Graham, *The Palaces of Crete* (1962)

Hansen, *Attalids*²   E. V. Hansen, *The Attalids of Pergamon* (2nd ed., 1971)

HSCP   Harvard Studies in Classical Philology

Hesperia   Hesperia

Hodge, *Roofs*   A. T. Hodge, *The Woodwork of Greek Roofs* (1960)

ID   F. Dürrbach *et al., Inscriptions de Délos* (1926–   )

IG   Academia Literarum Regiae Borussicae, *Inscriptiones Graecae* (1873–   )

*IG*²   Academia Literarum Borussicae, *Inscriptiones Graecae* (editio minor, 1924–   )

Isthmia   Isthmia, Excavations conducted by the University of Chicago (1971–   )
    1, O. Broneer, *The Temple of Poseidon* (1971)

IvPri   F. Hiller v. Gaertringen, *Inschriften von Priene* (1906)

JARC   Journal of the American Research Center in Egypt

JdI   Jahrbuch des Deutschen Archäologischen Instituts

JEA   Journal of Egyptian Archaeology

Jeppesen, *Paradeigmata*   K. Jeppesen, *Paradeigmata* (1958)

JHS   Journal of Hellenic Studies

JOAI   Jahreshefte des Oesterreichischen Archäologischen Instituts

JRS   Journal of Roman Studies

JSAH   Journal of the Society of Architectural Historians

Kock, *ComAttFrag*   T. Kock, *Comicorum Atticorum Fragmenta* (1880–8)

Koldewey–Puchstein   R. Koldewey, O. Puchstein, *Griechische Tempel in Unteritalien und Sicilien* (1899)

Korkyra   G. Rodenwaldt, *Korkyra; Archaische Bauten und Bildwerke* (1939–40)
    1, H. Schleif *et al., Der Artemistempel* (1940)

Krauss, *Athenatempel*   F. Krauss, *Die Tempel von Paestum* 1.1; *der Athenatempel* (1959)

Krauss, *Paestum*   F. Krauss, *Paestum, die griechische Tempel* (1941)

Lawrence, *Gk. Arch.*³   A. W. Lawrence, *Greek Architecture* (3rd ed., 1973)

Lindos   C. Blinkenberg *et al., Lindos, Fouilles et recherches*
    3.1–2, E. Dyggve, *L'Architecture* (1960)

LSJ   H. G. Liddell, R. Scott, *A Greek–English Lexicon* (9th ed., rev. H. Stuart Jones, R. McKenzie, 1940)

MAAR   Memoirs of the American Academy at Rome

MacDonald, *Architecture* 1   W. L. MacDonald, *The Architecture of the Roman Empire* 1, *Introductory Study* (1965)

Magnesia/M   C. Humann, *Magnesia am Maeander; Bericht über die Ergebnisse der Ausgrabungen der Jahre 1891–93* (1904)

Marsden, *Treatises*   E. W. Marsden, *Greek and Roman Artillery; Technical Treatises* (1971)

Martin, *Manuel* 1   R. Martin, *Manuel d'architecture grecque* 1, *Matériaux et techniques* (1965)

MDOG   *Mitteilungen der Deutschen Orient-Gesellschaft*

Meiggs–Lewis, *GHI*   R. Meiggs, D. M. Lewis, *Greek Historical Inscriptions to the End of the Fifth Century* (1969)

MetMusSt   *Metropolitan Museum Studies*

Milet   T. Wiegand, *Milet, Ergebnisse der Ausgrabungen und Untersuchungen seit dem Jahre 1899* (1906–)

   1.2, H. Knackfuss, *Das Rathaus von Milet* (1908)

   1.3, G. Kawerau, A. Rehm, *Das Delphinion in Milet* (1914)

   1.6, A. v. Gerkan, *Der Nordmarkt und der Hafen an der Löwenbucht* (1922)

   1.7, H. Knackfuss, *Der Südmarkt und die benachbarten Bauanlagen* (1924)

   1.8, A. v. Gerkan, *Kalabaktepe, Athenatempel und Umgebung* (1925)

MonAnt   *Monumenti Antichi, pubblicati per cura dell'Accademia Nazionale dei Lincei*

Nemea   B. H. Hill, C. K. Williams, *The Temple of Zeus at Nemea* (1966)

OlyForsch 1   E. Kunze, H. Schleif, *Olympische Forschungen* 1 (1944)

Olympia   E. Curtius, F. Adler, *Olympia, Ergebnisse der von den deutschen Reich veranstalteten Ausgrabungen* (1890–7)

   2, W. Doerpfeld *et al., Die Baudenkmäler von Olympia* (1892)

   5, W. Dittenberger, K. Purgold, *Die Inschriften von Olympia* (1896)

OpArch   *Opuscula Archaeologica*

OpAth   *Opuscula Atheniensia*

Orlandos, *Ylika*   A. Orlandos, Τὰ Ὑλικὰ δομῆς τῶν ἀρχαίων Ἑλλήνων (1955–8)

PAE   Πρακτικὰ τῆς ἐν Ἀθήναις Ἀρχαιολογικῆς Ἑταιρείας

Pennethorne, *Anc.Arch.*   J Pennethorne, *The Geometry and Optics of Ancient Architecture* (1878)

Penrose, *Principles*[2]   F. C. Penrose, *The Principles of Athenian Architecture* (2nd ed., 1888)

Pergamon   Staatliche Museen zu Berlin, *Altertümer von Pergamon* (1885–)

   2, R. Bohn, *Das Heiligtum der Athena Polias Nikephoros* (1885)

   3.1, J. Schrammen, *Der Grosse Altar, der obere Markt* (1906)

   4. R. Bohn, *Die Theaterterrasse* (1896)

Plommer, *Anc.Class.Arch.*   W. H. Plommer, *Ancient and Classical Architecture* (1957)

Pollitt, *Anc.View*   J. J. Pollitt, *The Ancient View of Greek Art* (1974)

Pollitt, *Art & Exp.*   J. J. Pollitt, *Art and Experience in Classical Greece* (1972)

REG   *Revue des Études Grecques*

RevArch   *Revue Archéologique*

RevEg   *Revue d'Égyptologie*

RevPhil   *Revue Philologique*

RhMus   *Rheinisches Museum für Philologie*

Richter, *Kouroi*[3]   G. M. A. Richter, *Kouroi, Archaic Greek Youths* (3rd ed., 1970)

RM   *Mitteilungen des Deutschen Archäologischen Instituts, Römische Abteilung*

Robertson, *Gk. & Rom. Arch.*[2]   D. S. Robertson, *Greek and Roman Architecture* (2nd ed., 1943)

Roux, *Argolide*   G. Roux, *L'Architecture de l'Argolide aux iv et iii siècles av. J-C* (1961)

Samothrace   *Samothrace, Excavations conducted by the Institute of Fine Arts of New York University* (1959–)

2.1, P. M. Fraser, *The Inscriptions on Stone* (1960)

3, P. W. Lehmann, *The Hieron* (1969)

Schmid–Stählin[6]   W. Schmid, O. Stählin, *Geschichte der griechischen Literatur* (6th ed., 1924)

SEG   *Supplementum Epigraphicum Graecum* (1923–)

SIG[3]   W. Dittenberger, *Sylloge Inscriptionum Graecarum* (3rd ed., 1915–20)

Snodgrass, *Dark Age*   A. M. Snodgrass, *The Dark Age of Greece* (1971)

Stratos   F. Courby, C. Picard, *Recherches archéologiques à Stratos d'Acarnanie* (1924)

TechCult   *Technology and Culture*

Tégée   C. Dugas, J. Berchmans, M. Clemmensen, *Le Sanctuaire d'Aléa Athéna à Tégée* (1924)

Tiryns   Deutsches Archäologisches Institut, *Tiryns, die Ergebnisse der Ausgrabungen des Instituts* (1912–)

3 K. Müller, *Die Architektur der Burg und des Palastes* (1930)

Travlos, *Pict.Dict.*   J. Travlos, *Pictorial Dictionary of Ancient Athens* (1971)

Vallois, *AHHD*   R. Vallois, *L'Architecture hellénique et hellénistique à Délos* (1944–66)

Wesenberg, *Kapitelle*   B. Wesenberg, *Kapitelle und Basen* (*Bonner Jahrbücher, Beiheft* 32, 1971)

Glossary

(Terms used only in a passage where they are defined are not included here.)

Abacus: flat, usually square member forming the top of a capital; see fig. 71.

Agora: market and political centre of a Greek city.

Anagrapheus: probably a template, used in specifying a design; see p. 55.

Anta: slightly thickened wall-end, usually terminating a colonnade (see fig. 72); its capital differs from those of the corresponding columns.

Archaic period: c. 700–480 B.C.

Architrave: lowest member of the entablature (q.v.), resting directly on the capitals; see fig. 71.

Cavetto: concave moulding, approximately quarter-round.

Cella: the main room inside a Greek temple, containing the cult statue; see fig. 72.

Classical period: c. 480–323 B.C.

Corinthian capital: an elaborate bell-shaped capital; in Greek architecture used with an otherwise Ionic order; see pp. 128–9, and fig. 55e.

Cornice: uppermost member of the entablature (q.v.) projecting to throw off rainwater; see fig. 71.

Dentils: blocklike projections in a band below the Ionic cornice; at first treated as an alternative to, later combined with, a frieze; see fig. 71b.

Doric order: conventional system of columns and entablature (q.v.), used originally in mainland Greece and the western Greek colonies, later throughout the Greek world. For the forms see figs. 31, 71a.

Echinus: lower member of Doric capital, its shape ranging from circular cushion to truncated cone; see figs. 41, 71a.

Entablature: the upper parts of a Greek order, carried by the columns—the architrave, frieze and cornice (q.v.); see fig. 71.

Entasis: slight convexity in the taper of a column; see pp. 108, 110.

Frieze: second element of the entablature (q.v.); see fig. 71.

Guttae: small peg-like projections from the mutules (q.v.) of a Doric cornice and the regulae (q.v.) of a Doric architrave; see fig. 71a.

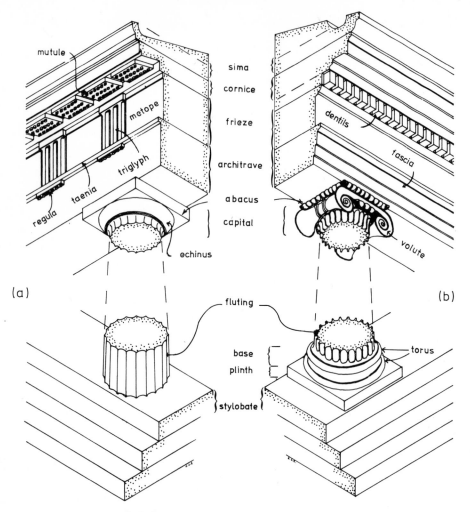

mutule

sima

cornice

metope

frieze

triglyph

architrave

taenia

abacus

regula

capital

echinus

dentils

fascia

volute

(a)

(b)

fluting

base

torus

plinth

stylobate

71   Technical terms: (a) the Doric order; (b) the Ionic order

Hellenistic period: c. 323–31 B.C..

Hypographe: outline, or drawing; see pp. 70–1.

Intercolumniation: distance from column axis to column axis; see fig. 72.

Ionic order: conventional system of columns and entablature (q.v.), used originally in Asia Minor and the nearby islands, later throughout the Greek world. For the forms see fig. 71b.

Metope: plain or sculptured panel between the triglyphs of the Doric frieze: see fig. 71a.

Mutule: slablike element projecting from the under face of the Doric cornice, one coming above each metope (q.v.) and each triglyph (q.v.); see fig. 71a.

Opisthodomos: false porch behind the cella (q.v.) in most major Greek temples; see fig. 72.

Orthostate: slab set on edge, usually at the foot of a wall; see fig. 12d.

Palaistra: building for athletic training and education, usually based on a colonnaded court.

Paradeigma: specimen of a part (e.g. a capital) to be repeated by the builders; see p. 55.

Pilaster: flat, rectangular projection from a wall, usually carrying an entablature and serving to enrich a plain wall face; it may be treated as an anta (q.v.) or as a flattened column.

Plinth: square slab below the base of some Ionic columns; see fig. 71b.

Pronaos: porch in front of the cella (q.v.) of a temple; see fig. 72.

Regula: projecting bar below the taenia (q.v.) of the Doric architrave, one coming below each triglyph; see fig. 71a.

Stoa: long colonnaded hall, used for general shelter and display in Greek sanctuaries and agoras (q.v.); see plate 2.

Stylobate: continuous platform on which columns stand; see figs. 71, 72.

Taenia: continuous band along the top of the Doric architrave; see fig. 71a.

Torus: convex half-round moulding forming part of the Ionic base; see fig. 71b.

Triglyph: grooved member alternating with metopes (q.v.) in the Doric frieze; see fig. 71a.

Volute: spiral forming the main feature of the Ionic capital (see fig. 71b), and occurring also in the Corinthian capital.

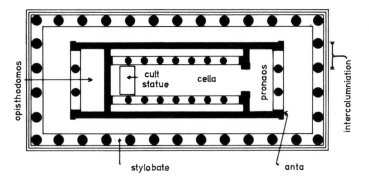

72   Technical terms for the normal Greek temple plan

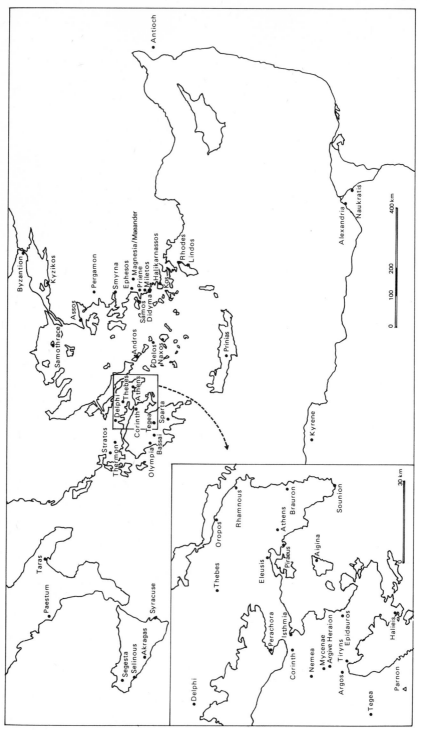

73　Map showing the main sites mentioned in the text

Index

References in *italics* are to figures in the text